BROA CLEARING

Stuart Broad was born in 1986, the son of former England opening batsman Chris Broad, beginning his professional cricket career for Leicestershire and appearing in all three international formats before making his Nottinghamshire debut in the 2008 season.

STUART BROAD

BROADLY SPEAKING

With Richard Gibson

**HODDER &
STOUGHTON**

First published in Great Britain in 2023 by Hodder & Stoughton Limited
An Hachette UK company

This paperback edition published in 2024

1

A CIP catalogue record for this title is available from the British Library

Paperback ISBN 9781399729444
ebook ISBN 9781399729437

Typeset in Minion Pro by Palimpsest Book Production Limited,
Falkirk, Stirlingshire

Printed and bound in Great Britain by Clays Ltd, Elcograf S.p.A.

Hodder & Stoughton policy is to use papers that are natural, renewable
and recyclable products and made from wood grown in sustainable forests.
The logging and manufacturing processes are expected to conform to the
environmental regulations of the country of origin.

Hodder & Stoughton Limited
Carmelite House
50 Victoria Embankment
London EC4Y 0DZ

www.hodder.co.uk

*To the wonderful cricket fans all over the world
& to the teammates I've had the pleasure of
sharing a changing room with*

CONTENTS

FOREWORD

My earliest memories of being around cricket were as a little boy of around four or five years old walking a yard behind my dad, hearing Nottinghamshire fans say, 'That's Chris Broad.' It was a privilege to be able to follow in his footsteps. I always wanted to emulate what he did. To hear strangers say his name was a weird feeling at first, but one I soon got used to, and later seeing BROAD on the back of his county one-day shirts during the early 1990s was inspirational.

I have always felt connected to Nottingham, and wherever I have lived, it is the place I call home. In childhood, Trent Bridge felt like a safe haven for me. Yes, it was an international sports stadium, but it was also my playground, and sitting here, reflecting upon my own career eight weeks after leaving the game, when I think about the ground, naturally it is the regaining of the Ashes there and taking eight for 15 to help England do so in 2015 that immediately comes to mind. However, it also makes my soul sing to recall images of the outfield at lunchtimes being full of kids playing with their parents. You don't get to do that at Wembley. Or at Old

Trafford football stadium. But it is how this journey I am now sharing with you began for me.

It was an ambition for me to play for Nottinghamshire. It would be trite to say that I would have played for the club for free, but the funny thing is that I technically did for fifteen of my sixteen seasons. When it came to choosing a new club as my contract at Leicestershire expired in 2007, I knew that playing at a Test ground was important to me, as was being part of a team that was winning consistently, because being surrounded by a number of other top-level players would improve me more quickly. I'd had a taste of international cricket by then but was not yet a dead cert pick in England teams. And so I looked around a few different places that met the criteria.

Of course, because of my dad's history with the club, I had my heart set on Nottinghamshire, but Warwickshire and Lancashire were my other suitors, and I could have seen myself playing at both of those counties. My mum, Carole, was from Bury, and Lancashire also rolled out Andrew Flintoff as part of their sales pitch, so these factors meant they were very much on my radar – and Nottinghamshire gave me a wobble because they made a much cheaper contract offer in comparison to the three six-figure ones from the other clubs, knowing how much my hometown connections meant to me.

Ultimately, I took a long-term view that if my career headed in the direction I wanted, the financial aspects would take care of themselves, and so I went with my heart and signed for Nottinghamshire on less money. As it was, I didn't receive a penny from them after my first season of 2008 as I was placed on an ECB central contract that superseded my county wage. It was a long-standing joke of mine with Mick Newell, the club's director of cricket, that I was his cheapest ever signing. I signed on the same day as Luke Fletcher and Alex Hales, and the three of us constantly reminded him it was the best transfer window he'd ever had.

To go from being the kid playing under the old scoreboard with dustbins as wickets to taking the new ball for the first team was special in itself, and I truly treasured every one of my appearances for the club. And so, you can probably imagine what a huge honour it was on 21 September 2023, when Mick and Lisa Pursehouse, Nottinghamshire's chief executive, asked me if I'd be willing to accept an offer from the club committee for the pavilion end to be renamed after me. The Stuart Broad End has a rather nice ring to it, don't you think? Trent Bridge is ingrained in our family's blood, and this will only strengthen the depth of feeling I have towards representing the county and the city of my birth. I am so proud that Nottinghamshire is my club.

My other 'club' was England, of course. The most prestigious of clubs of which to be a part. Before receiving my Test cap from Sir Ian Botham in Colombo, Sri Lanka, in December 2007, I'd heard a lot of people say, 'It's my dream to win an England cap.' Yet, it was never my dream just to get one. Even before debuting at the SSC ground, I didn't view it as an achievement simply to wear it once. I knew I wanted so much more.

I wanted to create winning memories and build a story with

that cap, and the Three Lions was never just a badge that I wore. To me, it was more like the cover of a history book, and when I look at the number 638, it blows my mind that in Test match cricket's great story only 637 Englishmen before me had received one. So every series I won with England, I poured a tiny drop of champagne onto my cap – to put memories and spirit back into this living, breathing thing.

Giving up the chance to record further glories wearing it was not easy, and yet I truly have zero regrets on leaving the sport that I dearly love. Two major events within the past twelve months have provided a feeling of true contentment: becoming a father to Annabella and accepting that playing cricket is now only to be spoken about in the past tense. The two are undoubtedly linked for me.

As a cricketer, it is the people around you, in the changing room alongside you or supporting you behind the scenes that are important. But life moves on and it is time for me to go the same way as others that walked before me. England will always be my team, and to have pulled on the same kit as my dad – representing the same county and country – has left me fulfilled.

Autumn 2023

CHAPTER ONE

FAST bowling is a gruelling job. Sometimes at the end of a day's play, there is nothing left in the tank. You are operating on fumes. But sometimes when you are striving for a wicket – the thing that provides such personal and collective joy – another energy source kicks in. When your body is screaming at you that it is spent, adrenaline takes over. This was one of those occasions.

Jelly-legged, I embarked on those six deliberate steps that build into my bowling run-up: the 16-yard dash to the crease that defined my working life for two decades. A journey completed thousands of times. My England team-mates estimated that I'd have been on the turf of Kazakhstan rather than Kennington at this point if they'd all been strung together.

Only on this occasion, the most familiar of runs felt very different. This was it. The moment. Just one ball to keep my place at the heart of this 2023 Ashes drama alive. Suddenly, I had been provided with a glimpse of what the end might look like after seventeen years competing at the highest level. This was scheduled to be my final delivery in international cricket. All cricket. I didn't like the vision that was forming in my mind of things fizzling out; slipping away quietly.

I couldn't face ending my career in this way. I so wanted to be the one to have the last word in my last match. To settle one final score with Australia by putting the finishing touches to a series-levelling victory.

Evening sun bathed The Oval, the stands were a-hum, and I could feel the warmth of the supporters that filled them – supporters who had roared me to the crease throughout the fifth and final day of the fifth and final Test. My final Test.

Yet as I placed one foot in front of the other, I knew I was now on my own, carrying with me a secret shared by only a limited few. Moments earlier, Ben Stokes, the England captain for the most enjoyable final fourteen months of my cherished career, had served notice that this was to be the last over of my spell, and he was turning to Mark Wood's extra pace in a bid to blow away Australia's tail.

I didn't want my involvement to come to a nondescript end. Certainly not right then, with another epic contest careering towards a thrilling conclusion. But with the Australians requiring 55 runs to win, two wickets intact, and 22 overs and one ball remaining of the match's over allocation, it was now or never. One ball of this tally was mine, regardless, and I badly wanted to make use of it. This was my glory shot.

On strike was Australia's bespectacled number 10, Todd Murphy, a player I had beaten outside the off stump with both of my two previous deliveries – the ball agonisingly close to the edge of the bat on each occasion. I desperately needed a change of luck. And so, after bowling the fifth ball of the over, I tapped into my mischievous side in a bid to alter these fortunes, switching the bails on the stumps for the second time in the match. This time, at the bowler's end, the Pavilion End.

It was an act that united two features that ran concurrently through my life on a cricket field but didn't always naturally align – a desire to enjoy myself and a desperation to win. After all, it had delivered instant rewards in the first innings, when I nipped in behind Marnus Labuschagne, facing at the Vauxhall End, fiddled with the furniture and stood back to watch – following a brief interlude in which he politely inquired what the devil I was up to – as he sliced to slip off Wood.

Detouring to the stumps at the bowler's end cannot be done covertly, of course, and so my second bail trick drew chuckles and cheers from the crowd, but when I got back to my mark, I went through my usual process, composing myself mentally, as I had done routinely for most of my previous 33,687 deliveries in Test cricket.

Then, desperately trying to get those legs pumping in my customary manner, I told myself with every stride of this particular approach to the crease: 'Hit the pitch hard and move the ball away.' I could barely feel those legs. The nervous tension must have been at its peak.

Throughout the later years of my career, I'd got into the habit of writing down observations and instructions in a notebook or on an iPad before play to be recalled once out in the middle. Little reminders of what would serve me well when the battle was at its fiercest. Trigger phrases to help me achieve my goals. This time, though, the words were not inked on paper but lingered on my breath and swirled in my head.

'Hit the pitch hard and move the ball away.'

The natural angle of releasing the ball from around the wicket meant it would be travelling into the stumps, and so my task was to redirect it.

This was it. I was into my delivery stride. The second-nature sweep of my right arm, the cocking of the wrist and . . . the ball could not have come out of my hand any better. It hit the pitch, hard. It angled away from the left-handed Murphy – and he bloody nicked it!

As the wicketkeeper Jonny Bairstow, moving low to his left behind the stumps, did the rest, there was pandemonium. Pandemonium. Everywhere. It was truly wonderful. The Oval felt like it was bouncing. My partner Mollie jigged up and down with our daughter Annabella in her arms. Alongside her on the balcony, where my family was gathered next to that of Jimmy Anderson's, my mum Carole and stepfather Nick were congratulated by Jimmy's parents Michael and Catherine, and his wife Daniella – they had all shared so many memories over the years. My sister Gemma stood arms aloft. Just along the row, my dad Chris smiled in disbelief.

If I write my own scripts, as has been claimed many times, this career-ending chapter was destined to be the most sensational yet. None of my loved ones or an audience of millions had been aware of the twist in the plot.

Surrounded by jubilant team-mates, my face told the story. The widest of eyes demanded: Did you see that? Murphy's disappointed trudge from the field left Australia 329 for nine. England required one more wicket to claim victory and seal the 2–2 draw our efforts deserved. The fairytale finish was on.

Crucially, I had also preserved the chance to finish on the highest of highs. From playground to Test arena, it is accepted cricket etiquette not to take a bowler off when they have just taken a wicket and so, in the knowledge that Stokesy would now resist the Wood move and allow me the opportunity to separate Australia's last pair of Alex Carey and Josh Hazlewood, I gave those bails a thank-you tap on my way to take my fielding position at mid-on for Moeen Ali's over from the Vauxhall End.

When I got the ball back in my hand at the Pavilion End once more, Carey was on strike, and our field setting high-lighted the predicament Australia's wicketkeeper-batter found himself in. We had men posted on the boundary's edge to limit his chances of whittling down the required runs quickly, and if he wanted to farm the strike, his chal-lenge was whether to attempt to hit me in-between or over those fielders for boundaries, or manoeuvre the ball into the gaps for twos.

With the ball swinging, it was also important to keep two slips in place, and I brought the outside edge into play with the fifth delivery of my next over – the ball flew at heel height towards Zak Crawley at second slip and despite a great improvised effort, he couldn't hold what was a really difficult chance.

As it was, my final act on a cricket field was inducing another nick behind the stumps in my next over at 6.25 p.m. on 31 July 2023, when England's 49-run win concluded in exactly the way Jonny Bairstow had predicted the previous evening.

Most of my deliveries to the left-handers had been leaving the bat through the air, but in the mayhem of the moment – with this brilliant England team coming back from 2–0 down to deny Australia a first series win on British soil since 2001, and me enjoying a fairytale finale – it went relatively unnoticed that the 604th of my Test match wickets was an in-swinger.

I had been bowling pretty wide of the crease, but on this occasion I got nearer to the stumps and tried to shape the ball back, aiming for a chop-on or bowled. The ball moved back slightly and Carey poked at it, managing to nick it through to Jonny, who took a smart catch.

Wicketkeepers see the angles best and he had followed the ball's trajectory all the way into his gloves. Funnily enough, he also had a pretty clear vision of this particular kind of dismissal a little under 24 hours earlier. Milling about in the foyer of the team hotel, I bumped into Jonny returning from a bite to eat with his family.

'You know what's going to happen, tomorrow? This match

is going to finish with a caught Bairstow, bowled Broad,' he beamed.

Now, as we hugged, and soaked in another electric atmosphere at The Oval, I reminded him: 'You called it!'

It was the most satisfying feeling, not only to end a Test match, but to say goodbye to my playing days. I felt fully content.

Calling time on a playing career is not an easy decision, but there is a saying in sport made famous by the All Blacks rugby team that you want to leave the shirt in a better place, and through all the peaks and troughs of my career that is what I attempted to do.

Whether I achieved that is up to other people to decide, but what I did know as I informed my team-mates of my news on the third morning of this most crucial of matches was that there has not been a better England environment than the one created by Brendon McCullum and Ben Stokes.

When I spoke to the other players and staff inside those private walls at The Oval, I was not only saying goodbye to international colleagues but dear friends. A truly wonderful environment was created when English cricket opted for that most dynamic of coach–captain combinations in May 2022. We have been what our Yorkshire trio of Joe Root, Harry Brook and Jonny Bairstow might call a 'reet team'.

I don't particularly like the word retirement, because as far as I'm concerned I am simply moving into a different phase of my life in cricket, but once I had informed Ben that I was 'done' the previous evening, I thought my friends should be the next to know. It was important to me that they found out from me directly and not second-hand and having reached a position of clarity, it was time for me to share things with them, even though the match still had three days to run at that point.

I knew the timing, mid-match, was not ideal. The last thing I wanted was for any personal news of mine to act as a distraction from the task at hand, or for the remainder of the match to become about me, but equally I knew how driven this group of players was and how determined everyone was to complete the team goal of defeating the Australians.

As the chairperson of the Test side's daily football warm-up game PIG, I began with a little speech of how much I'd enjoyed the position, but it was now time to pass it over to Ben Duckett. There was a round of applause as I handed him a new Premier League football, shook his hand and told him, 'Do it your way.'

Then I said, 'Look, guys, on the back of that, this will be my last game of cricket. It's been an absolute pleasure and privilege to share a dressing room with you SAS Rogue Heroes.'

I'd been watching the BBC drama chronicling the creation of the SAS throughout the Ashes and Stokes and McCullum reminded me of its two founders. Stokes is just so Paddy Mayne, with the way he looks to do things in ways not attempted previously.

I finished by saying, 'I know we're not a results-driven team, but let's do the business this week.'

People will no doubt query the timing, but to be honest I really wanted to go out at the top of my own game, bowling as well as I could remember, in an England versus Australia match, at the end of one of the greatest series imaginable. Ashes cricket brought out the best in me. I was proud to become the first Englishman to take 150 wickets in this most iconic of sporting rivalries. Something about playing Australia stirs things in me, just like it did for my dad in the Eighties. A post-Ashes exit felt almost perfect.

Almost perfect. What a feeling it would have been to be on that stage lifting the urn. Sadly, chiefly down to the Manchester weather the previous week, that wasn't to be, but as I mulled over things, the prospect of ending with a win at a ground upon which I'd enjoyed success against Australia before – notably, the five-wicket haul to set up a series-sealing victory in 2009 – still held great appeal.

I'd also come to realise how nice it was to have control over your destiny and that, at the age of thirty-seven, I was only a hamstring tear away from someone else telling me it was the end, rather than me dictating my own terms.

Even then, it was only when I went to Ben's hotel room at half past eight the previous evening, and shook his hand, saying, 'That's me,' that I felt completely satisfied it was the correct call. I knew that whenever I was to leave the field for the final time during that Test match, I would do so still loving the sport and that was important too.

Thankfully, those around me fully respected my choice. Ben certainly didn't try to change my mind, and that was a good thing as far as I was concerned, as I had not gone to him for a negotiation. When you feel, as I did, that you still have plenty to give, I guess there is always a chance of being talked round, but one good sign for me was that I did not feel one ounce of regret.

There were some emotional moments for me on that third day, beginning with a plan to let Jimmy Anderson in on my news before we began the journey to The Oval. Every morning throughout the series, a different player from our WhatsApp group volunteered to do the team coffee run and so I put it out there early that it was my shout, and sent Jimmy a message asking him to give me a hand carrying the drinks, as a ruse to get him one on one. So we crossed over Kensington High Street from the Royal Garden Hotel to Starbucks, and I'm thinking of bringing things up very casually – only to be scuppered by two fans refusing to leave our sides. They stopped us for a picture, began chatting about the game and wishing us good luck. But all I could think was: 'I'm moving away from the game and I want to tell my best mate before I get on the team bus.' I tried walking around the shop for some privacy, but we just couldn't shake them. Never were they more than two yards away, and so eventually I rushed onto the bus before anyone else, put the coffees down on the little table where me and Jimmy always sat and offered my hand, shaking his and saying 'That's me,' in much the same way I had to Ben Stokes. I could see he was shocked. He had no idea it was coming. I also tried telling Joe Root privately at the end of that journey across London and struggled to get any words out. In addition to Jimmy, I'd wanted to let him know ahead of the others, because I'd played alongside him for so long and he had been my captain for many years.

During the evening session, Moeen Ali gave me a glove punch as we crossed on the field. Our families have known each other since we were at school, dating back to an ECB (England and Wales Cricket Board) development team of Under-17s selected to play the Bangladesh Under-19s in 2003.

Further on my journey walking out to bat, Mark Wood told me, 'This is a great honour.' The partnership lasted all of four balls . . . preceding the most special aspect of being on the field in the hours immediately before my post-play public announcement – batting with Jimmy Anderson. Over the years, it has been our bowling partnership that has coveted attention, but in our first match as England team-mates we had walked off that other famous Oval, Kensington in Barbados, having sealed a one-wicket win over hosts West Indies in the 2007 World Cup. This felt like perfect symmetry.

International cricket had been my life for the past seventeen years and I made such strong friendships, none stronger than that with Jimmy. We shared similar qualities: neither of us ever wanting to let our standards drop.

When I was a kid, I loved the passion and drive of my sporting heroes like Stuart Pearce and Martin Johnson and I never wanted anyone ever thinking that I was not putting absolutely everything in. As I reflected during these final days, I was content that I had given my heart and soul every time I had pulled on the shirt for England, Leicestershire and Nottinghamshire.

The morning after my public announcement, the fourth of the match, it felt as if the decision had repaid me when I connected with a short delivery from Mitchell Starc, towering the ball over the head of the fielder at deep midwicket and into the stand beyond. It was a long time since I had struck a ball so cleanly, and with Jimmy dismissed by Todd Murphy at the other end, it meant I had struck my last ball in Test cricket for six. Not a bad way to go.

Was this another sign that I was destined to finish my career in spectacular fashion? I certainly hoped so. Deep down, I wanted to make eye-catching contributions to the end and finish at the very top of the game.

I had known for some time that in an ideal world I wanted my last bat and bowl to be in an England shirt, and for the majority of the summer I was uncertain when that might be if I called it quits in 2023. If you'd told me I would play in one Test match versus Australia I would have been happy, and so I was blown away to be ever present and finishing at The Oval. I certainly didn't think I would get picked for all five matches.

But under Stokes, McCullum and Rob Key, England's director of cricket, selection felt less of a long-term strategy and much more about the here and now. Rather than planning ahead, being clever and identifying certain players for particular games based on a second-guessing of a venue's conditions, and potentially skewing the immediate make-up of teams as a result, it was about picking the best available XIs for the game, taking form and fitness into consideration.

Even so, bearing in mind that this particular Ashes series

was scheduled over a period of just seven weeks, it felt unrealistic for any fast bowler to truck in for all five; so it was nice to hear Pat Cummins, the only other one to do it, say he was pretty knackered by the end.

The way I bowled on the twenty-fifth day of twenty-five told me I could have carried on, and that was a prospect I had considered at length. I was physically able to get through an unbelievably intense Test series and not let my standards drop. Ultimately, though, I'd always wanted to leave the game loving it. I still did. It was not something I could cast-iron guarantee in future.

For some time previously, there had been a bit of fear gnawing away at me whenever I turned my thoughts to hanging up the headband. It was the prospect of playing against an up-and-coming twenty-year-old and them saying, 'I heard he was okay, but he's rubbish.' And so, I wanted to hit the finishing line chest out, with those around me unequivocal in their belief I could still do a job. A couple of people inspired me in this regard.

Firstly, Alastair Cook – scoring a hundred in his final Test appearance against India at The Oval aged thirty-three. He has had several years of being told he had gone too soon, which is infinitely more preferable to being told you've stuck around too long.

Chris Read was the other. When he left Nottinghamshire, every single one of his team-mates were like, 'Oh God, you could definitely have done another year.' Sounds better than, 'You look done.' Don't you think?

Not everyone feels like they have plenty left in the tank when they opt out, of course. Indeed, I recall Nasser Hussain being invited by then England coach Peter Moores to address the team during the Test series in the Caribbean in 2015 – one of a number of such invites to past greats encouraged by Moores and something that appealed to me, probably because of my heritage as the son of a former England cricketer.

We've all heard Nasser talk passionately about cricket hundreds of times, of course, in his role as a Sky Sports commentator and pundit, but to hear him speak in this way about what it meant to him to play for England really stuck with me. In contrast to the way I was feeling in July 2023, when he retired immediately after winning his 96th Test cap, he said he'd given everything – there was nothing left in the tank.

It was the first Test of the 2004 summer at Lord's, he had just made runs to help win a match against New Zealand, but equally he knew his race was run and he could look himself in the eye in the knowledge that he'd squeezed out every last drop of talent. He was one of those players who always left it all out in the middle, and so being four appearances shy of a century was irrelevant. That day in Antigua, he urged us to consider our own endings, and not to think when walking away from an England shirt: Could I have given any more?

For me, though, there was another consideration in my deliberations. I thought not only about the present but the future. My target for the previous year had been the Ashes. Everything was designed for me to peak against Australia. It was my Everest. The ultimate challenge. I have always been someone able to motivate themselves for the heights of the sport. Equally, other mountains have not presented the same allure. If I'd opted to keep playing, my next assignment was due to be the tour of India six months further down the line. Then another gap to the 2024 summer featuring West Indies and Sri Lanka as the visiting teams. With all due respect to two fine cricket nations, it was not a schedule that excited me.

I have always been a goal setter, manufacturing specific challenges to drive my game forward. Throughout 2023, with this Everest expedition in mind, it had been preparing strategies to neuter Steve Smith and Marnus Labuschagne, Australia's two premier batters. Both of them are at their best when the ball is straight and they are able to work it off the stumps, and so I concentrated on the development of an out-swinger to ask them different questions. But what could be my special project in 2024? I couldn't pinpoint an answer. That added further weight to my conclusion: if you want to finish at the top, now is your time.

Also, the older you get as a fast bowler, the more susceptible you become to that cruel master of misfortune, injury, and my omission from the tour to the Caribbean in the spring of 2022 had given me a taste of what it was like to have an England place whipped away. It was horrible. This way, I maintained control of my destiny.

There was also a sense of responsibility to an England team I had served across 344 appearances. Although it was not something we had spoken about directly, it had become like an unwritten clause in a contract that Jimmy and I never wanted to finish at the same time. We didn't both want to leave and watch close to 1,300 wickets' worth of experience disappear out of the changing room with us. There had to be some overlap.

I had chatted to Jimmy briefly while playing golf at the leafy Cheshire course of Mere, the day before the Old Trafford Test match, asking how he felt, and what he was thinking with regards to the winter tour of India. He was very clear about wanting to carry on. Hearing him say how excited he was about events on the horizon solidified things for me. I could make a straight call on my own future.

We had been a bowling double act since before anyone else in the England team had made their debuts. Jimmy's eldest daughter Lola turned fourteen in January 2023, and watching me take those wickets at The Oval on that final day of the series, she burst into tears. Me and her dad had been playing cricket together her whole life.

Mollie and my mum were among those crying too, but the only time I got emotional was the following morning when I woke up to see a TV clip of headband-clad fans in the crowd celebrating a wicket. Wow, I thought, that's what it means.

Scanning the stands, I had spotted pockets of people wearing headbands during those two final days of the series, and there was another surprise awaiting me when I took our dog Alfie for a walk later that day. On the way to the local park, I passed a house with three headbands tied like ribbons around the railings at the front. I looked up and there were a trio of hand-made placards posted in the front window.

'Local Hero', one read.

'We'll Miss You', another.

A third, very simple: '604'.

It was nice knowing my efforts were appreciated by so many people.

Groups of lads had turned up in their Karate Kid accessories in honour of my late career attire, of course, and that was pretty cool. The headwear became an essential part of my match-day get-up, but for superstitious reasons rather than practical ones.

Truth is, you see, it was not something I had intended to keep wearing beyond Test cricket played in COVID regulations – when players putting saliva on the ball was first prohibited and we were instructed not to put sweat on the ball either. At that time, the headband halted my tendency of mopping my brow with my fingers, but when things went back to normal, I ditched it.

Only when I was not as prolific as I would have liked in a couple of subsequent matches did I revert back to wearing it – a bit like my 'Bail Mary' at The Oval, doing so in a bid for improved fortune. It appeared to have the desired effect, too. My bowling returns improved and it has stayed ever since.

In the hours after beating the Australians, I received hundreds of messages congratulating me on my playing achievements from far and wide, but it was the persistence of a caller from France that caught my attention. Over the years, habit has made me ignore the numbers of those I do not know, or show as withheld or private, so I let the first call go at around 9 a.m. but, intrigued, I picked up later on.

'Hi, Stuart, this is Elton.' Yep, as in Elton John. I couldn't believe it. We had an awesome fifteen-minute chat, and it was a real 'wow' experience. His supportive nature towards performers both in his own world of music and those in other spheres is well documented, and it was only on the eve of this year's Ashes that my dad was recalling how Elton sent champagne to the England team of which he was an integral part after they won in Australia in 1986–87.

I was just six months old then and becoming a family man myself in November 2022 undoubtedly altered my outlook on life. For twenty years, I had put cricket first, but becoming a father to Annabella changed my priorities.

Professional sport is a very selfish career, and although I totally understand those that say playing for your country is such a privilege – of course it is, I've said it myself enough times in the past – the dream life of travelling around the world is not a dream all the time. There are sacrifices you make to be on the road and I chose to re-examine my priorities in parenthood.

One of the things about me is that year after year until very recently, I placed my professional life ahead of my personal one, so focused was I on trying to be the best cricketer I could be, undoubtedly to the detriment of relationships. However, things changed when Mollie and I rekindled things in 2018. We had dated for a brief period in our mid-twenties, but our busy schedules meant it was not destined to last. I would be on one side of the world playing cricket for England, and she would be somewhere completely different fulfilling her commitments with The Saturdays. Spending time together was nigh-on impossible and although things fizzled out, we had enjoyed each other's company and vowed to remain friends.

Things were different, though, in our early thirties, with me playing in only one international format and Mollie also travelling less than previously, and we began dating again around the time she joined Radio 1 as a presenter. It became much easier to make things work around our respective careers, and I owe Mollie a huge debt for the part she has played in mine. She has been an awesome influence on me, and there is no mistaking that my performances got better in the final five years. She took the pressure off me completely, and I probably would not have played as long as I did without her. Nor enjoyed as much success. She has an unbelievable outlook on achieving her goals and it rubbed off on me.

But when I knew I was going to be a dad in late 2022, I wanted to break from the norm and put my family first. Being at Annabella's birth was so important to me that I asked England coach Brendon McCullum if I could be excused from the Test tour of Pakistan. Mollie's due date was in November, meaning that attending the pre-series training camp in the United Arab Emirates became impossible, and there was no way I would have been up to speed fitness-wise for the kind of physical work required in Test matches the following month.

Naturally, such a course of action came with jeopardy. I knew that if another of the seam bowlers excelled out there – and let's face it, no one was to come back from an historic 3–0 win with their reputation diminished – my position in the pecking order of bowlers might alter for the tour of New Zealand.

Following my omission from the away series in West Indies in March 2022, I'd had relatively recent experience of being passed over in selection. However, there was a different vibe around the England environment now and I knew future decisions would be based on the simple criteria of form and fitness, rather than next-generational planning, and so it was a risk I was more than prepared to take.

Mollie was the last person I spoke to before going to see Stokes in our High Street Kensington hotel. Ending our FaceTime call, I walked there immediately. She had always been good at motivating me to play, but less instructive now on the prospect of not playing, listening but ultimately telling me it had to be my call.

'Go with your gut feeling,' she said. Problem was that I didn't really have one, and so I simply had to go one way or the other. There was no point in procrastinating. It was either committing to another couple of years or put playing in the past. As I mulled it over, it still felt like a 50–50 call.

Perhaps subconsciously, the fact I had barely seen Mollie and Annabella for the two previous months swayed me. It definitely makes you miss home having a little daughter who is changing every day, and I want to be a dad who is there for her, takes her to school and watches her grow up.

Not that there was any sense of payback to the decision to end my England career. No sense of duty to move to a new phase in life. Crucially, though, there was something about having my two girls at home that made this decision feel easier as I walked along the hotel corridor towards Ben's room. It filled my heart with joy knowing that when this particular week in London was over, I would be able to spend more time with them.

It might sound flippant – given that I had many wonderful periods playing for England over seventeen years and enjoyed 90 per cent of it – to suggest that the final fourteen months represented the best time in my career. But the final fourteen months *was* the best time in my career.

Let's talk about Bazball. Only, let's not talk about it. For this brief reflection will be the first and last time I refer to it as such in these pages out of respect for Brendon 'Baz' McCullum. He hates it.

There was actually a very funny moment, when soon after returning to his role as our bowling coach, David Saker provided reflection in one of our post-play daily wraps at Edgbaston.

'That's what Bazball's all about,' he said.

'It might be your first day,' Baz smiled. 'But say it again, and it will be your last.'

None of the players called it that in the England changing room. To us, it was a style with no name, even though we all knew exactly what it was. Baz just didn't like the association with him, as a coach who always wanted the players to take credit. Not that he can escape it now. Even other sports are intoxicated by its spirit. Take Tottenham's Australian manager Ange Postecoglou professing his love for it on the eve of the Premier League season, having witnessed it first-hand at Lord's.

Cricket under 'Baz' McCullum was so liberating. When people talk about Bazball, they are not referencing game plans and strategies. They are talking about cricket in its purest form. An environment in which the usual pressures associated with international cricket are conspicuous by their absence. It was the freest I ever felt on a cricket field and playing with no fear of failure suited perfectly the stage I was at in my life. Arguably, it also helped that between the ages of thirty-five and thirty-seven I knew exactly how I wanted to bowl, and retained confidence in delivering it.

Other England teams taught me playing qualities that I adapted for myself, shaping the player I would become. In 2009, players like Andrew Flintoff, Kevin Pietersen, Andrew Strauss and Paul Collingwood showed how battle-hardened you needed to be to beat Australia. Without Andy Flower, the coach who took England to the number one Test ranking, an away Ashes win and oversaw a maiden global trophy success, I would not have developed the grit and never-say-die attitude. Under Peter Moores' tenures, I began thinking about the need to improve, searching for things to add to my game. Ways to get better became a relentless pursuit. Why? Because as I approached thirty, I always kept in mind that there was a 21-year-old with designs on my shirt. It was a thought that never left me.

These other eras played their own parts in building me as a player, but the finale at The Oval allowed me to put all these characteristics into practice.

As we all huddled in the middle of the pitch anticipating the moment of leaving the field together, I found myself next to Moeen Ali, the player in the team I had known the longest. Moeen is a few months younger than me, but he was always a prodigious talent as a young player with Warwickshire and so we had first been team-mates in representative matches twenty years earlier.

'If this is you, I want you to walk with me,' I said to him, anticipating that he would also be walking away from Test cricket.

Nothing had been said officially, but Moeen had only come out of retirement to feature in this epic five-match series – after receiving a text from Stokesy that simply read: 'Ashes?' – so my hunch was that he would revert to being a limited-overs specialist once more. He was providing spin cover following Jack Leach's devastating news that a stress fracture would keep him out for the rest of the summer.

Typically of Moeen, who has such a great demeanour and is much loved within the England environment for his gentle, laid-back attitude, he appeared unwilling to walk off with me. Knowing him, it would have been a typically selfless act, wanting me to take the acclaim alone, so I made it hard for him to say no, throwing my arm over his shoulder and pulling him with me towards the boundary rope in front of the pavilion. Given our history, that was special in itself.

Taking those last two wickets proved to me that I still loved the thrill of playing at the top level, and the atmosphere generated by the biggest sporting occasions. Running around like a headless chicken celebrating told me that I maintained the necessary level of emotion and love for winning Test matches.

I have also loved the interaction with the crowds and now came the chance to say my final goodbyes to some of the people who had paid to watch me play on the international stage since 2006. It was a lovely ovation as we got towards the rope. Sky Sports had sent a request through the England team's media manager Danny Reuben to interview me immediately, but I declined as there were other things more important to me.

Firstly, as there are few better feelings than sitting back down in your place after Test match victories, I wanted to climb the steps for one final time and enjoy it – while taking the chance to revel in the noise from the stands as we did so. The Oval was so loud.

The only thing missing for me was the match ball as a memento. Days later, as I was still trying to locate it, there was talk Down Under of it being under investigation by the

International Cricket Council (ICC) amid suggestions that it was from another year's batch of Dukes balls rather than those with 2023 stamps on them (something the ICC subsequently dismissed). Its whereabouts remained a mystery until early September when Wayne Bentley, the England team manager, sent it on to me. Sorry to disappoint the conspiracy theorists, but it carries a '23 marking.

I am not one for memorabilia. Only one previous item had been preserved from my career: the match ball from Trent Bridge in 2015 when I took my Test-best figures of eight for 15. But there were two things I wanted to keep from my final match: the bat with which I hit my final ball for six; and the ball with which I took the winning wicket.

Something I did take away with me from that day, however, was memories. As I sat among my team-mates to contemplate the perfect ending to an extremely emotional week, I peeled off my socks to expose the blood-stained strappings on my feet. Such is the fast bowler's lot. You have to get used to the blisters, the cuts, the bruises and the soreness. I wouldn't have swapped the aches and pains for anything. Hunched over, face to the floor, I experienced the most vivid moment. Playing cricket still gave me the same special feeling that intoxicated me as a boy. The pleasure it has given me is indescribable, but I felt fulfilled, content.

A fast bowler who had bowled his last, with his discarded boots alongside him. I did what felt appropriate in the circumstances. I picked them up and threw them in the bin.

CHAPTER TWO

MY mum Carole only ever wanted to know one thing whenever I played sport growing up. Was it fun? It was never about the runs, the wickets, the goals, the tries, the misses, nearlys and maybes. She didn't have much time for the incidentals.

Her attitude towards cricket was that you could score nought, fail to dismiss any of the opposition, drop a catch and still have a great day. 'If you didn't have a great day, you're doing the wrong thing,' she'd say.

This wonderful philosophy, which provided the backdrop to my youth, never placed focus on results. Everything was measured on level of enjoyment. Sound familiar? Let's call it Cazball.

My father Chris might have been an England cricketer with dozens of international caps, multiple Test centuries, and notoriety as Man of the Series in the 1986–87 Ashes, but my parents split up when I was three and with me and my elder sister Gemma living with Mum, she became not only my taxi driver but my go-to for advice.

Mum has always been my number one sounding board. With any sort of decision, really. Cricket or life. Someone who is quite reflective, not necessarily giving you an opinion straightaway, which is definitely an approach I inherited from her. She was always much likelier to say, 'Let me have a think and call you back,' returning with a carefully thought-out answer, rather than force an opinion on you.

I remember turning up to Leicestershire Under-10s and some of the other kids were already in the nets with parents piling on the pressure to impress, whereas when Mum was asked to fill in a form detailing where I had played the majority of my junior cricket, she wrote: 'Garden'.

The garden in question, our garden, was in Whissendine, a village in rural Rutland, and it was true enough that I did the majority of my learning either there or in the acres of greenery surrounding us. This is how my love of sport grew; alongside mates or on my ownsome. We were always playing something. Headers and volleys in the park, with jumpers for goalposts, would often develop into a bit of cricket. On other occasions, we might throw a rugby ball around.

David Collier, the former Nottinghamshire and ECB chief executive, lived in the same village, and his sons Simon and Mark, very good cricketers both, were my knockabout pals. There is a notion popularised by Malcolm Gladwell's book *Outliers* that to be world class at something, you should do it for 10,000 hours, and there's no doubt that we put in those kind of hours. Doing so provided huge enjoyment.

As far back as I can recall, out would come the tennis ball, taped on one side to accentuate swing, my Kwik Cricket set of blue bat and blue stumps, and off we would trek either out the back door or the front depending on the day's chosen venue. If on home soil, garden chairs would be placed in strategic positions like short leg and slip, increasing the jeopardy for batters – hit them on the full and you were out.

Sometimes playing club cricket you can get pigeonholed into being a wicketkeeper, leg-spinner or fast bowler from a young age, but we were creative, offering a smorgasbord of roles for anyone who wanted to try. We would alternate between leg-spin and off-spin, try bowling like Glenn McGrath or Andy Caddick, replicate the yorkers of Darren Gough, and look to emulate Brian Lara's stroke play with the bat. We were experimenting with whatever styles suited us.

When alone, I threw a spongy, elasticated ball against the shed wall, and hit it with a stump or a cricket bat, scoring as I went along. Games would be Test match length and recording deliveries over by over took hours. I played religiously. This was my happy place. Even retrieving lost balls from over the fence without being spotted by the next-door neighbours was a thrill. Although the video game era was in full swing, and Brian Lara cricket and Jonah Lomu rugby were both favourites of mine, I'd be in that garden if the sun was out. Sometimes even rain or cold would not deter me.

I was fortunate to have such an outdoor space, and it suited my nature to be active all the time. I wanted to be face down in the mud or running around with grass-stained knees. My dribbling of a football around the garden and even the corridors of the house annoyed Gemma no end, and in some ways I think everyone else was happier when the elements permitted me to get outdoors. Inside, I'd turn the cushions on the leather sofa upside down so the leather was on the carpet, then launch myself on top and slide along, scoring tries in the corner of an imaginary rugby pitch.

And whenever Gemma and I were with Dad, we were surrounded by cricket. Despite their split and the distance involved after he moved back to Gloucestershire, there was never any animosity between my parents, and whenever his schedule allowed we would go and stay with him. I have such vivid memories of the great West Indies paceman Courtney Walsh bowling at me on the outfield at the end of a day's play and being fascinated by the quirky Jack Russell's cricket coffin. Jack was an England wicketkeeper at the time and even at the age of seven I was aware that his kit was unique.

At both Nottinghamshire and Gloucestershire matches, the intervals of lunch and tea provided opportunity for us to play with children of the other cricketers. Although Tim Robinson and my dad were opening partners at Trent Bridge, they were very different personalities and didn't speak much, not even when batting in the middle, but that didn't stop me and Tim's lad Phillip being great childhood mates.

Down in Bristol, Neil Bainbridge, son of Phil Bainbridge, and I would leave the old sandpit area and run amok as soon as the umpires signalled it was time for lunch, and even now when I see kids at Trent Bridge running around the outfield, it makes me very happy. Thirty years ago that was me. There was a period when the authorities stopped the practice and I hated it, as that is a place of great learning.

Seeing grounds at the Ashes this past summer, with games bursting out everywhere, was fantastic. The same happens in South Africa and while cricket is a great sport to watch, which is the reason people are there, that feeling of hitting the ball, or getting a wicket when you are bowling, is what really makes you fall for it as a kid.

Naturally, I wanted to follow in my father's footsteps and play for England, and although as a teenager of fourteen or fifteen those feelings dwindled, due to a combination of some health issues and a period of self-doubt, the feeling never completely went away. If I wasn't playing, I would be watching videos of cricket. There was a series called *Cover Point*, presented by David Gower, which featured highlights of the English domestic season, and from being a tot I had been weaned on another VHS production, *On Top Down Under*. Other toddlers got to watch *Postman Pat*, but I had to endure Dad scoring his centuries against Australia in 1986–87 on repeat.

My parents always wanted me to be a cricketer and that is why I carry three initials – Mum and Dad going for two middle names because they liked the way that it looks on a cricket scorecard. The first Christopher is fairly self-explanatory, but the second John is in recognition of a very difficult start in life for me, and an extremely stressful one for them.

Although it is hard for some people to fathom of someone who is as close to seven feet as six, when I was born at Nottingham's City Hospital on 24 June 1986, I was nine weeks premature and therefore extremely underweight. At just 2lb 2oz, my entire body fitted in my dad's hand. Frail and with a couple of deficiencies relating to not being a full-term delivery, including one of my lungs not forming properly, I spent the first couple of months of my life in an incubator, thanks to a successful delivery carried out by a doctor called John. Hence the name. I lived because of him. The baby in the adjacent incubator did not make it. Recalling this, Mum cried on my twenty-first birthday.

I was not in decent enough health to travel that winter, but Mum and Gemma joined Dad on the other side of the world for a launch of the family business – special envoys intent on improving international relations with Australia. Mum wasn't necessarily keen on cricket before she met Dad at college, but she was sporty, very much into athletics, and went on to work as a secondary school PE teacher. But she got to know the game through Dad, then myself and Gemma, and grew to love it. I doubt very much she will be giving up her season ticket at Trent Bridge just because I've packed up.

It was Dad's family that was cricket-based. My paternal grandfather Kenneth was a really decent player for Long Ashton Cricket Club in Bristol and sat on the general committee of Gloucestershire, only stepping down once Dad signed professionally, He didn't want anyone to think that Dad playing for the club was in any way influenced by him.

Having family connections in the game can be as much of a hindrance as a help, and while Dad was known for scoring big hundreds, I could not score runs for Leicestershire Under-15s. At schoolboy cricket, I didn't necessarily feel any extra pressure from being Chris Broad's son, it was more an expectation of performance from those outside my family circle – whether it be team-mates, opponents, coaches or teachers – that being the son of a professional cricketer, I should have been doing better than I was. Because despite my deep love for the sport, I was not a highly talented young cricketer. Certainly not a standout.

But this is where Mum played a crucial hand once more, using her own experience of sport to encourage me to play as many different ones as I could. It is hard to get bored when you are experiencing such variety. It is also true that you can lose a love for something if it is all you know, and becoming accustomed to skills, tactics and temperaments in other pursuits felt really healthy. Some of the best cricketers I played with – such as Ben Stokes, Jos Buttler, Chris Woakes – were all brilliant at multiple activities. Focus on one sport from primary school age and you almost burn out.

Yes, I loved playing in the Thursday night Kwik Cricket League, in which everyone would move around a circled field waiting for their turn to bowl. But winters were spent playing for Melton Mowbray rugby club, winning my first ever trophy as Player of the Year when I was eight. Not the mini or tag varieties popularised this century, but matches on adult pitches. I recall thinking, oh my God, I am never going to make it, after one burst from the halfway line. And not that I claim to have possessed any great levels of natural talent when it came to football, but what I had was concentrated on playing as a striker for Asfordby Amateurs.

I pulled all these kits on with such regularity that when I reflect on how often I was being dropped off here, there and everywhere, it is a wonder that Mum managed it all. Saturdays and Sundays were wall-to-wall sport.

One thing about my endeavours as a youth was that they were almost exclusively in team sports, rarely if ever individual ones, and I would class going to the driving range as hanging out with mates. Playing something on my own never floated my boat, although I got a sense of isolation from hockey, which I only played at school, because I was a goalkeeper.

If cricket was undoubtedly favourite for me, my number one, it was hockey that was tucked in neatly at one and a half. At one stage, there was not a great deal of difference in the enjoyment they gave me, and I spent a lot of my youth in real hockey havens like Cannock and Bromsgrove, and travelling all over playing for Leicestershire and the Midlands. I even sat on the bench for England once without making it onto the field. You may be wondering how I ended up in net. The answer is straightforward. My efforts playing outfield were short-lived because of my being left-handed. Hockey is a sport exclusively featuring right-handers and as it felt so alien playing the wrong way round, I plumped for stopping goals rather than scoring them.

Me and my elder sister Gemma, two years my senior, spent time at the state primary school in Harlaxton and later at Brooke Priory where Mum taught, before I won a full cricket scholarship with Oakham School, in Rutland, aged twelve.

Sport at Oakham also included rugby union, but despite playing throughout my secondary education, I never made it to the first XV. I was never big enough until sixth form and in any case it was a pretty high threshold in terms of the quality required for you to be considered. In that side were Tom Croft, who went on to represent England and the British Lions, and Matt Smith, who played twenty years for Leicester Tigers.

I had been in the Leicestershire CCC set-up for a couple of years by the time I went to Oakham, and I was probably a pretty good cricketer from ten to fourteen, before I suffered an episode in November 2000 that stopped me in my tracks. It was a cold morning. I woke up and I simply couldn't breathe. During wintertime, the lung defect that I'd had to contend with since my testing start in life was always at its worst, but this felt so very different, like my chest was being crushed.

'Mum, I don't feel very well,' I tried to say, barely able to get my words out.

Mum rang for an ambulance, but was met with a rather direct response from the operator when she informed them of my symptoms.

'No time for that,' they said. 'Get him here straightaway.'

It was an acute asthma attack. Mum raced to the hospital in Melton Mowbray and I was treated immediately, the doctors placing me on steroids to reduce inflammation and swelling in the airwaves. I was kept on them for some time afterwards, causing my entire body to inflate – my weight ballooned and my skin became puffy. I looked like the Michelin Man. I was too poorly to play sport for several months.

Naturally, I lost confidence during this time, but thankfully asthma didn't affect me again on a sports field until the back end of my professional career. Yes, I struggled in polluted cities like Kanpur in India, but it was not until a storm was on its way to the Ageas Bowl during a Test match against Pakistan in the lockdown summer of 2020 that I was stopped in my tracks. Suddenly it went really humid and I had to say to Joe Root, who was captain, 'Look, mate, I have bowled a few overs and I can barely breathe.' He was brilliant, telling me to calm down and see the doctor.

That was the only time in my career when I felt I could not bowl due to my condition, but even then it didn't rule me out for the entire day. Once the atmosphere changed again, I was good to go once more.

It was upon my return from the first asthma attack that my physicality, or lack of it, became really obvious in my cricket. While everyone else appeared to shoot up in height between fourteen and sixteen, I stayed the same and although I had decent technique, it meant I lacked the strength or power to keep up with my age cohort.

Only later would I realise that this period did me a favour rather than harm, because once I did start growing – and boy, did I grow – I had the technical ability to be able to play the game, rather than relying on being a big kid.

In my GCSE years, I probably looked a nice player, shaped up and addressed the ball pleasingly, but I never put any performances on the board. I would score 30s opening the batting, but it would take me 130 balls. I wasn't making scores of 70 and 80.

Typically, Mum always steered me away from fretting over performances, though, with her broken-record questioning whenever I got into the car.

'Did you have fun?'

That was something I always had at Egerton Park, the club in Melton Mowbray of my stepdad Nick Joyce. It was a lovely little place to play. From those Thursday nights of orange balls and blue stumps, I graduated to the youth teams and then into men's cricket from the age of thirteen, batting at number 8, and bowling a few overs here and there. I always found the atmosphere at the club very welcoming, as if everyone wanted me to do well.

Egerton Park represented everything that is good about club cricket. After matches on a Saturday, all the kids would play cricket on the field while someone stoked up the barbecue. Heading down there felt like an addiction to me. I just wanted to be involved.

Everyone had little jobs to do around match days and mine was always putting out the boundary flags – suitably spaced to allow a game of bowls for those doing laps during the game, with each flag becoming the next jack. Getting the scoreboard open was another one I didn't mind landing, and there was always a communal responsibility to put up netting, because the ground backed onto a river at both ends – otherwise the ball would be in there with every four. In fact, depending on who we had in the side on any given day, it wasn't unknown for us to send in pinch-hitters to target the water. Opponents would come with only one new ball, and if you could get it wet early, all the better. It would be retrieved by a huge fishing net and thrown back to them!

The club's president days were my favourite. Even at fourteen or fifteen, I loved the sense of occasion, and these were the biggest games of the season. Past players would turn up in their club jackets and ties for a big slap-up lunch and watch whatever game had been organised for that particular year. It might be 1sts v 2nds, or an Egerton Park XI versus local rivals like Thorpe Arnold. A game with that bit of added pressure always got me excited and I used to really enjoy playing in front of the bigger crowds, even if we are talking fifty people as opposed to a dozen.

When I moved into men's cricket, I played a lot of games with my stepdad Nick, who bowled little leg cutters off about four paces. As an ex-Leicester Tigers second row of many years standing, his mobility wasn't world class by the time he was fifty, and while he was still dangerous on a green seamer, in the politest possible way I think he probably played for the social. He always enjoyed a beer after the game, or when he got out if we were batting second.

Another Nick, Nick Newman, was the senior player, and he was a bit of a role model for me as he had played Leicestershire second-team cricket back in the 1980s and would later play for England Over-50s. It was his style that made the most impression on me. Such a naturally talented cricketer, he would often try to hit a boundary first ball and would always put the emphasis on having a bit of a laugh.

Down there, I never went home feeling like it wasn't worth it. It was a great entrance into a wonderful sport, and I feel very lucky, because I know not everyone has that. Later, when Leicestershire asked me to move clubs to better myself, I refused.

Mum knew I played sport chiefly for pleasure and she was crucial in making sure it remained that way, because there are a lot of different pressures that circle sporting kids. How many goals have you scored? How many tries have you scored? What about runs? Obviously at that age it doesn't matter, but when you get to an age when it does, you need to retain a growth mindset of improvement, which in itself is triggered by enjoyment.

In those days, you would receive a letter on Fox-headed paper to inform you whether or not you had made the county representative team, and at Under-16 level I received one on the negative side of the selection equation. The person in charge of the decision was Keith Wright, father of Luke Wright, one of my best friends, who ironically enough would go on to become England's national selector in the winter of 2022–23.

I was disappointed but recognised it to be the right decision, because I hadn't really moved my game forward. Looking at things pragmatically, Keith had done me a favour, because if I had been picked, pressure would have grown on me to perform and I would not have possessed the requisite skills to do so. The fear at Leicestershire was that any struggle by me to contribute positively to the team would lead to chat of me only being selected due to being Chris Broad's son. This avoided such scrutiny during the long summer holidays and allowed me to concentrate solely on playing for Egerton Park.

When my chance came again at Leicestershire, I never looked back.

That was when I got picked to play for the Under-17s as a replacement the following year, having attended a few nets at Grace Road with a separate training squad in the interim.

I batted in what had become my customary position of number 7 in a drawn match against Cumbria just before my seventeenth birthday, but the sliding doors moment in my cricket career came three weeks later, when I received the proverbial last-minute call one evening, inviting me to open the batting the next day versus Derbyshire at Denby.

I was torn, but my gut instinct was that I didn't want to play. As usual, Mum urged me to have a think about it and said she would back whatever decision I made. Only play if you are committed to it and you want to be there, she advised, and don't feel pressurised. So I did commit to play, channelling the nerves positively to hit 190 in more than seven hours at the crease.

One of a sequence of eight hundreds in the space of a month, the surge in form had coincided with a significant growth spurt. The mid-teen sapling with a good technique suddenly had gears. Bear in mind, I had never scored one before. Talk about London buses. For so long, everyone was bigger and stronger than I was and I didn't think I was ever going to reach the standards of others, but there was one crucial aspect of this breakthrough display. Phil Whitticase, Leicestershire's academy director, was among those watching. The following week, he offered me a place on the Grace Road academy.

The summer of 2003 also saw things come to a head with hockey. Strapping on all that padding was a form of escapism that kept my mind fresh between cricket matches and practice, but it came to an abrupt end when I had to make a call following an injury.

My style between the sticks was best described as fearless; I would think nothing of throwing myself into challenges or hurtling out at a short corner. But while playing for Leicestershire Under-17s, from one such set-piece I rushed to make a save and the shot got undercut. Goalkeepers in hockey probably have the most protection of any human on a sports field and yet somehow the ball slid past it all and hit me flush on the kneecap.

I missed some cricket as a result, and people at Grace Road were asking: 'Isn't this now the time to focus?' After leaving the astroturf at Leicester City hockey club that day, I never returned.

Growing up, I had a poster of Glenn McGrath on my bedroom wall that I had cut out of *The Cricketer* magazine. Every issue in those days included a player-of-the-month photo and while others would come and go, stuck up there only a matter of weeks before being hauled back down, McGrath's presence was permanent.

He might have been an Australian fast bowler rather than an English one, but he was an inspirational figure to me, because I'd read that he hadn't had great opportunities as a cricketer when he was fourteen or fifteen, and his game developed much later. His story was much like mine. In an interview, he said that he came to bowling later, and that resonated with me. If the talent of the leading fast bowler in the world had been overlooked, I need not worry.

My issue was that although I bowled for Oakham School and for the first team at Egerton Park from the age of fourteen, I wasn't always thrown the ball when playing for Leicestershire's age-group sides. In my mind, McGrath was a perfect role model and I told myself that my time would come too – so I never felt stressed about not bowling for the county. Sure, when I got the chance to bowl in the nets or at winter training, I took it, but I never forced it.

Perhaps it was the fact that I was the son of a former England opening batter that influenced the way people at Grace Road viewed me; they thought that I should be following in his footsteps at the top of the order. But if you asked my two school coaches Frank Hayes and David Steele, both of whom were ex-internationals themselves, they would have told you that I was a bowler from the age of twelve.

Yet you could see why people pigeonholed me. Although it was true that I possessed some nice qualities as a bowler, like a nice away swinger, I was hardly blessed with other attributes. Yes, I could get some decent shape on the ball, but the problem was that it was coming from no height whatsoever. To reiterate, although I stood 6ft 6ins when I made my England debut at twenty, I was really no bigger than average height until midway through sixth form.

For that reason, perhaps you couldn't blame Gareth Williamson, the captain of my Leicestershire year group, for not believing I had the potential that Hayes and Steele saw in me. Or maybe I simply wasn't good enough for the next level at that particular time.

Moeen Ali still talks about those times every now and again, because when I was seventeen we played a development game together against Bangladesh Under-19s at Loughborough University. Two years later, we were teammates again, for England Under-19s, and he couldn't believe the cricketer I had become. The change blew Moeen's mind. I was a completely different player. In two one-day wins over Sri Lanka in 2005, I took four wickets on each occasion and there was a five-wicket haul in the 'Test' win at Shenley.

At school, I had bowled little away swingers with the keeper standing up, and now here I was wearing the three lions on my chest and playing matches televised live on Sky Sports. Although I was not quick, I got the ball to bounce and move away, and I could be a handful for plenty of opponents. In a flash I had gone from a part-timer able to contribute three or four overs at county age-group level to being the country's new-ball bowler.

* * *

To Australians, for whom I would become public enemy number one later in life, it might be a surprise to learn that it was my adoption of an Australian attitude towards cricket that coincided with my big improvement, and I will be forever grateful to a small enclave in Melbourne for the crucial role they played in my development. A season with Hoppers Crossing as a teenager really toughened me up.

Egerton Park had a link with Hoppers, which meant that during our summers they would provide the overseas player to our club and in winters we would reciprocate. It was a practice I was more familiar with than most, because for a couple of years Mum and Nick were the host family for a guy called Prashant Iyer. There was an age difference between us, him being about twenty-one and me in my GCSE years, but I loved his company. Frankly, I was in awe of this brash Aussie whom I viewed as a proper overseas pro, but in reality was simply over to experience England and play some weekend cricket.

When it came to their turns, players from our club generally did a bit of fundraising to pay for the flight Down Under, and food and accommodation upon arrival. This was where family connections kicked in for me, because Richard Hadlee, the legendary New Zealand all-rounder who played alongside my dad at Nottinghamshire, kindly agreed to come to Egerton Park for a Q&A one evening – the proceeds going to yours truly. I was so thankful for that.

When I got to Hoppers in the winter of 2004–05, I knew three or four people straightaway because they had played with us in previous years, and I remain friends with some of them to this day, including Mark Craig, who picked the eighteen-year-old me up from the airport. I tried to meet up with him for a drink whenever I was in Australia after that and always loved reminiscing about the old times.

The place itself is a suburb in the south-west of the city, near Werribee and towards Geelong. Aside from Fawad Ahmed, very few first-class cricketers have emerged from the club, as the Victorian Turf Cricket Association of which it is a part is a step down from the district cricket level that so many young county players have participated in over the years.

A lot of players that previously played grade cricket for the bigger clubs like North Melbourne or Richmond found their way back into turf cricket as captains or player-coaches, while others with ambition knew a good season might result in a move the other way. One thing was certain from my perspective, though. I was in the perfect environment, and playing the perfect standard from which to learn.

At grade level, with an established Melbourne suburban club, there would have been more expectation on me to perform and I didn't need that. The cricket was hard enough without facing the likes of Peter Siddle every week – a realistic prospect given that even the Australian internationals among the state players drop down to grade cricket at weekends. After all, I was on a career trajectory that incorporated a switch from being a schoolboy cricketer to a professional in the space of six months and I credited this Hoppers season for quickening my development.

Tuesdays and Thursdays were training nights and matches were played on a Saturday, which was my time to shine. I opened the batting and the bowling, and my job as the overseas player was to perform, something that I was comfortable with at that level. I thrived on the responsibility. Mark Mitchell, the captain, was brilliant to me, giving me so many opportunities. If I was up for it, so was he, and it meant that I went from being limited to six overs in a spell in England to bowling eleven. I just went out and played: bowling with different fields, in different conditions. It was a great education.

There were some life lessons, too. For a start, I bought into what it meant to be a proper club man, replicating the odd-job mentality at Egerton Park by helping to roll the pitches (it helped that I lived with the groundsman in this regard). Things were taken more seriously as well. Fail to train on both Tuesday and Thursday, and you weren't picked on Saturday. No exceptions. Turning up late was also a non-negotiable offence.

So, I could be found in the nets twice weekly, at the gym three or four times. During the day, I laboured for a landscape gardening firm, starting work at seven, mixing cement and laying paving stones around swimming pools until four. It was my job to go around with the spirit level to make sure puddles didn't gather if it rained. The disciplined lifestyle hardened me up from being a kid heading to the other side of the world wanting to be a professional cricketer, to feeling ready to be one by the time I boarded my return flight home.

It also helped my confidence that I contributed significantly to the team cause, winning the club champion award – their version of player of the year – without either scoring a hundred or taking a five-for. In twelve matches, I scored 374 runs at 31.2 and took 16 wickets at 24.4. I took pride in doing my bits for the team, whether that was fighting hard for draws or bowling over after over. There was a great team spirit.

It meant I came back from the trip having developed an edge to my game. A competitive streak had always been inherent when it came to me and sport, but I began to add other aspects to my character such as pride in performance. At training, I worked hard and experimented in equal measure. I liked the fact that high standards were expected in practice as well as match situations.

My transition towards a greater body of work with the ball came in the 2004 season, my last year at school, when I played three Second XI Championship games. Although I was still thought of mainly as a batter, and I remember bowling against Durham at Hartlepool with the keeper up to the stumps – how could I forget, given the number of times Moeen has reminded me – I was bowling first change and now showing promise as an all-rounder.

Enough promise, Leicestershire decided, to be offered a professional contract by the club's director of cricket, James Whitaker, in September 2004. I was buzzing. I was going to be a professional cricketer. The £5,000-a-year salary was immaterial. This was my dream.

Jumping in the car, I read the official letter top to bottom and intended to drive straight home to show Mum. But I got only halfway home when, so excited by this life-changing event, I pulled over at a golf course to call her.

'Don't sign anything,' she said.

As I have mentioned, Mum is someone that always likes to do things properly, digesting all the information and putting things into context before making any decision. She was excited for me. Of course she was. I am sure she loved the idea of me wanting to commit to being a full-time cricketer. It was just that I was due to go to university the following month, having been offered a place on a sports science course at Durham, and her advice was to keep all my options open going forward.

As a PE teacher and someone who had first-hand experience of professional sport, first through my dad's cricket career and then with my stepdad Nick, whose appearances in the second row for Leicester Tigers were second only to Martin Johnson, she knew both the merits of a good education and the need to take chances when they presented themselves.

When I got home, she said that although it had to be my decision, she viewed things this way. Treat the offer at Leicestershire as your apprenticeship, she said. Why not give professional cricket a go for a couple of years rather than do things the other way round? It was pretty standard in those days for talented cricketers to put off a move into the county ranks, attending university first before embarking on a playing career. Go into this like you're a plumber learning your trade, she told me, and if you don't like it two years down the line, or haven't made it, go to university then.

Mum said exactly what I wanted to hear. Even though I was potentially the lowest-paid player on the Leicestershire staff, I signed the contract with zero negotiation, because to me the money was immaterial.

Proud of the fact that I was arriving at Hoppers that winter as a professional cricketer, I logged onto the internet daily to check if my addition to the Grace Road playing staff had been announced on Leicestershire's website – a ritual that lasted all of two months. Nowadays X, formerly Twitter, and Instagram are instantaneous, but this was a time that pre-dated such apps, so it was a case of logging onto whatever technology was available in the hope of seeing if the day's headline story read: 'Stuart Broad signs.' Or some such.

The news was eventually released in early 2005 and when I came back for pre-season in March, it is fair to say that Leicestershire welcomed a different player from the one to whom they had offered the contract.

Physically, I had changed a huge amount and everyone was surprised by the transformation. I remember John Sadler, a young left-handed batter, saying I was a completely different proposition at one of the first net sessions, and it was down to the combination of events coming together over the previous twelve months: the growth spurt, the fact I had filled out a bit, bowled lots of overs in the winter, and was suddenly swinging it away at 85–87mph.

Hoppers Crossing was only an amateur club, but it was a

serious one. They weren't encouraging you to be on the other side of the world slobbing around, drinking beer. They gave me a gym membership, and I trained four or five times a week outside of cricket practice. It was no wonder I came back from Down Under a different specimen.

It was something I continued during my first summer on the county cricket circuit when, new on the scene, I was thrown into a house with the Australian-raised Jim Allenby, Chris Liddle, who later played for Sussex and became bowling coach with the Netherlands and Northamptonshire, and a lad called Nick Ferraby, who didn't get a first-team opportunity at Leicestershire but ended up playing international cricket for Jersey.

As you will realise from my salary, money was not a primary concern. Indeed, it was the little privileges afforded to you when you sign a first professional contract that felt special. Liddle and I were the youngsters and we played up to it, acting like kids. Able to go to the gym daily, we did so, making up little fitness challenges like throwing diving sticks to the bottom of the swimming pool and retrieving them, in the belief that this was the ideal activity in building our fitness.

However, while we were naive in thinking these voyages 20,000 leagues under the sea were worthwhile, it meant we encountered proper dedication to fitness in the form of our team-mate Ottis Gibson, the former West Indies fast bowler. Ottis could be found in the swimming pool every morning. He was in his mid-thirties by then, but was still the ultimate pro when it came to post-match recovery. I have always been inquisitive, watching what the best people do, and his swimming vigil lodged in my mind.

Leicestershire provided the perfect environment for me. It is arguably the smallest of the eighteen first-class counties, and its atmosphere resembled a halfway house between a serious club and a Saturday league one. I don't mean this detrimentally in any way. It felt homely, warm and bonkers. For example, my first nutrition folder carried a reminder not to overfill on scones at tea, especially if you were due to be bowling. It makes me chuckle to think how much the game has changed in aspects like this over the course of my career.

There was an all-hands-on-deck vibe around the place, too. The office staff would literally do anything to make the players feel more comfortable, and their above and beyond approach reached a wondrous level on one particular occasion.

In those days, I drove a three-door Vauxhall Corsa, my first car. It was not ideally suited to a lad standing six and a half feet tall, I grant you, and I used to have to lodge myself under the steering wheel in instalments. Until someone at the club came up with an ingenious idea. They would elongate the leg room on the driver's side by removing the ratchets that kept the seat in place, screwing them into a new position in the back. Needless to say I carried on as it was.

We had a renowned supporter called Lewis Springett. Well, I say supporter, he was more a club legend. Lewis was of Caribbean heritage, always wearing either a Leicestershire or

Hawaiian shirt and was present for what seemed like every moment of every game. He used to shout things out like 'Brandy time!' when a home batter scored runs, or 'If the cap don't fit, don't wear it!' if anyone played and missed. When an opposition player went out to bat, he would cheekily tell the stewards, 'Leave the gate open.' He was the most loyal fan you could ever wish to meet and he felt like a member of one big, happy family.

Even through the simplest of gestures, it felt that everyone at the club was desperate for me to do well, and to tell the truth, although I made a bit of an impression in pre-season, I wasn't expecting to break into the first team. I barely deserved to, based on my statistical returns for the second XI in April and May. There wasn't anything to justify my selection for the sixth County Championship fixture against Somerset at Oakham in 2005.

As it was my school ground, I had obviously bowled quite a bit there and was very used to the pitch. It might have been a bit of a PR stunt to play me, who knows? But it was clever, because making my debut at a familiar place felt comfortable, and I was coming into a team that was full of experience, particularly in a bowling attack comprising the international cricketers Ottis Gibson, Claude Henderson and Charlie Willoughby. I was very raw but very willing.

Comparisons with my dad were inevitable from 3 June 2005, when I finally stepped onto the field as a first-class cricketer (the first day of my career was a wash-out and we batted on the second). Had I featured as a number 6 or 7 batter who bowled the odd over, as had been the role for which Leicestershire signed me, such comparisons would certainly have lingered longer, but as I was carded at number 10 and clearly now considered a bowler, they died down quickly. Yeah, there might have been the odd 'He hits through the off-side, like his dad did,' but I faced none of the scrutiny that only adds pressure to a young player following into his father's trade. There was no judging of comparative records.

The full father-son judgement is arguably what happened when Liam Botham burst onto the scene. He was faced with the recurring question: is this English cricket's next great all-rounder? Whereas my skills were so diametrically opposed – aiming to be a Test match opening bowler and my dad being a Test match opening batter.

Somerset had Sanath Jayasuriya and Graeme Smith in their team. Forget the prospect of bowling at them, merely being on the same field as them was awesome. I didn't dismiss either of them, as it happened, settling instead for Michael Burns, now an international panel umpire, as my first wicket. I actually got him in both innings, something I remind him of regularly, most recently when he was among the match officials at the Edgbaston Ashes Test in 2023. Wouldn't want him forgetting about being nicked-off first innings and trapped LBW second now, would I?

I was as green as anything, and although I knew the technique of bowling through school and club cricket, suddenly I was up against overseas stars with thousands of runs and Graeme Hick, a player with more than 100 first-class hundreds to his name. Where was my learning curve? Answer: there wasn't one. It was like hopping on a sky rocket, clinging on and hoping for the best. Hick was a name to strike the fear of God into county seamers. An English cricket legend. Yours truly, yet to master hitting a length six times in a row or bowling a maiden.

Travelling at such breakneck speed suited my inquisitive and determined nature, however, and thanks to the generosity of others, I kept up. I had Ottis, Leicestershire's veteran opening bowler, as my guardian. Without sounding too cheesy, he made sure that I got the tiny little things that a break-through young bowler needs.

As the attack leader, Ottis ensured it was me and not him who bowled with the wind at my back, and was always encouraging the captain HD Ackerman to bring me on when a new batter arrived at the crease. He knew the right times for a young bowler to operate. This was a classic case of the senior pro looking after the next generation. A lot of guys were influential in those early months, but Ottis felt like my cricket dad. He would do all the hard yards, putting his body on the line, to make it easier for me. You don't forget that kind of thing.

Initially, keeping up with the physical transformation between the ages of seventeen and eighteen was tough and while I felt very free as a young player, able to play without stresses and strains, I did have to adopt a new bowling trajectory and I wanted to learn the more technical aspects of bowling as well. This was never a problem with Ottis around.

He was only too willing to pull me aside and go through techniques, as someone who had only recently returned to playing after qualifying as a coach. I had a West Indies international standard bowler, passionate about trying to improve other players, giving me the wealth of his knowledge. It was the ideal situation for me.

Ottis had a fiery, competitive streak as well, and if he was in a battle he would go for it. That was Leicestershire's trademark, really. Their wicketkeeper Paul Nixon, someone who did things his own way, was similar and the ultimate professional. Both those guys looked after themselves incredibly well.

While they were mentors to me from a playing perspective, Jeremy Snape was very much into the psychology of the game and the advice he gave me when I joined the staff stuck with me all the way through to that very last evening of my career. Remember, he used to say, the game can't start until the bowler's ready, so never rush. Make sure you're mentally ready to go. Simple but brilliant. Sometimes out on the field, you get thrown the ball all in a fluster. Calm down, he'd say. Get a routine that works for you.

Of course, things have gone wrong for me, sometimes drastically so, and I didn't always stick to the advice, because even players with the best intentions forget in the heat of the moment, or get distracted. But in the latter stages of my playing life, I came to realise that routines in sport are way more important than they are given credit for. Not that I was ever going to make people wait till 11.05 a.m. to bowl the first ball of a Test match, but I had to get through my mental routines first.

Three seasons of first-team cricket at Leicester provided a great learning experience and I will be forever grateful to James Whitaker, Phil Whitticase and Tim Boon, the three senior members of the coaching staff during my time at Grace Road, for that vital commodity for a young player – opportunity. All three were influential in giving it to me.

Every time a debut is awarded in competitive first-class cricket, other people are left thinking, how is he better? Or, how has he got the chance ahead of me? That is natural in a top-level environment, so there is an appreciation that they backed me. I hope my feeling that I did not let them down is justified.

With every move through the levels, of youth, school, recreational and professional cricket, I recognised an admirable common link. The best teams work together, back each other, nurture the young and develop great camaraderie.

CHAPTER THREE

Ashes series tend to be preceded by team bonding trips. It is probably to do with the fact that matches against our old enemy Australia are scrutinised to stratospheric levels when compared to those against other international rivals. When sport is at its most intense, understanding your team-mates and knowing that everyone has got each other's backs is essential. It was no different for the 2023 series, although this particular venture took on a lighter tone than some of its predecessors.

Of those gone by, the *tour de force* trip took place in the autumn of 2010 when the squad selected for the impending tour Down Under flew to Bavaria and was put through the most strenuous fitness drills by a couple of ex-army officers. Yet it was not only physical sharpening that was intended to take place that particular long weekend. Such gruelling treatment undoubtedly added to our mental toughness too.

The only blip on this particular trip was when Jimmy Anderson drew the short straw in the boxing competition, picking out the behemoth that was Chris Tremlett, 6ft 7ins of fast bowler, and departing German soil with a cracked rib. When the media found out that his chances of making the first Test in Queensland were in jeopardy as a result of a spot of Queensberry Rules, it went down like a cup of cold sick, but all was well that ended well – Jimmy won his fitness race and we had discipline drilled into us.

High demands were placed upon us. One night, we were woken at 4.00 a.m. and made to lug bricks and logs on a trek; we had to refer to each other formally at all times, so we became Mr Broad, Mr Bell and Mr Pietersen, and if anyone was heard slipping into the use of nicknames like Broady, Belly and KP once more, it was a compulsory 100 press-ups for the entire group: the number of press-ups each of us did over four days hit 1,000. There might have been some grumbles, but we committed.

In 2009, Andy Flower had arranged a trip to the First World War battlefields of Belgium, where we laid wreaths at the Menin Gate Memorial to the Missing in Ypres, and visited cemeteries in the region. It opened our minds and placed a focus on leadership.

Then there was the 2013–14 version, which cannot be described as anything other than an unmitigated disaster. It was designed to be a surveillance operation, but it was destined to be a farce from the moment we sat in a classroom in Stoke being prepped for a role-play scenario by two ex-SAS officers. We spent hours driving round the city, using walkie-talkies, working as a team to track and eventually apprehend a criminal.

I was paired with Ben Stokes in a Ford Focus, and at one point in the early hours we found ourselves parked outside a house when a bloke leaned out of the bathroom window and lit a huge joint. When he spotted us, he quickly slammed the window shut and turned off the lights. But we weren't on a drugs bust. And the mission that we were on failed after the perpetrator we were observing in a pub among a dozen Saturday afternoon drinkers evaded Jonathan Trott, the look-out, as he exited. Trotty said he'd been signing an autograph.

When Trevor Bayliss came in as coach in 2015, the away days took on a much more relaxed feel. Organised by Andrew Strauss in his capacity as the ECB's director of cricket, it was a kind of getting-to-know-you excursion as much as anything in the Spanish resort of Desert Springs, and while there was a focus on catching while we were out there, there was some cycling, running and golf too. As Trevor was newly appointed, it also provided a relaxed environment in which to discuss his view on how he wanted the team to play.

Brendon McCullum's pre-series getaway was even more relaxed than the Desert Springs version and came several months ahead of the first ball going down at Edgbaston on 16 June. One of the issues that Brendon was acutely aware of when he agreed to become England's Test coach in May 2022 was that from the start of the 2020 summer until that particular juncture, we had faced such heavy restrictions on socialising that playing for England felt lonely at times, and more akin to an individual pursuit than a team game.

Long-term COVID restrictions had completely changed the complexion of our dressing room.

None of us were looking for sympathy, and of course we get paid handsomely for what we do, but a lot of the joy associated with being part of an international sport was taken away. The pandemic had sucked out our team spirit in one sense. For example, during the tour of Australia in 2021–22, we were limited to going out in a maximum of three and could only sit outside. When Melbourne was struck with a city-wide outbreak of COVID, the extra restrictions imposed felt debilitating. Forget not having our families around, at times we were even apart from each other.

Baz's philosophy on how to turn things around for a team that had struggled to one win in seventeen was therefore to get everyone back together and spending time in each other's company again. Throughout the 2022 summer we would eat together a lot as a team: local players would host the rest of us at their houses, we would go out in little groups for food during matches, and if it was a room service night, we might pop in for coffees, chats and a game of cards rather than sit in alone.

So, the culture was already changing when he organised a week of events for the tour of his native New Zealand in early 2023. He wanted us to experience a different side of his country, so we spent a bit of time in Queenstown on the South Island, were invited for an evening at his great mate and renowned horse trainer Peter Vela's place, and were dropped off at Lake Taupo and told to have a beer and play golf the next day. Cricket was what we were there for, but he wanted us to get together as a team and make sure we bonded as tightly as we could.

Although this took place in early February, as soon as you enter a year featuring a home Ashes series, the focus tends to be on little else. Every cricket story tends to have an Ashes slant placed upon it and this can engulf you if you let it. Not that Baz is someone to let that kind of thing distract his teams. One of his sayings is, 'Play where your feet are.' In other words, concentrate on the here and now rather than look too far ahead. But there is no doubt that the relaxed nature of that social week in New Zealand – ahead of a 1–1 drawn series that demanded attention for more unbelievably gripping Test cricket – possessed longer-term properties and is looked back upon with great fondness by the group.

Not long after the sixteen-man Ashes squad was announced on 3 June, we embarked on another jaunt, this time to Loch Lomond in Scotland. For two days there wasn't a bat or ball in sight, and once again its purpose was for the players to spend time in each other's company, having golf lessons by day and eating barbecue food at night. Naturally, there was criticism from parts that maybe this was not the best preparation for facing an Australian team that had just been crowned Test cricket's world champions by virtue of victory over India at The Oval.

Grist was added to that particular mill whenever no-balls or dropped catches followed, but to focus on such minutiae was to overlook the bigger picture. Under the captain-coach duo of Ben Stokes and Brendon McCullum, the England team had created a culture of which it was awesome to be a part.

The England management are all too aware that with other tournaments now sprouting up here, there and everywhere – SA20, ILT20 and Major League Cricket all established a place in the global market from the start of 2023 – if players don't enjoy playing Test cricket they have plenty of other options. So, why not make playing for England the ultimate dream? One in which players are creating memories and forming lifelong friendships. Getting the same level of pleasure they once did when they became besotted by the game as boys.

Test cricket may no longer carry the greatest financial rewards, but it is still widely regarded as the most personally rewarding by the players – the pinnacle of the sport. Treat it as so, they appeared to be saying. Fun has become the essence of the England dressing room.

A big reason for the happy mood has been the style in which the team has been encouraged to play. The simplest way to describe it is to say that it champions the taking of positive options at all times, and being true to that policy certainly reaped rewards across the first twelve Tests under Stokes and McCullum. During that period, leading up to the English summer of 2023, we had scored at a run rate of 4.76 per over – considerably faster than any other team in the history of the game. The Australian side that dominated Test cricket either side of the millennium scored at an average of

4.12 runs over a ten-match block in 2003, but in the greater scheme of things these two rates are not even close.

It was enjoyable from a player's perspective, entertaining for fans of the game and effective in terms of results. Ten of those dozen fixtures were won. And yet, one claim kept being repeated. We couldn't possibly play this way against Australia and hope to succeed.

Others were openly mocking us, as if playing with a greater freedom of expression was heresy. On a tour of Sri Lanka in July 2022, Cricket Australia put out a video clip of Steve Smith batting in the nets ahead of the second Test in Galle in which he ran down the pitch and, launching aerially over the bowler's head, shouted 'Bazball!' and laughed as he did so.

'I'm just intrigued to see whether it sort of lasts, whether it's sustainable,' Smith said. 'If you come up on a wicket that's got some grass on it, and Josh Hazlewood, (Pat) Cummins and (Mitchell) Starc are rolling in at you, is it going to be the same? Things can turn around pretty quick.'

This idea that we had constructed a game plan designed to fail, and fizzle out, went in the face of the evidence we had provided. Yes, in Australia we would be facing Test cricket's premier team, winners against India in the final of the World Test Championship in early June 2023, but claims that it could not possibly work against the best teams or the best bowlers were worth reflecting upon. As far as we were concerned, these were neither accurate nor new. Nothing motivates a team like being written off.

The previous summer, South Africa captain Dean Elgar had declared that it would not work against his bowling attack. Agreed, Kagiso Rabada, Anrich Nortje and Marco Jansen are no mugs. The same can be said for Jasprit Bumrah, Mohammed Shami and Mohammed Siraj of India. Two sets of bowlers whom it certainly did work against. It would not work in conditions the England team would encounter in Pakistan, either, apparently. A first-ever whitewash of the Pakistanis by a touring side followed.

This playing ethos had suited us just fine since its first airing in the 3–0 victory over the then world champions New Zealand in 2022, and despite being subjected to claims to the contrary, we were confident it would succeed against their successors too. And to the Australians who claimed they did recognise in our play the concept of the B word, I offer another B word in response. What absolute rubbish.

All this debate over its effectiveness and suitability was, of course, missing one rather important point – the paying public loved it. Not only was it enjoyable to be a part of, it was a joy to watch, as emphasised by the fourth and fifth day full houses of the previous year. As Ben Stokes often reminds us, we are in the entertainment business. And so, we gathered at Edgbaston, united as a team, fully invested in our method and ready to put on a show.

There was one other issue that seemed to be getting people, particularly those of antipodean associations, worked up as the series was shaping up to be the most intriguing between the two countries since the iconic 2005 matches. During an interview with the *Daily Mail*, I said that I had personally voided the 2021–22 Ashes because of the tour experience.

To me, Ashes cricket is highly competitive, involving players at the top of their game, but for that previous away series we had nothing like the preparation for such high-level sport. Our practice ahead of the five-match series was almost completely washed out and we spent weeks of bubble life away from family and friends. So, in my own mind, in order to cope, I voided it.

I was certainly not saying that the 4–0 result should be expunged from the record books. And I am not sure how Australian commentators on this issue had a leg to stand on, either, because their national team did not play a single away Test during the pandemic. In fact, I will never forget Pat Cummins speaking in Hobart at the end-of-series presentation and bemoaning the fact that COVID meant they'd been unable to play any volume of cricket. Our players looked at each other in disbelief. We had committed to being locked in hotels to do so and we went there to keep the game alive, while they did not leave their own shores.

What I did know was that I was now match-ready for international cricket, having had a really good lead-in to the one-off Test versus Ireland with four County Championship appearances for Nottinghamshire. The older I got, the better I seemed to be at judging how many games I required to be both physically ready for the demands and in rhythm to perform. Although the start of a county season is packed with four-day action, and can be heavily fatiguing for those trying to turn out every week, I had the luxury of picking and choosing when and where I played, meaning that I had a schedule of one week on, one week off.

It also contained the added bonus of featuring an away fixture against Middlesex at Lord's. As I was hoping to play for England at least once before June was out, I viewed getting match practice there favourably. My other three games were at Trent Bridge, meaning I was bowling exclusively at Test venues too, and while a tally of 15 wickets at 28.4 runs apiece did not necessarily do my work justice, I was certainly content with form I knew would be up to the task at the top level.

To be frank, I had no expectations of what might happen selection-wise from the Ireland meeting onwards. The challenge I set myself was to make sure I stayed in the present, looking to deliver one game at a time. Easier said than done when an Ashes series is looming, but the short-term view had served me rather well since I had been recalled twelve months earlier, following what I perceived to be an unjust axing for a tour of West Indies.

Now, with six Test matches inside a matter of sixty-one days, I envisaged that we would require a pack mentality when it came to the fast bowlers. Each of us would be needed at some stage, I figured, and when it came to facing Australia I was determined to have as big an impact in one Test as I could manage in five, if that was my lot. I was just delighted to be in the mix, and whether my chance was to come at

Edgbaston in the first match or at The Oval in the last, I truly believed one thing – I would deliver.

The reason for such confidence was my record against Australia. Lots of players have opponents that bring out the best in them and for me it is the Australians. Statistically, my numbers were no different to those I managed against the rest of the international field, but something about the history and heritage, and the heightened atmospheres that meetings of the two teams guarantee, were contributing factors in three Player of the Match awards: two series-sealing wins in 2009 and 2013 preceding those career-best figures of eight for 15 in my home city of Nottingham in 2015.

If selection didn't come my way, I vowed to give my full energy to those out on the field, something made easier by the environment created by our two New Zealand-born leaders in the twilight of my career. As my thirty-seventh birthday approached, I felt free and whether I was to play one more match or twenty in my career, I was happy.

It became clear around this time that Jofra Archer would not be included in our bowling armoury for the summer. It was desperately sad news that Jofra would miss out following yet another stress fracture of the elbow, after returning home prematurely from the Indian Premier League. When it comes to injuries, he has not had the rub of the green.

I was also on the field with Olly Stone when he hobbled off against Lancashire with a problem that was destined to keep him out of consideration too. It was one of those really unfortunate ones. Late in the afternoon, cold and wet, at a time when we were constantly on and off the field. He had been bowling great, but then in his follow-through, his right hamstring pinged.

With Archer and Stone suddenly unavailable, it left us a little shy on X factor and potentially over-reliant on Mark Wood for express pace. Such an ingredient had not been necessary the previous year when six wins out of seven were completed with a bowling attack including myself, Jimmy Anderson, Matthew Potts and Ollie Robinson, a quartet able to make best use of that most essential facet in English conditions – movement. Equally, though, the 90mph option is always a decent variety in a bowling group and so it was with this in mind that the selectors called in Josh Tongue as a late addition for the Ireland match with injury niggles bothering squad members Wood, Anderson and Robinson.

I had actually contributed to Jimmy's setback in a round-about kind of way, defying Lancashire for fifty-five minutes at the end of the match in which Stone was injured. On what was a pretty dead pitch, they managed to make light work of the Nottinghamshire top order, leaving the tail to secure a draw, nine wickets down. Being up against my mate gave me that little extra incentive not to get out and while he kept pounding in, I kept blocking.

In the end his twenty-over contribution to Lancashire's second-innings total of 67 on the final day suggested he'd been slightly overbowled. He had certainly worked bloody hard in coming so close to securing the 16 win points for the visitors, so I was gobsmacked to discover, having walked off the field with him in Nottingham on the Sunday evening of 7 May, that he'd taken the new ball again versus Somerset the following Thursday morning – after just three days' rest. He was to play no further part after tweaking his groin before lunch on the opening day.

Tongue had not been rewarded for his performances with Worcestershire *per se*, although one aspect of his relatively modest collection of eleven Division One wickets had stood out. He was the first bowler to dismiss Steve Smith, trapping Sussex's temporary overseas signing LBW at New Road. There had been a lot of talk about Australians playing County Championship cricket to warm up ahead of their World Test Championship final meeting with India and the first Ashes Test at Edgbaston, but I was not in the anti-Aussie brigade on this occasion.

Why not? Well, simply because I didn't see that it was going to affect whether Smith scored runs against us or not. My view was that it was a fantastic development tool for our young county players to come up against Smith, Marnus Labuschagne, Michael Neser and Marcus Harris at that time of year. Tongue, however, owed his first full international call for the impression he'd made with England Lions in Sri Lanka earlier in the year, when he charged in despite the unresponsive nature of the surface to claim a five-wicket haul.

Most people assumed that Chris Woakes would return to the XI for the first time in fifteen months, particularly given his record at Lord's of 27 Test wickets at an average of 11.33

– but Tongue was preferred in the knowledge that the England side might need some of that X quality at a stage in the summer when stakes were higher. Everyone knew what Woakes at thirty-four could do, it wouldn't make any difference to an experienced professional whether he played or not, so it was a logical call to provide a man nine years his junior with some exposure to the top level.

Tongue showed great signs in the 10-wicket victory over Ireland, seamlessly switching between plans to swing the new ball and bowl hostile bouncers with the older one, taking five for 66 in the second innings of a game completed inside three days. My figures of five for 51 in the first represented only my third such innings haul of five at the ground, and meant I felt ready for the Australians, selection pending.

I fear I would have been left out at Edgbaston had Mark Wood been fit, but he had not featured in any cricket since mid-April after quitting the Indian Premier League early to witness the birth of his second child. He had not been able to get matches in for Durham and so needed building back up to full fitness carefully.

Yes, I would have been disappointed to miss the start of my ninth Ashes series, but I had developed a much-changed attitude towards the selection of England teams under the watch of Rob Key as the ECB's men's director. Baz and Stokesy are very good communicators, whose opinions on the game are ones I fully trust, and I respected the fact that they would pick the eleven players for the job. There is no doubt I've had times in the past when I have not trusted others' opinions on the same subject.

They made some of the hardest calls in my time as an England player, and never harder than preferring Jonny Bairstow to Ben Foakes behind the stumps for the international summer of 2023. I was gutted for Ben, because he'd done absolutely nothing wrong, keeping superbly, scoring runs, and being a fantastic team-mate for four years. Unfortunately, though, in piling up a huge 681 runs, Jonny Bairstow averaged 75 in the home season of 2022 with a strike rate of 96 and was pretty much the embodiment of how the team wanted to play.

Would you choose Jonny over Ben to keep wicket? Probably not, but once Jonny declared himself fit there was only one place for him to slot back into the team. You certainly couldn't have dropped Harry Brook, after the most unbelievable start to an England Test career imaginable, or leave out one of the openers, so it was the wicketkeeper position at number 7 that best fitted the Bairstow characteristics as a cricketer.

Sure, the pressure is on when it comes to Ashes cricket and Jonny's mobility was nowhere near 100 per cent in terms of where he would have wanted it to be. In fact, Professor James Calder, the orthopaedic surgeon who operated on him following the freak golf course accident of September 2022, later said that repairing a severe lower-leg fracture dislocation, multiple broken bones in his leg and his ankle, as well as ligaments, was 'like putting Humpty Dumpty back together again'.

Medical opinion was that he might not play again given the extent of the damage, let alone make the start of the season with Yorkshire in his race to be fit for 16 June 2023 in Birmingham, but once he had ticked the boxes to be on a field again, it would have felt wrong to overlook him. After all, it was such an horrific piece of misfortune he had suffered and the timing was truly awful too, coming immediately after his bat had fuelled the early days of this high-octane revolution. But it did come with some risk, I guess.

How can you expect a player who has not kept wicket for three years to come into the most high-pressured series of them all and pick it up like he'd never been away? The ultimate hypothetical question is would England have won the Ashes with Ben Foakes behind the stumps? During the first Test, it was one many were debating.

This England team has generally thrived on the freedom given to it through consistency of selection, and players sticking together, backing each other. We have come to appreciate players for what they do within the bigger picture of a successful collective, which is why no one within our environment envisaged Zak Crawley being under pressure for his place despite a Test average of only 28.26 and the outside noise created by that.

To be honest, the selectors' backing of the players creates more solidarity within the team, because you're not constantly looking over your shoulder. If you know others are being backed, it rubs off on you and you're not worrying about getting a score to keep a place, but relaxing and buying into exactly the reasons you were picked in the first place. Again, there was a lot of pre-series hot air about how few deliveries Crawley's opening partner Ben Duckett attempted to leave in a typical first-class innings. It was as close to zero as any opening batter in history has ever got, but he is at the top of our time for the balls that he strikes. He has an incredible ability to hit the good ones for four.

Team culture is so important and that meant you were now much more likely to get a pat on the back for attacking the ball than prodding and poking at the start of a Test match. The messaging had always been extremely robust – it is the attitude rather than end result that makes the team successful. As an example of this, take Ollie Pope when he brought up his double hundred against Ireland at Lord's by marching down the pitch to the off-spinner Andy McBrine and hitting a six. He was stumped next ball and Stokes declared, meaning he got roared into the changing room.

I guarantee you that if he had been caught at long on for 199, or stumped the ball before, an even bigger cheer would have greeted him. Why? Because of the monumental way he wanted to bring up such a landmark. Actions like that are the living proof that a fear of failure has been removed from England's Test cricket.

It takes a bravery from everyone involved to back the process and style rather than what appears on the scorebook.

Sometimes it might be a cameo innings, just a couple of boundaries or a foiled attempt to change a contest's tempo, but if you are playing in the England style when the pressure is on, you will receive plaudits.

Take fielding. We never talked about catching, or dropping catches, because those things happen in the field regardless. The number one goal for this team, fitting in with the mantra of chasing victory until the end, has always been to throw yourself at the ball because that's the way you emphasise commitment. No one intends to put down a chance, but not everyone maintains full intent in the field, so you are judged on that and nothing else.

You will no doubt recall Jack Leach's launch into the boundary Toblerone in the first match of the McCullum era. I know concussion is awful, but to put in such an effort to save four was exactly what the coach wanted to see. Baz is very authentic. It is what he believed in as a player, and he wants his players to replicate the buy-ins. It is all about the mindset.

There is something about the final few hours before an Ashes series that feels different. In terms of pressure and excitement, the bar goes up several notches.

The evening before, although it wasn't a full roll call, the majority of the team ended up in Nando's around the corner from our Malmaison hotel in Birmingham, as much to get out of our rooms as spend a bit of time together, making sure that we weren't just sitting there thinking about the game. It can consume you, and, as had proved over recent months, this England side plays best when relaxed.

Controlling nerves is something that you get better at doing over time, but you never totally master it, and half an hour before the toss, Jimmy Anderson and I were bowling on the warm-up pitch at the edge of the square.

'Oh, my God. My legs feel so heavy,' I said to him. 'My hamstrings are tight. I feel like I've already played three Test matches.'

We put it down to the crescendo of expectation that consumes players ahead of England v Australia matches. Being aged forty and thirty-six respectively is no antidote to that, and although you normally move into calmer territory once the match starts, I was quite happy when the coin landed in our favour and it allowed us to put our feet up.

The first ball of an Ashes series sets its tone. It also tends to be memorable and the 'crack' that this one made off Zak Crawley's bat to begin the 2023 voyage is one neither I nor the other 25,000 people in the ground that morning will ever forget.

Edgbaston had fallen into a hush of anticipation as Australia captain Pat Cummins approached the crease to unleash the first delivery, and there could not have been a greater contrast in volume once bat met ball in the biggest and most glorious of cover drives. As it bolted its way to the boundary, accompanied by an ear-splitting roar from the crowd, our changing room erupted.

Previous Ashes openings have not been good from an English perspective. Take the previous series in Australia, where Rory Burns was bowled around his legs, or 2006–07 when Steve Harmison sent down a delivery so wide it found its way into Andrew Flintoff's hands at second slip. This, though, was a real statement of intent.

Zak playing that glorious shot relaxed us all into the series and stamped our style and authority on it from the off. It also highlighted the stark difference in style between the two teams. His approach exemplified the mindset with which we wanted to approach every innings. There was no demand to score at a certain rate. Only a request to be faithful to what you do. What Zak Crawley does is hit sumptuous cover drives for four – it's his shot, and so if he got out playing it, fine. If he started prodding and poking, that would be a different matter.

Australia, meanwhile, started with a field that featured a deep point. There could not have been many previous Test matches, if any, in which they'd done that. By the second over, there was extra protection on the boundary. I had played against these guys a lot over the years and it was in their DNA to put markers down at the start of a series, so it really surprised me that at the very start of this one they were employing tactics that would best be described as un-Australian.

It showed that they had thought long and hard about what we were going to do as a team and how they were going to try and stop that. But I was amazed that a country whose cricket has been renowned for its assertiveness were willing to be reactive from ball one; that they did not let things play out for ten overs and then review. Regardless of what was to come, their tactics that morning provided us with a psychological edge. It was already obvious that we would do all the running and the Australians were happy to chase us.

The extent of this pace-setting became clearer in the evening session via a move that was to trigger hours of debate.

When Ben Stokes declared on Friday night, none of the rest of the team knew he was entertaining any such thoughts, but as he has shown on so many occasions, he is a captain who acts on instinct. If he has a gut feeling about something, he may mull it over quickly in his head first, but generally he just goes for it.

This decision had caused him conflicting thoughts. Moments after Joe Root brought up his thirtieth Test hundred, going past a certain Sir Donald Bradman in the process, Ben said, 'Something inside me says declare tonight, but maybe we should take the runs.' Then he went, 'Nah, I've thought about it, we are going to have a bowl. I've said I want to stay true to how I play the game. Let's go and stamp our authority on things. It doesn't matter if we get any wickets or not, but actually us declaring on Australia is quite a powerful move.'

Root and Ollie Robinson were scrambling Australian brains with their ninth-wicket stand, and eighteen had just come off Nathan Lyon's over, but the Stokes policy throughout his first full year of leading England had been to commit to such feelings, and ultimately he knew that pulling out at 6.04 p.m., with the scoreboard reading 393 for eight, would give us two cracks with the new ball – one of four overs that evening and one the following morning in what the forecast suggested would be helpful overhead conditions.

People were scornful of us leaving first innings runs out there, but the response of our team was simply, 'Okay, cool.' We always backed the captain and bought into his belief that we would simply score them in the second innings instead. In that kind of situation, statisticians would tell you that the percentage chance of us winning the game from there dropped, because with an in-batter we had the chance to score another 50–60 runs.

However, I am sure the Australian batters would rather have avoided the kind of awkward fifteen-minute session to which they were now being subjected. Most opening pairs would. And if it took them by surprise, they clearly had not been watching England closely enough in the build-up. This was hallmark stuff: opting for the unconventional and consigning established cricket logic to the past.

It was all quite last-minute and as I changed into my whites and pulled on my bowling boots, Ben wandered up to me and said, 'I want you to have the first ball at Davey.' That's how he operates. In the immediacy of now, rejecting over-analysis. He knew that nipping out a couple of Australians before the close would make it the greatest decision ever, and I was about to renew acquaintances with David Warner. I didn't need reminding, but neither did I mind being told in the build-up that I had dismissed him seven times in the previous home series of 2019.

But it was obvious that the pitch upon which I was keen to extend his misery was not the fast type that McCullum and Stokes had stated they wanted at the start of the summer. It can be a fool's errand trying to second-guess how a playing surface will turn out, but the general consensus among our players when we first witnessed it 72 hours before the start of play was: it's ready to go now.

When it looks like that, generally any pace and bounce it may have contained is zapped out of it pronto, and Pat Cummins and Josh Hazlewood – two of the best bowlers in the world – had hardly fizzed the new ball through to their wicketkeeper Alex Carey. In the trade we call them 'chief exec' pitches: ones that are designed to keep chief executives happy by ensuring the match features five days of hospitality.

The pitch's sluggish nature was obvious within the first four overs as Australia closed on 14 without loss. This particular England team's bowling attack was one that hit a challenging length consistently and moved the ball both ways, bringing the slips into play, but you also need some zip off the pitch to make that a successful policy, and so that position on the field was redundant.

Yes, there were some enjoyable periods in the game, but equally lots of dull patches when it was hard to remove the Australian batters, particularly Usman Khawaja, whose relative comfort was emphasised by him batting on every day of the match. In conditions like that you have to be creative with both skills and tactics, and we held our heads high that we took 18 wickets – the same number taken by Australia. It was certainly easier to prise opponents out when they were playing a few shots.

In the circumstances, I had an impulse to look elsewhere for help when play resumed next morning. As I revealed earlier, over the final five years of my career I had taken to writing down my thoughts in an iPad notebook: little cues to be recalled when on the field. On this particular day, I wrote: 'Engage the crowd?' To emphasise its importance, I gave it the pink highlighter treatment.

As an England player, the crowd at Edgbaston is a notoriously good one to connect with, and I am sure it can be an equally intimidating venue for opponents because of their partisan support. I am someone who lives off the singing of songs and general shouts of support, and I was prepared to take any help I could get on this surface. Together, it felt like we were creating a real energy during that first hour of the second day.

The atmosphere was simply electric when David Warner chopped one of my wider deliveries into the stumps in the seventh over of the morning. We were only too aware as a team what a dangerous player Warner has been in the past, and despite his troubles four years previously, he can take games away from you, so it was great to get him early.

With the Eric Hollies Stand still in full voice, a couple

of policemen then did me a favour when they managed to get in Marnus Labuschagne's eyeline as he set himself to receive his first ball. The delay slowed things down a bit for me, allowing me to refocus on delivering a specific ploy to him. You see, his dismissal moments later was probably more of a mental than physical success for me, because in the series build-up, I had deliberately made a lot of the fact that I'd been working on an away swinger for both him and Steve Smith.

Wobble seam is my favourite delivery, and I always think nipping the ball back onto the top of off stump is best when a batter arrives at the crease, but trying to beat players on the inside edge on slower pitches can be really tough. Three of the four County Championship games I'd played for Nottinghamshire earlier in the season had come on very slow pitches, which gave me the chance to put into practice the out-swinger I had been working on with the club's bowling coach Kevin Shine.

What was a bit naughty of me was to disclose exactly why I had been making little tweaks to my action during my training sessions. There was no need to mention names, but in doing so I was taking a punt. Let's face it, my record against both of those two fine Australian players had been pretty average previously and I concluded this was because my main attacking weapon was trying to get the ball angling back into the right-handers, while these two were both batters you would consider to be edgers rather than LBW merchants. Hence, I thought I may as well try to plant little seeds in their minds. I wanted them to think that facing me this time would be different.

I considered my kidology to be something straight out of Glenn McGrath's pre-series playbook. McGrath loved placing doubts in the minds of opponents, particularly English ones, and the tactic reaped its rewards. For Labuschagne now to nick the first ball I bowled to him, one that swung away slightly, was glorious. One of the reasons I ran around like a man possessed was because it is not often that things like that pay off . Certainly not so quickly. My horseshoe-shaped dash behind the stumps, receiving high fives from team-mates along the way, ended in the vicinity of the Hollies Stand, where the atmosphere was spectacular.

It was disappointing then, after creating a chance for my third Test hat-trick, that my execution was zero. The world's number one Test batter had been replaced at the crease by the number two. I twirled my finger above my head, signalling to the crowd like a conductor to his orchestra, and set off with a plan to surprise Smith with a yorker or low full toss. With two leg gullies, in addition to a bowled dismissal, there was a chance of him flicking it straight into someone's hands. Unfortunately, though, it was a leg-side dud.

However, an inability to threaten Smith first up was nowhere near the level of frustration I felt later that evening when I produced an absolute Jaffa to pin back Khawaja's off stump with the second delivery of the second new ball, only for his dismissal for 112 to be chalked off. Quite simply, I should never be close to overstepping the line, let alone over it. There are no excuses for the seven no-balls of that day, other than to say that during the first innings of a series against Australia, you are probably striving a bit more, trying to run in as hard as you can, and the outfield was spongy, which only serves to make a bowler over-stride in trying to create their own energy into the crease.

Confirmation from on-field umpire Marais Erasmus that Khawaja should abort his slow walk off and Australia were not 264 for six, but 265 for five, came on a day in which we made more errors than we would have liked. Jonny Bairstow's catch to dismiss Labuschagne low to his right was world-class, and he had shown his value with the bat when he counter-attacked with 78 on day one, but two misses standing up to the stumps only served to emphasise the fact he had not kept wicket regularly for three years.

Cameron Green survived on nought when Moeen Ali lured him out of his ground and that squandered stumping was followed by Alex Carey being gifted a life on 26, in the over before my no-ball wicket. There were four chances spurned in all, but I was as guilty as anyone and we had fostered a no-blame culture. What will be, will be. That attitude helps to keep people relaxed when the next catch comes along, and if you talk about dropping catches, it leads to people questioning themselves.

Another of my jottings that morning read: 'We're not a results driven team. It's way more important to relax, have fun, smile, and stay upbeat.' Our successes had come from dwelling on positives, not negatives, and the end of the second day was a time to think about the damage we had inflicted, not those Australia had avoided. Australia were still 82 runs behind, five wickets intact and there were questions to ask of them. Not least, whether Labuschagne would now be thinking about the threat I offered courtesy of the ball leaving him. I hoped so.

In typical fashion, we were still considering ways to win. In years gone by, this match would have been a nailed-on draw when, after securing a slender seven-run lead on first innings, two-thirds of the third day was lost to rain and our openers Zak Crawley and Ben Duckett were lost in a passage of bowling in floodlit murk that was as testing as any period of the match. But continuing to push the game forward on day four allowed the opportunity for the crowd to witness a result one way or the other.

No one better summed up the attitude of this England team than Joe Root, who was unbeaten on one overnight in a second-innings score of 28 for two.

'I'm thinking the reverse ramp is the way to go first ball,' he said, as we got ready that morning.

Obviously, for all the *joie de vivre* brought by being part of this team, having played more than 150 Tests previously, I still had some of the thinking of the traditional cricketer left inside of me. I found myself conflicted. 'This is crazy, forget being funky, get a hundred, please,' said a little bloke on my left shoulder. But I gave my head a shake, suppressed any old-school advice and simply said, 'Yeah? Go for it, then.'

You can't pick and choose when to buy into a method like

I spent the first few weeks of my life in an incubator after weighing just 2lb 2oz at birth.

With the caps my dad acquired on England's 1986–87 Ashes tour of Australia.

Rocking the 2023 bucket hat look, batting right-handed with my hands as a leftie.

My elder sister Gemma with the 'little cricketer'.

Despite being the son of an England player, I had to settle for pillows as pads.

Playing rugby for
Oakham School

I would spend hours
re-creating Test matches,
playing on my own and
recording every single
delivery in a scorebook.

With Gemma, sporting my usual dress sense – Nottinghamshire jumper and Gloucestershire cap.

In my Leicester Tigers kit, kicking three points. Kicking was my favourite part of rugby, which tells you all you need to know!

Fully kitted out at Trent Bridge, a Test match venue but my childhood playground

From a young age,
I clearly wanted
to emulate my
dad Chris.

n the way to Twenty20
nals day glory with
eicestershire in 2006; I
as picked for an England
ebut on the back of it.

Celebrating hitting the winning runs with Jimmy Anderson after securing a one-wicket England win over hosts West Indies at the 2007 World Cup.

this. If it was on his mind, he had to do it. And as a team-mate, I had to encourage him. After all, it's Rooty's shot. He nails it more often than not. On this occasion, he didn't. Pat Cummins' delivery narrowly missed the off-bail and became the most talked-about dot ball of the summer.

That second innings turned into a bit of a scramble, but once we had set Australia a 281-run target we knew there was a chance of taking a 1–0 series lead, despite the limited modes of dismissal available. Other than bowled, potentially from players chopping on, or a fine nick, the only other way to prosper as a bowler was from the mistiming of an assertive stroke, and for that to occur, we knew we had to leave Australia a fourth-innings score they believed they could make. To encourage them to take risks and play shots. Had they come out to block, saying, 'Right, you're going to have to move us,' they would have been very difficult to shift.

Chipping away with regular wickets on the fifth day, I thought the game was ours when Carey was caught and bowled by Root, or else that Australia would shut up shop. But fair play to Pat Cummins and Nathan Lyon for taking us on and securing the two-wicket win.

Philosophically speaking, maybe it was not our time to win that game. Evidence of that came when Lyon hooked me in the air straight into a 10-yard gap at deep square-leg. For a moment, Ben Stokes looked like he was going to produce a replica of his famous World Cup back-handed catch against South Africa four years earlier, but this time he just couldn't claw it in. But for his nearly moment of brilliance, the ball was destined to lob into a gap plumb in-between fielders and sometimes in cricket you have to accept it is not your day.

There was one regret on our part, however: the taking of the second new ball with 27 runs required for Australia to win. Throughout the series we would find bowling with the new ball was tougher than any other as its harder nature negated the slowness of the surfaces and brought it onto the bat quicker. Generally, it was easier to score off, and so if I had my time again, I think I'd have stayed with the old one and continued with the bouncer theory, which had made it difficult for them to score without taking a really big risk.

Only Ollie Robinson and I were fit to bowl – Ben Stokes had done a great job to fill in with some overs, but his troublesome left knee was sore, Moeen Ali's spinning finger had ripped on his return to Test cricket following a near two-year absence and Jimmy Anderson had a bit of a twinge in his quad that, if aggravated, had the potential to put him out of the series. So we gambled.

Essentially, it was my call. When making decisions out on the field with his bowlers, Stokesy instigates conversations along the lines of: 'What are you thinking?' I told him that the bouncer felt threatening, but we were waiting on them to make a mistake. Whereas the new ball could help us bowl them out.

It was nip and tuck. But, as a new-ball bowler, I would always back myself to produce something to dismiss a number 10 and 11 with two dozen runs to work with. I regretted it, because it didn't work. Then again, if we had lost the game retaining the old ball, even more question marks would have been asked about why we didn't take the new one.

I am not an overly emotional person. I only tend to cry at family bereavements. Yet, when we sat down to reflect on what had just happened, I did so publicly outside of such occasions for only the second time in my adult life. The first was also Ashes-related: a response to the news that I was out of the 2010–11 series due to injury only two matches into the 3–1 win. This time, it was an embrace from Ben Stokes that set me off.

Emotionally and physically drained, struggling to accept that we had lost a match we felt we should have won, I was perched forward, palms on temples, when I felt the presence of Stokesy next to me. The hug he gave me said, 'Good effort, mate.' It also opened the tap to my waterworks. I began to sob. Taken by surprise and unsure if others nursing their own disappointments could see, I pushed the sun hat on my head forward to a position where its tilt covered my face.

CHAPTER FOUR

No one really tells you how to prepare for the pressure moments as a bowler. It tends to be a case of learning on the job. Cricket is a team game but it has a tendency to expose the individual, and I was to suffer from its cruel lessons on 19 September 2007. The night my career truly hit the skids. The place: Durban, South Africa. Opponents: India. My tormentor: Yuvraj Singh.

Such a chastening experience might have been the breaking of some people, but being the first player in Twenty20 internationals to be struck for six sixes in an over was the making of me. Of course, I wish that the 19th over of a World Twenty20 match between England and India at Kingsmead had never happened. And, initially, it was a hammer blow to the pride of a twenty-one-year-old cricketer, but later I reflected upon it as the most influential moment of my career.

Why? Because of how I reacted to the experience. Not only did it encourage me to develop a steelier edge to my game, it got me thinking more deeply about preparation and sharpened my post-match analysis. I certainly would not have developed into the fierce competitor I became without it. I know that Ben Stokes feels similarly about his pounding at the hands of Carlos Brathwaite in the 2016 World Cup final. Climbing out of the troughs can be more educational than scaling the peaks.

Frankly, I was ill-prepared. When I was selected in the summer of 2006, I was England's youngest T20 cricketer – a title I held until another Leicestershire player Rehan Ahmed made his debut in 2022, more than sixteen years later. I was the junior member of the bowling attack and yet here I was, thrown the ball by captain Paul Collingwood for the penultimate over of an innings against a powerhouse team like India with their muscular duo of Yuvraj and Mahendra Singh Dhoni at the crease. Until this point, I'd had no experience of bowling at the death domestically, let alone against this kind of batting artillery. I was on a hiding to nothing.

England recognition had come via my performances with the new ball for Leicestershire. My role throughout 2006's Twenty20 Cup was simple: bowl four overs straight at the start of an innings, hit the pitch as hard as I possibly could and try to pick up wickets as a result. My numbers were outstanding. My economy rate was just 4.5 from 32 overs, and no one else who bowled 20 overs in the competition went under a run a ball. I also took some big wickets, but being a one-trick pony didn't teach me any other skills – for example, developing variations that could serve a bowler at the death.

In one way, I was a victim of my own success. While I

was keeping opponents' top orders in check, or getting them out, why did I need to change? The game plan of sending down four straight through was broken only on a couple of occasions, and one of those was in the competition's final.

Leicestershire winning a trophy was a bit of an upset, even though it was the club's second T20 title in four years. We had a decent side based around the spin of Jeremy Snape, Claude Henderson and Dinesh Mongia, and very clear plans. Barring a last-ball loss to Lancashire, we won all our home fixtures with a method that suited our personnel. Darren Maddy whacked it up top, HD Ackerman would anchor things alongside him and Paul 'Nico' Nixon would come in and play reverse sweeps. It all felt well-planned and routine, but playing in front of 5,000 people tops in the familiar surroundings of Grace Road was a different proposition to a sold-out finals day at Trent Bridge.

This was to be my first experience of big-day nerves and pressure. I needn't have worried. Jeremy Snape, our captain, went on to become a sports psychologist, which was unsurprising to those of us party to his brilliant motivational and communication skills.

When we woke up on the Saturday morning, fake newspapers had been shoved under the doors of each of our hotel rooms. The front-page splash read: Foxes are champions! It was a full write-up of all the positive things that could happen during the day. Even though it had no bearing on reality, it put our minds in a really good place from first thing.

Stephen Fleming got off to a bit of a flier, but as soon as he went for 53, I came back on for my fourth and final over, with 70 needed from seven, and took the prize wicket of David Hussey. That whole experience taught me how clarity plays such an important role. I nailed what I was asked to do, but then I had nothing to fall back on for different types of scenarios.

One of my first proper verbal battles took place on the field that day during the semifinal in what was a mismatch from an age perspective. While I was at one end of the career spectrum, my adversary was Ronnie Irani, Essex's gun in T20, who had enjoyed success up the top in T20 cricket, planting his foot down the pitch and whacking it straight past the bowler.

It was a bit of a collision course, in truth. He targeted me as the young player that he could put off, and I was targeting him as their most dangerous batter. He was aiming to demolish the new ball in my hand and so here we were, me aged twenty, him pushing thirty-five, having a ding-dong.

'Yeah, the rumours are true, you're as big a prick as your dad,' he said.

I came back with, 'Well, you're old enough to have played against us both.'

Not only having the confidence to respond but perform told me that I was ready for this battle. I wasn't simply going to lie down. It also made it quite clear that he was coming at me, and Nico had said to me before the game, do not dare let him hit me over my head. So when charging in, all I was thinking was: you can pull me, you can hook me, whatever, but you won't be getting anything full.

After every delivery, I stared at him. He was staring back and chirping, and it was brilliant theatre and drama. Obviously, I was nervous. Properly on edge, if I'm honest, but I had set my target to dismiss him and cared about little else. He got a seven-ball nought, caught behind off me by a buzzing Nico – the plan had worked. Opposition dangerman, removed. Tick.

We won that semi-final comfortably and rather cleverly, then went away from the ground rather than hanging around all day, which can have a tendency to make you feel lethargic. Back at the hotel, I slept for a bit and chilled, and returning to Trent Bridge later, we treated the final against host county Nottinghamshire as a completely new event.

For 95 per cent of its duration, the showpiece match was a real edge-of-your-seat affair. But when it came to the crunch, I loved every minute, and if you asked every professional cricketer about pressure games like this, not all of them would say the same. I also revelled in having a major influence at a crucial juncture in proceedings, sending back Dave Hussey to make it a wicket in consecutive overs. Nottinghamshire got off to a good start through Hussey and Stephen Fleming and it meant for once I did not bowl my four overs off the reel, instead returning for my fourth immediately after Jeremy Snape dismissed Fleming, and it arguably nudged us in front.

Things ended in pouring rain and controversy when, with 11 required off the last delivery of the match, Jim Allenby sent down a waist-high full toss. We had hurried through to get the game done, so everyone could get off the field, and what happened after Will Smith smoked the ball for six reflected that. My immediate reaction from square leg had been, 'Ooh, that's high.' Had it been called a no-ball, Notts would have needed four from one to win, but Nico cut off any hypothesising when he pulled the stumps out celebrating, and the umpires weren't brave enough to tell him to put them back in.

Medal round neck, lifting the trophy, celebrating with my team, this is what I want to do, I thought. I want this kind of game to be my everyday. Yes, I'd felt nerves, but I didn't have any fear of this kind of occasion. I had loved being there.

A couple of weeks later, I was picked for England.

While I'd experienced what a big day felt like – the Sky Sports cameras, the expectation of the crowd – an international debut brings a whole different challenge. Bowling some warm-up balls in Bristol between innings of a Twenty20 match against Pakistan, I could not feel the ball in my hand or my arms generally, because of the tension. My entire body was tingling.

Luckily, though, just as Ottis Gibson had done when I came through with Leicestershire, here was Darren Gough looking after me as I made my way with England. Ahead of sharing the new ball, Goughie came to me and said, 'It's your debut, I want you to feel as comfortable as possible. It's a howling gale – you bowl with it.'

To hear that felt pretty cool. Gough was one of my heroes, and the reason I would go on to wear the number 8 shirt after he retired. When I started, I was number 39.

Despite the hiccup at halfway, I was fine once the innings got going, replicating what I did for Leicestershire – holding the seam up and hitting the pitch as hard as possible on a length. My first over contained five dot balls and then in my second, I trapped Shoaib Malik LBW with one that nipped back. When Younis Khan gloved a short ball on its way through to Chris Read, it meant my debut was to feature a hat-trick opportunity. Shahid Afridi proved a party pooper: trying to hit me out of the ground, he cleared long off. Just.

Pakistan won their maiden T20 international by five wickets, but from an English perspective the one-off contest and one-day series against the Pakistanis that followed was played against a backdrop of more important off-field issues, such as whether the likes of Andrew Flintoff, Steve Harmison and Jimmy Anderson were going to be fit for the upcoming Ashes series. Would Michael Vaughan be on the plane as captain?

England coach he might have been, but I honestly don't think Duncan Fletcher knew my name. I am not sure he even knew who I was. He gave me absolutely nothing. I can't ever remember him speaking to me in the games I played, even in the World Cup the following year, and yet when I had a beer with him in Hermanus, South Africa, in 2020 following the Cape Town Test, he could not have been warmer. He had arranged for myself, Zak Crawley and Paul Collingwood to have a round of golf, and we met up afterwards for an hour of fun and laughter.

My observation of Duncan Fletcher's time as England coach was that there was an inner sanctum, of which Colly, Marcus Trescothick, Ashley Giles, Geraint Jones and Andrew Strauss were a part. Flintoff, Harmison, Anderson and Liam Plunkett were not. Me? I don't mean this disrespectfully, but I think I was an irrelevance. As I say, Fletcher was preoccupied with getting his first-choice bowling attack back ASAP. There were bigger fish to fry but that did not bother me. I was still going to energise, charge in and try to make an impression playing for England.

Some sports people will say they felt that they belonged from the moment they got onto the field, but that didn't apply to me – not by any stretch of the imagination. It felt like an unbelievable step up from county cricket. Here was me, charging in and thinking I could rush Inzamam-ul-Haq, when the reality was he could pirouette five times and hit me through midwicket. I couldn't get him to play a false shot.

Yes, I picked up a few wickets, as you tend to in ODI cricket – a format that involves batters taking more risks – but I didn't leave that series reflecting on being an England cricketer. I left it with the little man on my left shoulder telling me: boy, you've got some work to do.

Yes, I had shown promise with Leicestershire, but I wasn't like Harry Brook in 2022–23, transferring his county form of hundred after hundred with Yorkshire onto the international stage. I took some three-fors with the ball, but I was still learning my trade.

Ultimately, though, I would not have developed as I did without that exposure. Learning at twenty? Wow. It was amazing. My work ethic changed, and so did my style of work, no longer practising the same thing over and over again, but seeking to add the new and the different. That was the only way to improve. The one thing I had not mastered, though, was bowling at the end of an innings.

I actually made my first-class debut before I played for England Under-19s. I had not been on the national radar whatsoever until the summer of 2005, and had not really deserved to be, so I was very much plucked out of nowhere when I did get picked. I would be very surprised if any England scout or coach had talked about me much before then, despite Mark Nicholas telling me in subsequent years that people around Hampshire had said to have a look at Chris Broad's son because the flow of his action was something to watch.

It wasn't all roses, though. The return match versus Somerset at Taunton, my first ever trip there, proved a baptism of fire. Graeme Smith got a triple hundred on the second day and I returned first-innings figures of 20.3–0–119–3. It seemed that wherever I bowled, the ball disappeared for four. When we came off at tea, Dave Masters, who had been omitted for that game, told a despondent away dressing room, 'If you'd played me, I'd have just run the ball from middle stump across him and nicked him off!' It was brilliantly delivered and very funny. Only it turned out he was serious. Then Paul Nixon, who wasn't captain, gave his analysis.

'It's pretty simple in my mind,' Nico said. 'We've got to bowl Championship lines and one-day lengths.'

What the hell did that mean? Championship line? So that's fourth stump, right? One-day length? What's that? A yorker? So, the way to get Smith out was a fourth-stump yorker. This was a classic example of a fine player scrambling the minds of an opposition team.

Smith had an unbelievable presence about him at the crease; he definitely made my top five when it came to players I hated bowling at. Whenever I did so, I tried to exploit the theory he would fall over and be hit on the pad, but he never was. He just whacked it. No batter made a short ball seem slower than him either, although I would still love to have bowled at him with the skills I developed later in my career, when I went around the wicket and moved the ball away. He didn't hit through extra cover particularly well and employing those tactics would have brought his outside edge into play.

Somerset were one of only two teams to finish below Leicestershire in Division Two that season, but the away fixture was a brutal experience. Twenty-four hours after the Smith masterclass, I faced Andy Caddick. It was a bit of a wake-up facing an England bowler of his quality. The graph line of a young cricketer's early progress looks more like a pendulum than a horizon. It shoots up and shoots down, and this was one of those occasions when it shot down.

Caddick bowled bouncers the like of which I had never faced before. They weren't even that short, yet the ball kept flying past my ear at a rapid rate.

'How am I ever going to cope with this?' I asked myself. 'How am I ever going to be able to hit deliveries like that?'

There was another England bowler awaiting me up north. Jimmy Anderson got me out the first time I played against him, although I had the last laugh as Leicestershire won a game of mutual squeaky-bum time at Old Trafford by four runs. It was the final game of the season and incorporated the first sign of needle I had witnessed on the pitch.

There was no Jimmy Anderson End in those days, as the Old Trafford pitches were the other way around and the sun set behind the bowler's arm. That regularly became a problem. On this occasion, Mark Chilton was not happy with the position of the sun and all the Leicestershire players, myself included, were at their wits' end as he dallied between deliveries.

Come on! Get on with it!

So, when I induced an edge, I gave him a bit of a send-off. The celebrations were even louder when Jimmy was last man out, caught at slip off Indian all-rounder Dinesh Mongia's left-arm spin.

I didn't play every single Championship match between June and September due to my England Under-19 commitments, but still ended with 27 wickets in eight appearances, plus the scalps in a tour match of the Australians Adam Gilchrist – not a classic dismissal, despite effectively being bowled through the gate – and Brett Lee. In the final month, we took on Hick's Worcestershire for a second time – and this time I dismissed him. At eighteen years of age, it felt amazing.

It was the summer of that historic Michael Vaughan-led Ashes win and there was a feelgood factor to English cricket. I was so glad to be a part of it. The England team had risen to the top of the sport and I had started to develop my own aspirations. Every one of my wickets felt like a cherished moment, an isolated event to be celebrated, and was recorded in a little book for posterity. It was actually way beyond my 100th first-class wicket when I stopped writing down who I got out, and how, along with other match details.

Pleasingly, the ones noted the following summer were strung more closely together as I began to turn in consistent, match-winning performances. It was my first sign of real career progression.

In between those first two seasons, I'd been chosen for the ECB's Loughborough academy intake, alongside some big names in the game like Rob Key, Owais Shah and Luke Wright, and I began to get a taste of what my peers thought about me when we were asked to complete an exercise that involved us assessing our team-mates. Each of us was handed a card and we were asked to put our name on the top and pass them around so observations could be made by the others.

When my card was returned to me, the comments were like 'hugely competitive, really talented, great work ethic', but also, 'rates himself, don't think he's going to struggle with confidence in his ability'. The general tone of this was fine, but some of it did make me cringe, because I hope I've never been an arrogant person. I don't feel as if I have been. Equally, though, self-doubt has never been an ailment, and sometimes one man's perception of confidence is arrogance in the eyes of others. Throw me the ball and ask me to have a crack, and I am going to have a crack. I've always been that way. Even as a teenager with only ten first-class matches of experience I wasn't intimidated by being among the country's next best players, preparing for an England A tour after Christmas.

That winter taught me how cool some of the people are in our sport. I've always found that friendships in cricket can be forged really quickly. And bonds can be strong. This was certainly the case with one I made in October 2005. Matt Prior, a young lad from Sussex, is not someone I would have met in life outside of the sport, but thrown together as roommates in the university accommodation, we got on like an absolute house on fire from the off and he ended up being one of my best mates through my England career.

The following spring, after Jimmy Anderson and Alastair Cook were summoned to India, I made my England A debut in the Caribbean. That feeling of getting the new box of kit has always given me a buzz. And I was now the recipient of my first England bag with a number on the side.

Midway through the following home season and I was on the full team's radar. I had done well across all formats, but it was my performance on Twenty20 finals day that earned me my first international recognition. Of that, I am 100 per cent sure.

At the end of the 2006–07 Ashes, I was called into an injury-hit England squad for the best-of-three finals of a triangular series, flying over from a spell at the MRF Pace Academy in Chennai. I didn't play, but two matches as twelfth man notified me of my place in the queue with a World Cup looming.

In fact, at one point I was on my way to Heathrow to fly out and join the fifteen-man squad, after Jimmy Anderson broke his finger. The tournament kit arrived at my mum's house and, all packed, she was driving me to the airport to send me off. But we were forced to turn round when David Graveney, the chairman of selectors, made a second call to advise I was no longer required. Jimmy had decided to have an injection and play through the pain.

Following that false start, I eventually arrived in the Caribbean not long after the infamous 'Fredalo' incident with Freddie Flintoff in St Lucia. I was there as a replacement for Jon Lewis, and ended up playing in England's last game of the tournament against the hosts West Indies – one that I would not forget for several reasons. Not only did it represent the farewell of the great Brian Lara, it brought the curtain down on Duncan Fletcher's tenure as England coach, and also featured yours truly hitting the winning runs from the penultimate delivery in a chase of 301, completed nine wickets down. My last-wicket partner was Jimmy Anderson. It was the first time we had played together, beginning a wonderful friendship and partnership.

For the initial period of my international career, that pendulum I mentioned earlier swung as violently as a Bryson DeChambeau drive, and there was no bigger contrast in the two extremes than two experiences three weeks apart in 2007.

During a one-day international at Old Trafford in August, I found myself in a duel with Yuvraj Singh, the man who would soon become my nemesis. Paul Collingwood, the England captain, mindful of the short boundary on one side, told me to drag the left-handed batter outside off stump with a series of wider deliveries and then – when he inevitably looked to compensate – go for the leg-stump yorker. I executed it to the letter, and Yuvraj's bowled dismissal formed part of a first four-wicket haul in one-day internationals for me. Then I doubled-up on career bests with an innings of 45 not out that included the hitting of the winning runs. It was comfortably my best performance to date.

Three weeks later, Durban happened. Talk about penthouse to outhouse.

I had just come out of rather a sexy summer. I'd been named in a couple of Test squads and was an ever-present in the 4–3 one-day series win over an Indian team captained by Rahul David, and also including Sachin Tendulkar and Sourav Ganguly. I was pretty cool, earning a bit of money. I am not saying that I was floating around thinking I'd made it, but my focus was just off. International cricket is like a motorway, and the more you can take in, the straighter you drive, but I was perhaps getting distracted, taking my eyes off the road and careering left and right.

I didn't need as extreme a circumstance as being hit for 36 in an over to tell me I still had my L plates on. Rest on your laurels for a moment, and the top level can be brutal. You go through massive peaks and troughs over the course of a career. No one is immune. Even my good friend Ben Stokes, with his superman feats, can reel off a low for every high, and ultimately it's the bouncebackability that counts, because over twenty years, you have a lot more bad days than good.

The match in question was a dead rubber at the inaugural World Twenty20, but against a team that would be crowned champions only days later. I was no death bowler, yet here I was at this tournament, the youngest member of the England team, being asked to fulfil the role for the first time in the format. I'd had some mild preparation during the one-day series against the Indians earlier in the month and had done okay, coming on at The Oval with India needing 27 off 18 balls, and bowling Mahendra Singh Dhoni in a 48th over that cost four – but I was unable to defend 10 off the last. Ironically, India had been challenged to knock off a score in excess of 300 after Dimitri Mascarenhas closed our innings by hitting Yuvraj for five consecutive sixes.

I had bowled the 18th over of a T20 international against West Indies at The Oval in June 2007 and the 20th of a comfortable win over Zimbabwe at the start of this competition. But in the bigger challenges that followed, against South Africa and New Zealand, I had gone for a dozen runs apiece in the 19th and 20th overs of the respective matches. At a World Cup things tend to get more serious as time goes on. And in years to come this would be remembered as one of them.

World Cup? Everything about the day screamed village green knockout. Fail to prepare, prepare to fail, they say. It was the only time in top-level cricket that I bowled without properly marking out my run-up. Even in league cricket, I always went through the pre-match rigmarole. But on this occasion, there just wasn't time.

South Africa had defeated New Zealand on the same Kingsmead pitch and when that first game of the day was delayed, it ate into our warm-up. They didn't want to delay the start of the second match because of TV schedules, so I hurriedly measured out my run at just one end of the ground – the one I knew I would be starting off from, not the one that would thrust the name Broad into cricket's history books for ignominious reasons.

Twenty20 cricket was still very much in its experimental stage when this first global tournament was arranged. It didn't feel massively serious. To sum up how disorganised we were during that tournament, we kept two close catchers in the first six overs because it was a requirement in our domestic T20 Cup. Only at the start of the following year, when we played against New Zealand at Eden Park and kicked off about their disregard for such a rule, did we discover this. When the fourth umpire informed us it was not mandatory for internationals, we thought the best policy was to keep quiet.

Our squad reflected the experimental nature. Darren Maddy opened the batting with Vikram Solanki, who also kept wicket, and the spinners were Jeremy Snape and Chris Schofield. We beat Zimbabwe, but it was an isolated success, and we struggled to switch tempo from the 50-over series we had just concluded against the Indians back home.

India got off to a rollicking start through Gautam Gambhir and Virender Sehwag, and my initial three overs cost 24 runs, which was a pretty admirable effort given the flatness of the pitch and the wind howling towards a tiny boundary on one side of the ground. Unfortunately, I was about to have these dimensions and elements turned against me.

Yuvraj got himself on strike for the 19th over with a single off the last ball from Andrew Flintoff's 18th, and the pair appeared to have plenty to say to each other – not that I was aware of any incident with an ability to cause a flare-up or there being any niggle in the game. We were already out of the tournament, so there was none of the extra tension a knockout situation invites.

What transpired over the next five minutes was something I avoided watching back for the remainder of my career. I knew only too well the mistakes I'd made, and did not need to see re-runs of the deliveries to remind me. Instead, I put up the barriers and created a TV blackout that even stretched to turning off the adverts during future T20 World Cups. I did everything I could to avoid being subjected to it.

Avoiding replays occasionally involved a great deal of effort. They would appear suddenly on dressing room TVs, especially in the subcontinent, and as recently as February 2023, after England beat New Zealand in Mount Maunganui, ground staff provided a memory refresher on the big screen as both sets of players enjoyed a few drinks on the outfield. Other eyes were attracted by the spectacle. Not mine.

I went into the over intent on hitting my yorker. Bear in mind that I was twenty-one years old and if I was practising ten yorkers, I'd probably nail only three. The percentages were not in my favour from the get-go. Even the process of thinking that six yorkers was the way to go lacked sense, especially to a left-hander hitting to a short boundary, and by the fourth ball my mind was scrambled enough to accept the advice of the captain Paul Collingwood to bowl around the wicket, wide. I had never bowled around the wicket in my life, and this was not an ideal time to start experimenting.

A full toss was dispatched over backward point with an upper-cut slap, clearing the biggest boundary – not that any of Durban's dimensions are what you would term big. It was an unbelievable shot. The best of the lot. If I was going to bowl a wide yorker, it should probably have been over the wicket, because then I would have had the angle working in my favour. Bowling around the wicket allows the left-hander to free their arms. That was the ball I knew I was in trouble. Dry-mouthed, I licked my lips repeatedly.

Yuvi's an amazing hitter of the ball anyway, but most of the balls were on a plate and what I was to reflect upon later was an alarming lack of clarity in my thought. From my point of view, there was no getting to my mark and thinking, right, what ball am I trying to bowl here? My mind was in a spiral. The final two from over the wicket were also launched into the South African night sky. With an Indian-dominated crowd it was bedlam. Yuvraj's twelve-ball 50 took India to 218 for four, a total that would prove 18 runs too many for us.

As I walked off the field, Luke Wright, one of my best mates, put his arm around me and gave me a bit of a hug. A nervous smile hung on my lips. I was embarrassed.

Ottis Gibson, my bowling guru, called me once the dust had settled and said it had surprised him that someone he regarded as a thinking cricketer had not tried to do something different. He asked me a question that sounded more like a statement: 'You bowled six of the same ball. A ball you weren't nailing?'

I had no answer because it still felt a bit of a blur, and I would imagine if you ask Ben Stokes, Kolkata 2016 is a blur too. He tried to bowl the same ball four times. I was watching at home, shouting through the telly to my England colleagues, urging one of them to tell him to do something different. I knew exactly where his brain would be, and it would not be promoting clear thought. In Durban, not once did I think, or anyone else suggest, bowling a slower ball or an off cutter. Didn't once think: bouncer.

In some ways, it was easier for me to cope. The reality was that my mauling didn't knock us out of a tournament. It didn't cost us anything much apart from a hit to my confidence, and one of the reasons I have got so much admiration for Stokesy is the fact that his hammering came in a World Cup final in a game in which the England team had their hands on gold medals. It showed incredible resilience for him to come back from that. I certainly feel that if my experience befell someone without similar levels of mental strength, it could easily have been the end of them.

What undoubtedly helped was the fact that we flew to Sri Lanka the next day for a 50-over series. The most important thing in this kind of situation is getting back out there as quickly as possible. Don't let this sound flippant at all. To be playing for England, living the dream and getting hauled down to the bottom of the ocean was awful, but I now had to find a way of swimming to the surface. People talk about difficult ordeals hurting their pride, but it was more than that, it hurt my reputation.

As an England player I had a standing in the game, and it took a bit of balls from the England coaching set-up at the time, led by Peter Moores, to stick with me for a bit. I was second top wicket-taker in that Sri Lanka series. Mum has a

24-hour rule for sport – mourn or memorialise your performances for this period of time, but once it has passed, move on. I gave myself 48 hours for this one. But as soon as we began net sessions that week, I went to Mooresy and said, 'I'm never bowling six balls the same again. I need to have an array of different ones at my disposal.' That was music to his ears as a coach. His response: 'Let's work on a leg cutter.'

I didn't have a leg cutter at the time, but incorporated it into my repertoire pretty soon afterwards, shifting the cricket focus from dwelling on a painful past to a brighter future. I reviewed how I wanted to bowl going forward and being Yuvraj-ed probably put me off yorkers. I never really committed to being a yorker bowler, because I reasoned it was quite a difficult task for someone of six foot six. All the best yorker bowlers of my generation tended to be a bit shorter – Waqar Younis, Darren Gough, Dale Steyn and Jasprit Bumrah.

It led to other forms of analysis from me, too. I compared it to footballers missing in a penalty shoot-out. When you are sweating in front of a crowd and a worldwide sofa audience, having to turn and go, then execute your skill. My problem was that it was turn and go, turn and go, turn and go. Not once did I try to control my breathing or slow things down, bringing some calm to try and figure out how to combat the onslaught. I was spinning and going, spinning and going. Later, when I realised these pressure moments were developing, I developed a coping mechanism, always looking above the stands to take myself momentarily out of the heat of the battle.

So, in some ways it was one of the best things that happened to me. It made me realise the level I needed to be at to perform on the highest level. The attributes required to be successful as an international bowler. As Freddie Flintoff said in the aftermath, diamonds are made under pressure. I don't think that I'd have been able to deliver under such pressure like I did in my later years without this experience. But that is not me saying I'm glad it happened. In other ways, it made things more difficult. My subsequent tours to India regularly featured people shouting abuse at me, some of it pretty vile on occasion.

Do you know what really helped me? Two years later, I was back in South Africa for the Champions Trophy, and the big screen at the Wanderers was flicking through the best and worst figures in T20 and one-day internationals on the ground. Shaun Pollock, one of my heroes, topped the worst, conceding 52 runs versus West Indies. He was one of the best bowlers ever. It made me think. Who cares? You know what, it is what it is.

As I write this, I am still third on England's list of T20 wicket-takers, and proof I recovered quickly came when I was part of the winning team in 2010's World Twenty20 competition. Holding that trophy was a balm to the pain of those six sixes.

Our team operated like clockwork out in the Caribbean. Everyone put their own signatures on what was a brilliant collective effort. The particular point of difference I offered to the bowling effort had been developed during the 2009 event held in the UK, which was indifferent from an England perspective. In practising yorkers, I discovered that I got them into the blockhole better from around the wicket.

I am not sure you would call me cricket's greatest innovator – Bail Marys notwithstanding – but this was something I started that other people like West Indies all-rounder Dwayne Bravo latched on to. Others continued with it going forward too, but Andy Flower put paid to me doing it not long after, because he felt it reduced the chances of taking a wicket – reasoning that the angle I was creating took the stumps out of the equation.

Some late selection changes, including a new devil-may-care opening duo of Craig Kieswetter and Michael Lumb, meant we were quite a new group. The openers were followed in the order by the best batter of the tournament in Kevin Pietersen. His form guaranteed us runs on the board, easing nerves in numerous chases, and although none of our bowlers lit up the tournament, we bowled pretty much the same overs to the same plan every game.

Ryan Sidebottom would look to swing it early, I would bowl cross seam into the pitch, and then come back in the middle and along with Tim Bresnan try to bowl slower balls into the wicket, trying to get opponents to hit into the cross-winds, which are so prevalent in that part of the world. We lost count of the number of opponents fatally hitting cross-bat into the breeze.

During the middle overs, the spinners Graeme Swann and Michael Yardy wheeled away, giving nothing. In contrast to the slap-dash approach shown in South Africa in 2007, there was a great deal of tactical nous from the bowling unit. No team managed to score 150 against us. Our preferred method was to bowl first, restrict and then knock the runs off, doing so in four of the five consecutive wins we enjoyed from the group stages onwards.

One thing that always makes me smile was an incident before the final, England versus Australia in Barbados. The mascots arrived when we were waiting in the tunnel and a little girl held our captain Paul Collingwood's hand.

'Hello,' he said. 'What's your name?'

'Lucky,' came the reply.

Turning round to the rest of us, he went, 'It's our day, boys, our day.'

So it proved. It wasn't necessarily redemption for me, but having that winner's medal and playing for England's first ever champion limited-overs team, felt really cool and it was a special tournament to be a part of. Luke Wright was one of my great friends in the game and I became very close with Michael Lumb on that trip. Cricket in the West Indies was something that I had watched on TV all my life: Curtly Ambrose, Courtney Walsh, the flavour, the carnival atmosphere. Behind Ashes wins, it was hard to look past lifting a trophy there as my major career moment.

By that stage, I had also enjoyed an ascent in Ashes exchanges. To set the scene, it was lunchtime on day two of the fifth and final Test at The Oval. Australia were 61 for none, and I was yet to bowl. Rain had brought an early conclusion to the morning session and Andrew Strauss came to me as we left the pitch, saying, 'Be ready. I want you to start off this afternoon. Don't worry about runs, just charge in and try to get me some wickets.' Cool. Yeah. Right. Focused.

In those days, if I knew I was bowling at the start of a session, I would go out to the middle five minutes before the bell and warm up. The idea being that it exponentially improved the chances of my first ball being right on the money. I used to like to be sweating at the top of my mark. On this occasion, I planned to go out with our bowling coach Ottis Gibson, and I was in a frame of mind that this was my time to shine. I was intent on having an impact.

The series was locked at 1–1 and I'd been worried that I wasn't going to play in this game. I would miss out on the chance to help England reclaim the urn. I'd had a pretty average series, and although I got a six-for at Headingley in the previous Test, also scoring a rapid half-century from number 7 in a fun-filled finale alongside Graeme Swann, we lost by an innings. When Freddie Flintoff was declared fit to return after a knee issue, I thought it was me he would come in for.

But I got the nod to play, and doing so provided me with one of the routines that would become a feature of my everyday pre-play rituals. Gibbo was like, 'Come on, mate, we need to go,' as I was pulling on a shirt in readiness to go and have that warm-up bowl. Oh God, I thought, that doesn't smell the best. Evidently, it was one I had used previously for batting, and so, wary of the pong, I grabbed the aftershave from my bag and gave myself three sprays before I went out – *doosh, doosh, doosh*.

I went out and took career-changing figures of five for 37. In the circumstances, the three sprays had to stay and so for every single session of my Test career afterwards, whether we were batting or bowling, whether it was morning, afternoon or evening, I repeated the trick. From the Paco Rabanne 1 Million of that special day south of the Thames, there was an evolution of aftershaves, with changes coming whenever I felt a bit low on wickets.

First, I flipped to Paco Rabanne's Invictus, because the bottle looked like a trophy. Then one Christmas, my mum bought me Chanel Bleu and I liked the fact the blue matched my England cap, so that one stayed for about seven years. Then, during the most recent Ashes tour of 2021–22, the late Shane Warne gave me some of his aftershave. If it's good enough for Shane Warne, a bowler with 700 poles, I thought, it's good enough for me. Many an umpire paid me the compliment of being the best-smelling cricketer on the circuit.

In those early days, commentators like Sky Sports' David Lloyd, Michael Atherton or Nasser Hussain would reference the fact that when my legs were pumping on my approach to the crease, I tended to bowl well. I quite liked the idea that other people recognised when something good was happening, not least because I knew it was my time to shine.

Problem was, it didn't seem to last. Those knees would be

up nice and high one afternoon, but I couldn't necessarily repeat it three days later. There was no consistency there. It wouldn't even be a weekly occurrence. The fact that the leg pumping took place on 21 August 2009 at The Oval is indisputable – but at the time I didn't clock the significance, or the connection between it and success. I was a typical young cricketer, not sure why I'd done well, but pretty happy it had happened all the same.

In subsequent years, the England backroom team identified the traits of my best form and it came down to the fact that when my knees pumped upwards, it kept my stride pattern short, so that when I landed, my delivery stride was shorter, instead of being long and stretched. When I got long and stretched, my front arm waved to the side as opposed to coming through its perfect arc. If my stride pattern was short on approach, it would create a short stride pattern on delivery, which in turn gave me whip, bounce, power and balance.

Everything would be in unison. We connected the fact that my run-up was key to my threat as a bowler in 2014, and so I began working on improving my running technique with Phil Scott, the England team's strength and conditioning coach.

As a young bowler, there appeared no obvious correlation to my running being perfect or otherwise, but playing to an international schedule meant you were less fatigued some days than on others, and if you were fresher and bouncier, the running might be spot on. Sometimes, I could be at an end that I particularly liked bowling from, on others it could be the direction of the wind that helped my approach. But the infrequent nature was a bit of a double-edged sword.

Some people would revel in the glory of the days when I was 'on'. Equally, all the criticism of me during my early days on the international scene was that I was someone who relied on hot streaks. It could be used to highlight a lack of consistency and suggest I wasn't reliable – and an average of 40.21 with the ball across my first twenty Test matches suggested I was *not* reliable.

If I had been more aware of what made me good, success may have come earlier. Bowlers who come into the England fold a bit later like Ollie Robinson do so when they have worked out what makes them tick, and are therefore able to deliver it on the big stage immediately.

Back at The Oval in 2009, though, I was destined to come up smelling of roses, or more accurately woody spice, and not only because of my aftershave. Australia had reached 73 without loss in their first innings, when I trapped Shane Watson plumb LBW: fullish, the ball was just angled in and would have hit the top of middle and leg. Soon afterwards, Australia were reduced to 85 for two when Ricky Ponting was undone by what the television commentators called an off cutter that had jagged back and found its way onto his stumps from an inside edge. I subsequently nodded along whenever anyone promoted this delivery's quality. Truth is that I just landed badly, the ball came out badly and it ended up where it did. It might have looked like one, but I certainly wasn't trying to bowl an off cutter. If anything it was pitch variation.

Michael Hussey, the middle of three wickets in as many overs, was my favourite of the lot, because we knew that his plan was to leave the ball, leave the ball, leave the ball early. It made it imperative for me to try to hit his off stump, and I would have struck it at the very top but for me hitting him on the knee as he tried one of his con shots – leaving the ball while faking a forward defence. On this occasion, it didn't matter who he was trying to kid as the ball landed in line with the stumps and angled back.

Michael Clarke's was a really good bit of captaincy from Andrew Strauss. We had talked in the bowlers' group, after Clarke scored 93 at Headingley, about his tendency to hit aerially, so we agreed that if the ball was swinging, we would position a close catcher at cover and throw the ball up there, in the hope he drove off-balance early in his innings. You wouldn't normally see a low chip to that position, where he was caught by the debutant Jonathan Trott, celebrated anything like as enthusiastically, but this was different. It always felt awesome when a team plan came together.

The fifth was spectacular, but Brad Haddin made it look like a Jaffa by simply missing a full straight ball, providing the illusion that it had swung away, turning him around in the process to knock back off stump.

It was a magical middle session, and just as Yuvraj had discovered twenty-three months earlier, when it's your day, it's your day. This was mine, and walking down to fine leg at the end of that over, doffing my cap in acknowledgement of figures of five for 26 at that stage, the stands erupting around me, it hit me that for the first time I was now having to cope with a completely different feeling as an international bowler: the adulation of 25,000 people. And I realised having a crowd like that upright and raucous in ovation brought the best out of me. I wasn't cagey, shy or embarrassed taking the applause. I was like: 'Yeah, make this louder, rev me up and I'll go again.'

CHAPTER FIVE

THE second Test in the 2023 Ashes series was a match that began in a haze of orange and ended in red mist. The common protagonist in both incidents was Jonny Bairstow, although it should be said in mitigation that it was primarily down to the actions of others that he took centre stage in the drama.

For controversy, it is hard to think of anything comparable in 139 years of Test cricket between England and Australia at Lord's. The chorus of boos at the start triggered by Just Stop Oil protesters intent on disrupting the opening of the latest encounter in a proud history. The cacophony of indignation during its closing stages reserved for Australian players who in the view of the paying public had tarnished it, prioritising a desire to win ahead of adhering to a moral code.

Between the moment Bairstow stepped over the boundary edge with a protester in his clutches five minutes into the match's first day and him leaving the field for a final time on its fifth, following a highly contentious stumping appeal upheld by the Australians, it is fair to say we had not given our best selves as an England team. Yet, there was an argument that the latter flashpoint was the catalyst for ensuring we did so for the remainder of the series. The fire was lit.

Ben Stokes's immediate response was to produce another astonishing innings, rivalling the unbeaten 135 that secured the glorious one-wicket win over the Australians in that famous Headingley match of 2019. This time, however, there was simply too much for one man to do, and his 155 would be filed in a different category: outstanding performances in a losing cause.

Like Leeds four years previously, Stokes had headed into the final day unbeaten, this time on 29, with the scoreboard reading 114 for four. All of us knew a couple of our players were going to have to play out of their skins to secure victory on this occasion, but this England team was different to those that had come before in one crucial aspect – it contained an inexhaustible supply of belief. Stokes has everything to do with that. Thinking that anything is possible really is quite liberating. We had felt that way when the fourth wicket went down at 45 the previous evening. We still felt it now.

With 257 more runs required, some might have argued a bid to level things at 1–1 was simply a case of blind faith, but this side had developed a pleasing habit of responding to adversity. Earlier in the year, we had been three wickets down very early in a Test match in Wellington, but the mood inside the changing room was never one of panic. Everything was calm, and that comes from the anticipation that someone, or more accurately two people, will deliver on each day. On that occasion, Joe Root and Harry Brook scored big hundreds. There was also the fact that four of England's eight highest fourth-innings run chases had been completed since the previous June.

We were not in unfamiliar territory. Quite the opposite, in fact. This is what we did. Causes looking lost, some even irretrievable, brought out the best in us. Now on the fifth morning of this match, as the coach made its half-hour journey from our High Street Kensington hotel to Lord's, I turned my mind back twelve months to the final Test of the previous June when at Leeds, we were 55 for six in the first innings, still 274 runs behind New Zealand. We managed to win by a comfortable seven-wicket margin, chasing 296.

Although we had not played as well as we'd have liked in this particular match, there was still a chance. After all, Stokes, whose history of remarkable feats also included the Player of the Match knock on the same ground in the 2019 World Cup final, was set, and at the other end was Ben Duckett, the player who had struck the ball better than anyone else in the match.

That Duckett was still there came down to one of the match's other highly contentious moments. He had been in the process of walking off the field the previous evening for his overnight score of 50 – after top-edging a cross-batted stroke off Cameron Green to a sprawling Mitchell Starc at fine leg. However, when replays of the catch were viewed, it immediately became obvious that this was no regulation dismissal, but one requiring an adjudication from the third umpire Marais Erasmus.

It appeared clear that while Starc had obtained complete control over the ball, it was equally indisputable that he had not obtained complete control over his own movement, as Law 33 also requires. To do so, he had cushioned his landing by pressing his left hand down, rubbing the ball along the turf as he slid along it.

From my understanding of the rule, the ball is not allowed to come into contact with the ground. We've all played in matches in which a catch is attempted with a fielder's hands facing upwards and in the process of diving, the elbows hit the ground and the ball pops out. Starc's actions provided a barrier against such an eventuality, because if you catch the ball and turn your hand downwards, grinding it across the grass, it can't pop out. If that was a legal way of catching, we would all be doing it.

Erasmus came to the only plausible conclusion from reviewing the footage: the ball had clearly been floored in the act of the catch taking place. The officials had made a call using the laws of the game, but the Australians were not happy, taking out their frustrations over the final minutes of that fourth evening on the reprieved Ducky, whose response was understandable: 'What have I done wrong?' Nothing, was the answer. He had made his way to the pavilion in the belief that it was a fair catch. Only when directed by instructions to do so from the match officials had he remained inside the field of play.

Cricket is full of these kind of opinion-dividing incidents because, even though a sport's rules and regulations are set out clearly, human nature leads to further interpretation of them. All of Australia thought Duckett was out and the catch had been completed somewhere along Starc's journey. All of England, not out, that it was not completed within the laws.

Sometimes, though, the search for a black-and-white answer on dismissals is futile, and to my mind this was never more apparent than on the fifth morning when this Test match contained arguably the biggest Lord's rumpus in Ashes history – Jonny Bairstow's stumping by Alex Carey. An issue debated for days afterwards, and one that even led to the country's prime ministers Rishi Sunak and Anthony Albanese weighing in. Sunak said he wouldn't have wanted to prosper in such a way; Albanese suggested it was time to 'harden up'.

According to these same laws of the game applied for Ducky's reprieve from the Starc catch, the ball was not technically dead when Bairstow left his crease at the end of an over in the final quarter of the morning session, as the Australian wicketkeeper Alex Carey simultaneously lobbed the ball towards the stumps, even though the action of people around it suggested it was.

The umpires had not called 'over', but a glance at the footage of when the stumps were broken by Carey's under-arm throw showed that one umpire had the bowler's cap in his hand, the other was looking at the ground, walking in from square leg.

Was the ball still live because Alex Carey catches it and throws it? Probably. Did a full stadium of people think that ball had been and gone? Yes. On the BBC's *Test Match Special* commentary, Jonathan Agnew had already moved on from the calling of that particular delivery – an innocuous Cameron Green bouncer that Jonny had casually ducked under.

The crux of the matter to me was whether Jonny was looking to gain an advantage. It was clear that he had let the ball go through to the wicketkeeper; he scratched his mark within the crease in a little show to the opposition that he had been in his ground; he was off for the kind of routine end-of-over chat with Ben Stokes that takes place dozens of times in a day's play. Clearly, he was in search of no advantage.

This was in direct contrast to an episode earlier in the match when, in his guise as wicketkeeper, Jonny himself had thrown the ball at the stumps, doing so because Marnus Labuschagne was batting outside of his crease. A move designed to increase the probability of being outside the line of off stump in the event of being struck on the pad, thus taking the LBW dismissal out of the game. In other words, seeking an advantage.

Video clips of Colin de Grandhomme being run out in the Lord's Test match of last year would later circulate on social media, but that was the most ludicrous comparison ever, because he got hit on the pad coming down the pitch, searching for a run, and Ollie Pope threw down the stumps from gully. Again, he had been trying to gain an advantage.

Arguments and counter-arguments sprung up instantaneously, but I was not in a position to discuss the situation. The decision to leave out Moeen Ali, still nursing a sore spinning finger, and accommodate Josh Tongue as an extra seamer for this match, meant I was on the way to the middle as the team's number 8 consumed by my own thoughts. My emotions were probably heightened more than anyone else's, because I had walked out of the changing room and therefore wasn't around the team to discuss it or listen to Brendon McCullum saying, 'Let's all calm down, lads.'

At 193 for six, Ben Stokes was waiting for me in the middle. You may not have believed it watching my behaviour for the next three hours, but the thing I've worked hardest on throughout my whole career is to control so-called white-line fever. But that was it, as far as I was concerned. All bets were off. This was a classic case of the red mist descending, and me not wanting to filter it. Australia's decision to take a wicket in what I considered an underhand way had incensed me, and shouts of 'That's a disgrace!' as I made my way through the Lord's members and onto the pitch served as the petrol to my fire.

I was intent on using this sense of injustice to my advantage. As I am always at my best when I get into a fight with someone, I often select an opposition player to engage as my adversary. But as Ben Stokes would later chuckle, this time I chose the entire Australia team. Batting is not my strong point, but with Stokesy at the crease, I knew I had a huge responsibility and so asked myself, 'How can

I best help him?' The answer: 'Get into the battle.' I needed to be in my best possible frame of mind to support the England captain. I wanted to stop thinking about anything technical.

Striding across the outfield, I sensed the anger of the crowd. The hum of disbelief bordering on disdain. I rode on the same wave of emotion. As Jonny's dismissal had come from the last ball of the over, it was the start of a new one, therefore I took my place as non-striker while Pat Cummins went to his mark to prepare bowling from the Pavilion End. I just let him have it: 'I can't believe you're a captain. And you've just made that decision. I can't believe it. It's ridiculous.' Of course, I'd had no real time at this point to analyse the decision, but I had seen it once on the big screen.

'You're hardly the example of the spirit of cricket,' he snapped back, no doubt in reference to a decision I made not to walk when I edged the ball in a Test match at Trent Bridge ten years earlier – which I believe is common practice in Australia, where you take your luck with an umpire's decision. I'd guess a thousand batters had not walked in the interim. I can't think there were many that had been dismissed like Bairstow, and certainly not in a Test match, with the eyes of the world on it.

I had engaged Cummins immediately, and he'd nibbled back. Not long after, when he was in the outfield at long on, I kept shouting reminders to him: 'Pat, these boos are for you, they're all for you!'

During this pantomime performance, which I might come to look upon differently in years to come, I tried to use every single opportunity to let the Australians know exactly what I thought of their actions. It also inspired a steelier resolve to my batting than I could recall. When I got on strike and took guard, as Cummins stood at the top of his mark, all I could think was: I am not getting out to him.

'This is all you'll be remembered for,' I told Alex Carey, as soon as he was near me.

Under the helmets as close catchers were Marnus Labuschagne and Matt Renshaw, and I made sure they heard every word when I joined in with the singing of 'Same old Aussies, always cheating.'

Some of what I was saying got picked up on the stump mics, ensuring people watching at home were party to a lot of what was going on, but I can genuinely say that such a prospect never even crossed my mind. Yes, it was petulant behaviour on my part, but it had its purpose. My goal was to create carnage and cause chaos. We were way behind the eight ball in terms of the game situation, and my ultimate aim was to get the Australians off what they were thinking. To use the maelstrom developing around the action to the England team's advantage.

It may have been a bit silly, but these distraction tactics also included me shouting 'in' every time I crossed the crease line with my bat, doing so in the most elaborate manner possible, and drawing more cheers from the crowd. It annoyed the Australians for the final half-hour of the morning session.

Stokesy said very little to me when I joined him, other than instructions to do as he said. 'If I call two, it's two. I go, you go.' It was very focused. Just like his batting. In the five overs that spanned that period, we put on 50 together. My contribution, a single.

When we went off for lunch, there was a huge ovation from the Long Room for Stokes's hundred, and as it is courtesy for the other not-out batter to hang back in such a scenario, I walked in behind him, with the Australians following. The boos for them from the MCC members were insanely loud, and lasted all the way up the stairs to the lunch room. MCC later apologised unreservedly to Cricket Australia after some individuals crossed the line with their behaviour. Three of its members were suspended amid allegations of verbal abuse. Now I'm not condoning MCC members shouting at players, but having toured Australia four times, I don't think hostile behaviour towards away teams is unusual.

At lunch, Jonny was goaded into challenging the Aussies' decision not to call him back. Screens between the two tables split the lunch room down the middle and as the England players settled into their places, Zak Crawley, in the knowledge that our opponents were taking their places on the other side, said, 'Do you think they're happy with that, Jonny? You should ask them if they're happy with that.'

Within a nano-second, a fired-up Jonny went for it. 'You happy with that, lads?'

David Warner came straight back with, 'Yeah, we're happy with that, mate. Yeah. All good.'

I wasn't there, because when you are one of the not-out batters you tend to eat in the changing room. In here, the general consensus was a disbelief – in light of what Australia had been through in terms of regenerating their image following their use of sandpaper on the field on the tour of South Africa in early 2018 – that they had actually upheld the dismissal. Pat Cummins, as his predecessor Tim Paine had done before him, was overseeing a cultural change and this was an opportunity to enhance it by rescinding the appeal.

The comments in our changing room regarding the Australian team's image were in my mind when I decided to head down to the pitch a couple of minutes early for the resumption of play. I went alone, not wanting to get into Stokesy's bubble, because he held the key to us winning the game. His targets were the Mound and Tavern Stands. He kept launching the ball into them. Mine, the Australian players just beyond the picket fence, waiting in that familiar huddle teams get into before the umpires go out. Suddenly, I found myself a yard from them all, and couldn't help myself.

I looked at Usman Khawaja, but was directing my message to all of their players when I said, 'I cannot believe, looking around this huddle, with the amount of cricket you lads have played, that not one of you, not one senior player went to the group and contested what you were doing out there. That no one said, "I'm not sure this is a good decision. I don't think we should uphold this appeal." That none of you consider it to be a crap way to get a batter out. I can't believe it.'

In the aftermath, I was reminded of the dismissal of Henry Nicholls at Headingley in 2022, when he whacked the ball down the ground off Jack Leach and it ricocheted off the middle of the non-striker Daryl Mitchell's bat into the hands of Alex Lees at mid-off. Sure, that's not a great way to be dismissed, extremely unfortunate in fact, but it was nothing to do with the fielding team. That was simply a case of his own team-mate getting in the way.

There are loads of examples in cricket of odd dismissals. But what could not be disputed was that Jonny Bairstow started in his crease to face Cameron Green, finished in his crease after negotiating the delivery, and when the ball was thrown, Carey could not say he was going for a run out, because he didn't know Jonny was going to leave his crease. All in all, it was a lame way for an Ashes wicket to fall, and I mean that for both sides. A bit lame from Jonny that he wandered out of his crease, but properly lame from the Aussies.

I like Pat Cummins a lot, he's a lovely man, but in the heat of the moment – for argument's sake, let's say the moment lasted a couple of hours – I just kept on at him with all the verbals I could. I wanted to undermine him, and it was very noticeable that he was bowling at the Pavilion End, with the wind going to the left-handers' off-side, while Mitchell Starc and Josh Hazlewood were bowling at the Nursery End, where the wind was aiding hits towards the short boundary.

Tactically, Stokes used this to his advantage, targeting that side of the ground for his boundaries when opportunity presented itself and biding his time when it didn't.

'This is interesting, lads, isn't it? You know the captain's bowling the best end. Meanwhile, you guys are stuck down here, taking the punishment. But I'll tell you what, it will be you that gets dropped, not him!'

Each six Ben hit was met by a *woo-hoo* from me at the non-striker's end. One of the sixes felt like it was close to striking Father Time – the famous Lord's weather vane on top of the lift shaft between the Mound and Tavern Stands – and my response to it was an extra-deep exhalation of breath. Despite the highly charged atmosphere, Ben later claimed that was all he could hear. Were the Australians cracking under the pressure? Mitchell Starc's response said so. At one point, he looked straight into my eyes and said, 'Oh, just **** off!'

This was not how I played my cricket throughout my career. I was not a wind-up merchant. Not intentionally at least. A lot of my success was based on me performing rather than derailing the opposition, but on this occasion everything was bubbling up and we were in the ascendancy. It was amazing to be alongside Ben Stokes when he was in one of those moods. Suddenly, I knew exactly how Jack Leach felt when he made Test cricket's most famous one not out in that thrilling victory over Australia at Headingley in 2019.

For the majority of our 108-run stand in 20 overs, the Australians had disappeared. They weren't saying anything.

They were walking around, heads down or staring into the distance, not helping each other at all. Cummins was struck on the hand in his follow-through by a booming drive, and Starc fumbled one over the boundary, the second of three consecutive sixes off Cameron Green that took Stokesy to his hundred. Then Steve Smith put down the only genuine chance offered in the first over after lunch, and for that period of time, despite us still being behind in terms of the match position, I don't think anyone could have argued that this combination of my defiance and Ben's clinical batsmanship and ball striking was not working.

At the start of my innings, I opted for a real over-my-dead-body mentality to my batting. I was determined not to get out before Ben. I will wear it, I thought. I will get hit and there will be bruises. But I will do everything to stop this ball hitting my stumps. My job was to face two balls at the end of the over and block them.

Jimmy Anderson reminded me later that I had done something similar in that Championship match against Lancashire at Trent Bridge, when during the final session of the match I finished unbeaten on three off 50 balls, saying that when he was bowling at me that evening he could tell he was not getting me out. 'You weren't looking to score, you weren't thinking anything about your feet,' he recalled. 'You were just looking at me as if to say: you're not getting past.'

I was going to get peppered regardless of my histrionics, as by this stage in the match everyone knew that the short ball was the most dangerous on a pitch lacking life on a length, and so I wore one on the shoulder, another in the ribs and, as Joe Root thoroughly enjoyed, the middle of the back. It's not a part of the body you normally take a blow as a batter and I am not sure how I got into such a contorted position to do so, but suffice to say I got belted.

At the other end, everything Stokesy tried seemed to come off, with his tactical use of the slope as a left-hander when the ball was moving into him, almost helping it on its way to that side of the ground. However, his undoing came as a result of a drinks break, which gave the Australians a chance to regroup and revise their own game plan.

Following a get-together of their senior players, it appeared they had calculated the need to keep the ball out of Stokes's hitting arc by bowling wider, and in only the second over of the resumption they induced a mistake through its implementation, when Josh Hazlewood angled a delivery across him and wicketkeeper Alex Carey steadied himself under a skier. Hindsight is a wonderful thing and sometimes when you're in such a rhythm it is not necessarily a good move to change things, but with all nine fielders on the boundary, there were singles all around the ground.

It is a pleasure to be out there with Stokesy when he's in one of those moods. I had the best seat in the house. In those situations, he is so clinical in choosing the balls he wants to face and what he wants to do with them. The cleanliness of his striking towards the leg-side can be extraordinary, both hitting sixes over the fielders and placing fours between them. On this occasion, sadly, it would not be in a winning cause.

With Stokes at the crease, and 70 required, England were favourites to win according to WinViz, the match prediction tool used in Sky Sports' commentary, but the balance of probabilities altered drastically with his departure. In the knowledge that there was no longer an onus on simply surviving, my innings of 11 concluded when I helped my 36th ball to fine leg, shortly after Ollie Robinson had departed to another short ball. On a pitch that had proved so tricky to score on whenever the ball was banged into the surface, the result now had an inevitability about it.

Although we were 'off' in delivering our skills, it was not due to a lack of effort, and we showed our willingness to fight on the penultimate day by committing fully to the most hostile form of bowling there is. With Australia holding the advantage, resuming 221 runs ahead with eight second-innings wickets standing that morning, we resorted to a clear and purposeful plan that had some comparing our tactics to the infamous Bodyline series of 1932–33. But with so little to work with in the pitch whenever a seam bowler pitched the ball up, it was a needs-must situation. We had to try eking out as much as we could with the old ball, and that meant reverting to a very deliberate plan of bowling bouncers.

When examining the upturn in fortunes of the England team after Stokes took over as captain, people tended to focus on the exploits of the batters, and how encouraging them to be positive in their stroke play had been key to the transformation. But equally important was the change in the bowling group mentality over my last fourteen months as an inter-national cricketer. Essentially, thoughts about biding time and building pressure, traits encouraged in previous England teams, were consigned to the past and everything was now about taking twenty opposition wickets – something we managed in the first twelve Test matches and a sequence only halted when Ireland batter James McCollum retired hurt in the thirteenth match.

Not that such a pursuit was based on uniformity. As a bowling unit, we were constantly being asked to unearth ways of dismissing opponents taking into consideration the condi-tions. The key to bowling well was to bowl the ball that suits your field. And the field was always one that included fielders in catching positions. Not necessarily conventional ones, but catchers nevertheless.

In this instance, they were put in position for mishit cross-batted strokes as the entire attack – which for a mara-thon spell of 12 overs from the Nursery End was led by Stokes himself – committed to the policy we believed best served our ends in dismissing the opposition. It was a long haul, once again taking us more than 100 overs to bowl Australia out, but we bought into the physical requirements and claiming the final eight wickets for 92 runs was reward for sticking with and fully committing to that plan. It was all very different to our tactical outlook on the first morning.

Sometimes in cricket, though, things don't play out as you might expect. The atmospheric conditions on the first day at Lord's were almost perfect – as long as you weren't a batter. Walking out to the middle at 9.45 that morning, I was excited and passed Ricky Ponting, who had just done an on-field chat with Sky Sports.

'You've got a spring in your step,' he said.

'These are great days to bowl at Lord's,' I replied, with a glance towards the cloud hanging above us.

Traditionalists would tell you that if a captain has any doubts about what to do when winning the toss at the start of a Test match, they need to think for a second and bat. Those who require further thinking time, take another second – and bat. The historical rule of thumb for a five-day game has been to put runs on the board and dictate the pace of the game, with an added bonus that in the event of the pitch deteriorating, the most difficult time to bat will be in the fourth innings. However, Ben Stokes had shown a willingness to flip such traditional thinking on its head during his initial matches as England captain, inserting the opposition and making use of one of the team's strengths – chasing down scores.

At Edgbaston, he had followed the traditional method of batting first when presented with sunshine, but with the grey overhead that I had alluded to during my brief conversation with Ponting, and the threat of showers and mizzle freshening up the pitch throughout the day, this was a 100 per cent bowl-first decision and so there was only positivity from our team when we won another toss.

Under the circumstances, we were not prepared for what

you would probably have to say was our worst day of this Ashes summer. It had a stop-start beginning when, with me preparing to bowl my first ball, a couple of Just Stop Oil protesters attempted to disrupt play by staining the pitch with their orange powder paint. Who knows how long the delay would have been had they succeeded in their quest?

Thankfully, however, there was no need for the contingencies the Lord's ground staff had made in the event of the match pitch being damaged. Further along the square, they had prepared a reserve strip for proceedings to continue on. The increasing number of attempted intrusions at sporting events in the previous weeks had made such a move prudent, but thankfully there was no need and no delay beyond the five minutes it took to restore calm, thanks to the quick-thinking and obstinacy of members of our team.

Pre-match, players from both sides had been advised not to attempt to apprehend pitch invaders, leaving the security personnel to deal with such incidents instead, but Jonny Bairstow is someone who acts impulsively. He had also been more than a little worked up by the actions of the JSO lot a fortnight earlier when, having been sidelined by injury for nine months, they threatened to delay his return with a slow march ahead of our team coach on its way to Lord's for the opening day of the Ireland Test – posting a video on social media to warn people we might be late.

Anyone doubting Jonny's strength should try picking up another man and jogging them 70 yards, as he did. With the accomplice shepherded away from the playing area by Ben Stokes, David Warner and others and apprehended by a net of blue-bibbed security closing on the square, we were back under way once Jonny had returned from a dash into the pavilion to change his soiled shirt.

One of the strengths of this particular bowling group had been to strike when conditions suited, down to sharing information as quickly as possible out in the middle. I owed my five first-innings wickets against Ireland at Lord's earlier in the month to recognising the ball would swing, and with the floodlights on during that opening day it was moving laterally through the air once again. It soon became clear, though, that striking with the new ball was imperative, because when it moved off the surface, it did so slowly, making it difficult to force Test match batters into playing a false shot even when it did deviate.

The two early chances we did create went down: Joe Root reprieving Usman Khawaja on one when failing to scoop up a low chance to first slip created by Jimmy Anderson, and then Ollie Pope putting down a thicker edge that would have meant I dismissed David Warner for the eighteenth time in Tests, when he was on 22. We kept the ball full, trying to draw the Australians forward and extract movement, but the zip off the pitch just wasn't there because of the lack of grass, and we got driven more as a group of bowlers than I could recall. Not that myself, Jimmy and Ollie Robinson were enamoured with our own performances, either, as Australia closed day one on 339 for five.

The one bowler who did deserve credit, though, was Josh Tongue. As the senior bowler, I'd had a few conversations with Josh in his debut match against Ireland. I am a big believer in sticking to your strengths when starting off at international level, so I told him to bowl exactly how he would for Worcestershire. I was to learn that he had several strengths, not least adaptability.

It was his first ever game at Lord's, and it is a unique place to bowl because of the famous slope. From the Pavilion End, you can get dragged back into the stumps and it can be very difficult for some people to hold the line outside off stump as a result. Equally, at the Nursery End, you have to fire the ball in at middle stump if you want to challenge the outside edge of the right-hander.

You can get over-emotional and overawed by international cricket, but playing against the Irish was a good way to break Josh in and he showed great temperament and character in response, refusing to worry about going wicketless in the first innings. He simply did everything that captain Ben Stokes asked of him, including roughing up the opposition with some short stuff, and later he gained his rewards with five in the second innings. Here, he produced a couple of Jaffas that shaped through the defences of the Australian openers – Khawaja on the stroke of lunch and Warner after it.

One of the things that convinced us that moving away from the swing policy was the correct course of action was reflecting upon Steve Smith's interview following his innings of 110. Smith averages 73 in Lord's Ashes Tests, and made a comment that it was just about the easiest pitch to drive on that he'd ever experienced. When our top order went out and batted on it next day, they agreed and it was significant that after we progressed to 188 for one in response to Australia's 416, it was Australia's tallest bowler Cameron Green who altered the momentum of things by going to the short stuff and having Ollie Pope caught in the deep.

When Ben Duckett, two runs shy of a hundred, and then Joe Root also departed to cross-bat shots soon afterwards, their feedback was that while from a length they could hit the ball anywhere of their choosing, it was an altogether different proposition when it was clattered in halfway down the track, because some deliveries were coming out of the surface quickly, others slowly, and that made controlling shots quite difficult.

When it comes down to it, Test match cricket is about adapting to the conditions set in front of you, whether they be constant or changing, and the statistics thrown up showed that we had beaten the outside edge thirty times on the opening day, suggesting that despite general dissatisfaction with our performance, we had been unfortunate.

It had been a similar story on the third day when trying to make use of the new ball. But you must also stick to your principles and not base your reflections purely on outcomes, so while we were disappointed with a third-morning session in which we lost six quick wickets for 47 runs, it was partly due to the attacking mindset we had championed – sometimes it will work, sometimes it won't.

Some of the external criticism felt unjust, because although the dismissals that plunged us to 325 all out might not have been conventional ones for Test cricket, you can't cheer when Harry Brook gets 150 on a green pitch versus New Zealand at Wellington and then cry on another occasion when he gets caught in the outfield. The two go hand in hand. Sometimes it can look ugly but it is a process we believed in and one that generally worked. On this occasion, it was not the easiest pitch on which to whack the ball.

Frustration for me came in the form of spending two hours of my Friday evening being checked over in hospital after being struck by a Green bumper that I simply lost sight of. Unfortunately, the ball caught me under the grille, striking me in the neck and going up into my jaw. Although it was sore, I was not too concerned about getting an X-ray until the end of the match, because I was going to be bowling regardless of whether I had a break, but the team doctor Glen Rae was worried about the swelling and the chance of a bleed in the artery, persuading me to seek the all-clear.

I was also disappointed with my reward, or lack of it, at the start of Australia's second innings, because I'd bowled much worse and contributed multiple wickets to the team cause. During an evening session that lasted only an hour due to rain, I was convinced that I had sent Marnus Labuschagne back LBW for 16, but somehow we relinquished the chance to review after comparing it to another shout that umpire Chris Gaffaney had turned down from the ball before tea.

On that occasion, after deliberating whether to review, we opted against, which was shown to be the correct call as the ball was sliding down the leg-side. But, having made a decision to get tighter into the stumps after the interval, when I struck him on the pad again, I knew it was out. I just couldn't get others to believe me. That's how DRS works. Very rarely do we go for it if only one person thinks it is out. Thankfully it didn't hurt us too much because Marnus, who also successfully challenged a leg-before review, chipped one to point soon afterwards.

This was an isolated success, however, and the pursuit of conventional dismissals had come at such a slow rate of return on day three that we changed tack on day four. Anyone who thought we should be bowling Australia out for 160 to get back into the series was being overly optimistic, given that our opponents had their own agenda and were not going to be overly attacking.

In truth, they didn't need to be. They had opened up a 91-run lead on first innings and armed with a 1–0 series lead were intent on playing the long game. In 45 overs of attritional cricket, they lost two wickets and had advanced their advantage to 221. Typically, it drew a proactive response from us. As Australia weren't looking to be positive, we had to be, embarking on a period of relentless short-pitched bowling.

With the scoreboard frozen for periods, we pounded away, hoping to engage the Australian batters in much the same way their bowlers had managed to engage ours the previous day. It did not bring reward initially, but after I had induced a top edge off the previously unflappable Khawaja in my first over of the day, Australia's patience proved thinner.

According to Sky, 98 per cent of our deliveries post-lunch were short, the most concentrated grouping in history, and while some questioned the bouncer barrage ploy, it highlighted the versatility in our approach to finding ways to win. Steve Smith skied one off Tongue. Then I had Travis Head caught at short leg in a flurry of three wickets for 10 runs.

With all the fielders set back in the deep, Australia became strokeless. So I played my own shot to break a 20-over impasse. Cameron Green had been very subdued, and I decided to play on his ego.

'Wow, I'd heard you were an exciting player, but . . . you're boring everyone to death. Listen to how quiet Lord's is. No one's even watching you, you're that lifeless,' I told him.

Soon afterwards he nailed his first pull shot straight to deep square leg.

It might have been physically demanding, leaving us bowlers sore ahead of a three-day turnaround for the third Test in Leeds, but tactically it was the way to go on that pitch and we all bought into it. Typically, Stokesy put in the hard yards too. He is not a captain to ask something of someone he would not do himself and so he kept running in despite discomfort, defying a sore left knee that had limited his capacity as an all-rounder for the best part of a year.

Commitment runs through the England team. Frankly, it was ridiculous that our vice-captain Ollie Pope was out on the field in the second innings at all after damaging his right shoulder in an innocuous manner, diving to make a stop in the covers in the first. The match officials accepted that as it had been an external blow that had forced him off, he could bat in his customary position of three, but it was later suggested after he did so that he would now be expected to field too.

Ollie argued that what he was being asked to do required a completely different physical skill, but was told that England would have to field with ten men if he was not fit enough to be out there – a decision that left him and the rest of us bewildered and angry. Ollie has had surgery previously, after dislocating his left shoulder twice in 2020, but after falling awkwardly for a second time attempting to save runs for the team in this match, he would now require an operation on his right one, ruling him out of the remainder of the series.

Two-fifths of the way through the series, we were hurting as a team, too. Suddenly, our style of play was being put under the microscope by some of the people that had previously championed it. Thankfully, one of the great strengths of the changing room was to stick to our beliefs. Only the opinions of the inner sanctum really mattered to us and we had built enough credit in the bank over the previous thirteen months to know that this adventurous approach paid greater dividends than its more cautious predecessor.

It had worked for us at Edgbaston, where we won pretty much every session apart from the final one. We were ahead of the game, and deserved to win, but Australia to their credit got over the line. At Lord's, they started better with the bat and they out-bowled us. There were no qualms with the result. Until the amazing drama towards the end, which might have seen us pull off another fourth-innings heist, Australia had been on top. They had deserved it.

But the post-match debrief focused on what a difference an individual can make. If Stokes had been out for 10 and we had lost by 300, there would not have been many positives to take with us, but because he had driven the game forward, he'd given us a chance of victory despite everything that had gone before. It made people view things clearly. Although we hadn't been great, we only needed to be slightly better going forward to put a completely different complexion on things. Turning the series around would take some doing, but it felt very plausible nevertheless. We knew we could do better, and the message was that England 3 Australia 2 was still very much on.

Australia must have felt that they had this series nailed down, but we were confident we could win three games back to back. Why? Because we had won three in a row against New Zealand in 2022. We had won 3–0 in Pakistan the previous winter. Our recent history told us it was possible. This had now become a three-match series for us and it was our task to turn up at Leeds three days later and hit the Australians hard.

My own analysis told me something similar. Stokes's brilliant effort with the bat gave us a fighting chance and when you finish a Test match, and lose by 43 runs, you look at everything that has happened and think: where could we have got those 43 from? To be four wickets down for 45 in that second innings and get so close to a target of 371 was very impressive, especially losing Jonny Bairstow in the manner we had.

Ultimately, the match result may have come down to the dismissal of a player who, with his displays of 2022, had shown himself to be the master of the fourth-innings hunt. That grated.

To repeat, it was not the act that annoyed me, it was the fact Australia upheld the appeal. As I say, Pat Cummins is a really great guy and I'd be amazed in years to come, if he doesn't sit back and think, 'I got that one wrong,' even though his bottom line at the time was winning a Test match. The whole thing felt a little underhand, to tell the truth, and if the series needed any more juice, I think that incident provided it.

CHAPTER SIX

ON-FIELD conduct was always important to me, and something that I actively tried to improve after recognising I had overstepped the mark in a Test match against Pakistan at Edgbaston in 2010. Throwing the ball at an opponent was a sign that I was unable to control my emotions fully. Something needed to be done about it.

So, I sought help from Mark Bawden, the England team psychologist, who came up with Warrior Mode, a mindset that I was to slip into every time I walked onto the pitch from the end of that summer to my last as a player. It would develop over time, new things added and others removed when appropriate, but its origin was a set of detailed bullet points reminding me of the need to be fiery and aggressive as a fast bowler, engaging in the heat of the battle, but keeping honour in the fight rather than allowing pure emotion to turn me into a thug.

Channelling things in this prescriptive manner became a necessity when I hurled the ball inappropriately at Pakistan's Zulqarnain Haider on day three of the second Test at

Edgbaston, an action resulting in an ICC code of conduct breach and a £3,000 fine – half of my match fee.

It was an incident born of frustration after Haider had survived a caught-behind appeal on review. Matt Prior, the wicketkeeper, and I were extremely confident, but the nick was too faint to show up on Hot Spot. The throw shortly afterwards struck the Pakistan batter on the shoulder on its way to the intended destination of Matt's gloves. It had been unintentional, coming at the end of the over when the ball was effectively dead, but was wholly inappropriate and I therefore pleaded guilty to the level-two charge laid against me by the match referee Ranjan Madugalle. Even at the age of twenty-four, as an England international I was aware of the need to set good examples and become a role model to others by respecting my opponents.

Dad said that I would not be his son if I wasn't passionate about the game and sometimes that boils over, but I knew that once I crossed the threshold of the boundary rope, sobriety was required. It had not been in supply on this occasion, and I placed it down to an inability to separate my sporting sphere from my personal one.

When Miche, my stepmum, was diagnosed with Motor Neurone Disease the previous year, we had no idea how it would grip her and how quickly it would take effect. I went to the World Twenty20 in the Caribbean in late April 2010, and she looked pretty healthy, but when I came back three weeks later I was stunned at how she had changed. Although she still felt 100 per cent on the inside, she couldn't even crack a smile – striking a victim's body but not their mind is one of the traits of the ghastly condition that took her from us aged sixty, just hours before the Trent Bridge one-dayer against Bangladesh on 8 July.

I was still trying to process Miche's deterioration when I was hit by her death and because Dad and I were in the midst of such busy schedules – he was match referee for the Pakistan v Australia series held in the UK – her funeral was not until after the first Test of four against the Pakistanis in Nottingham. Everything was raw for me. We certainly never expected her to pass away as early as she did. There wasn't time to grieve.

Miche had written a note to say she wanted me to play that game against Bangladesh. She didn't want life to be affected. But I wasn't able to focus on the cricket at all, which was a pretty natural reaction while grieving, and throwing the ball in frustration towards Zulqarnain was a further example of not being able to control my mind at a particular moment.

As I sat with Ranjan Madugalle to discover the terms of the punishment, I wasn't thinking about the discipline or the fine, but the fact that I had lost a bit of control in delivering my skill. I had lost focus on being the best I could be with the ball, and then a couple of overs later I missed a run-out chance.

It also forced me to re-evaluate my behaviour generally and what influenced it. I was never someone to back down if engaged verbally by an opponent, and so I ended up in

Mitchell Johnson's face while batting in the 2009 Ashes Test at Edgbaston.

Teams do tend to target younger players, looking to undermine them in the hope that doing so affects their performance, but I think that was one of my strengths. I did stand up for myself. There were times when it was good to let opponents know you were not going to be a pushover. But there were others when I needed to keep a lid on things or react to situations in different ways, particularly if catches were dropped or a team-mate's misfield had cost a boundary off my bowling. Every bowler suffers from that initial frustration in such instances, but back then I lacked the ability to let it go, instead holding on to it for a whole spell or a full hour, allowing things to fester as a result.

There is no doubt that I used to put too much pressure on myself to take wickets, too, a common trait for a young player trying to get into international teams and stay in them. Cricket is a statistics-based sport and the scoring of runs and taking of wickets is essential to selection. However, if your focus is solely on the end result of the numbers, you cannot relax and being less tense is often what has helped you get into the performance mindset to deliver them. I needed to be less uptight and invest in the process of bowling, taking the evaluation away from outcomes to what was most likely to get me there; things like whether I had created chances, or acted as a leader in the bowling group and performed in a communicative way.

I knew I had to start building a barrier around me to stop these frustrations manifesting themselves on the field. It was a key time, really. In terms of years I was still young, but I was not inexperienced, having accrued 100 caps and taken 200 wickets across Test and one-day international cricket. I just needed to deal better with the ups and downs such a journey presented. Hence, the chats with Mark on how to create a more robust demeanour. Warrior Mode provided a series of checkpoints – reminders to ramp up my emotions to get into the battle and ways to dampen them down if an external issue triggered them.

Essentially, it was designed to create an on-field character that was calm but clinical. The aspiration being that if someone was watching on TV, they wouldn't necessarily know if I had gone for four or dismissed a batter the previous ball. It is not a phrase I like, but I needed to *get into the zone*. To deliver what was required for the team on a more consistent basis.

As I played in all international formats, we also created a variation on the theme: Assassin Mode. Designed for limited-overs cricket, it focused on the process of bowling and personal performance, rather than whatever the batter might be doing. In white-ball matches, where every ball counts, the frustration of going for runs or team-mates misfielding increased, so Assassin Mode concentrated on keeping calm. The red flag was going too far the other way: being too calm and as a result giving off the impression that you didn't care.

Eventually, when white-ball cricket and I separated, the two modes blended into one in an attempt to strike the balance between the best points of each. Whereas Warrior Mode was about being relentless, aggressive and hunting for wickets, one-day plans were often about role clarity in different phases of the game, without becoming a robot.

My ultimate goal in all this, of course, was to turn down the dial in terms of my on-field mannerisms. At the start of a day's play, I would remind myself of the HeartMath – a coherent breathing technique to encourage calm that I incorporated into the pre-ball routine Jeremy Snape had set me as a teenager with Leicestershire – and I would question myself at its end, checking that I had stayed within the parameters of the mode.

Mark also made me consider the kind of individual I was by creating a personal profile that marked me down as 'an adaptable realist'. Someone that liked structure and systematic processes. I had to agree with his assessment. Whenever confronted by a proposed change from a coach, either in technique or tactics, I would always question why. Provide me with evidence, I'd say. I've always been someone who knows the importance of detail within the process.

There was another aspect that was beginning to bug people about my bowling – the 'celebrappeal', a slang cricket term that became synonymous with me. For the uninitiated, it is celebrating a wicket before the umpire has raised his finger to confirm it. Often, it involves a complete disregard for turning around at all, proceeding instead arm aloft to teammates gathered in the slip cordon.

One of the people it bugged happened to be Andy Flower, the England coach. He wanted me to eradicate it ahead of the 2010–11 Ashes tour, so he asked Mark Bawden to come up with a series of preventative measures for me to work on alongside my mindset material. Accepting that it was not a good look, particularly given my dad's standing as an international match referee, I willingly went along with all that was proposed.

Bawds emailed me a four-step plan to tackle the habit, encouraging me to:

1. Get a reference point by accessing video from the team analysts of myself appealing to the umpire.
2. Put an umpire in place every time I bowled in a net session and turn to them whenever I thought the batter was out.
3. Visualise myself running into bowl in a particular Test match or at a particular ground and turning to the umpire, and appealing.
4. Have a visual cue to focus on, e.g. 'look for the umpire's eyes'.

Great in practice, poor in theory. I simply could not kick the habit and so video reels of my best (or worst) instances – depending on your viewpoint – did the rounds on the internet for a decade. Bowling in the nets, the part of turning round in practice was fine, but for those ten seconds on the field when you believe someone is out, I couldn't control my emotions. When the excitement kicked in, that was it. I could not persuade my brain that I needed to turn round if I hit someone on the shin. On every occasion, I would say sorry to those involved.

My dad had warned me about it during that Pakistan series too, yet I was still doing it ten years later when in the COVID summer, I placed him into a compromised position. As an international match referee, he could not sit for England games until that year of 2020 as ICC regulations demanded neutrality. Only the effects of the pandemic changed that and he was therefore appointed for a home series against West Indies, in which I performed my trademark transgression of article 2.1 in the ICC Code of Conduct, which forbids 'celebrating a dismissal without appealing to the umpire when a decision is required'.

I was bowling with the wind going across the ground at Old Trafford, and I was bowling outside off stump to Roston Chase. I'd been talking to Chris Woakes at mid-off about replicating the tactics that he had employed to Chase in the previous Test, bringing the batter across his crease with a wider line, before firing in a slightly quicker one that came back in. For nine deliveries, Woakes kept telling me 'patience, patience', and so when I tried it and it hit the pad, I got carried away. When a plan comes together like that, it's a slightly different level of excitement.

Umpire Richard Kettleborough gave Chase out, but only after my celebrations had begun and it led to a bit of a nervous wait. It wasn't one of my favourite moments, but I think Richard and Dad gave me the benefit of the doubt on this occasion. Or like everyone else, they'd simply given up on me changing!

One thing I would never apologise for is showing natural passion, because I would hate to think someone was watching me and thinking: I could do better in that shirt. We're all fans at the end of the day and one of my pet hates when I watch my favourite sports teams like Nottingham Forest, Leicester Tigers or the England rugby team, is saying of a player: tackle, chase back, run. Those things should be an absolute given in top-flight sport, so I was always conscious of projecting my effort levels, never being someone who just swanned around.

If people didn't regard me as the player to throw the first punch, at least I wanted to look as if I was punching back. The sports players I loved watching as a kid were like that. The Forest and England footballer Stuart Pearce would give every last ounce of energy he had to prevent the opposition prospering and drive his own team forward. And you always knew what Martin Johnson, the Leicester and England captain, was about when he ran out with a rugby ball under his arm. I used to love sports people who not only refused to shy away, but would actually instigate things. I would hope as you share this journey with me now, you do not have a memory of me when you thought: Come on, Broady, put in!

To be honest, I never cared what opponents thought of me – as long as they knew they'd been in a scrap. I suppose that was how I wanted the teams I played in to be like, too. The bare minimum was to compete, and I never wanted a county team to come to Trent Bridge and think Nottinghamshire were an easy team to play against. We had occasions particularly during the 2019 season when we became that team. It was really frustrating, not least because I couldn't put my finger on why.

Once I crossed the white line, I would much rather be thought of as a horrible team to play against than a nice one and, on an individual level, I wasn't bothered if Michael Clarke or Ricky Ponting were going around making it known I was a bit of a prat, as long as they were also saying, 'He's always at us, he's always on the money. He's always coming for us.'

Until Edgbaston, I had cried only once while wearing an England shirt. Dealing with injury is a fast bowler's lot, but its wicked nature, striking sometimes without warning and often at the most inopportune moments, leave emotions susceptible. This was the case when I tore an abdominal muscle during the Adelaide Test of the historic 2010–11 Ashes series in Australia, when England won 3–1. It was devastating.

We had travelled to Australia with extremely high hopes of becoming the first England team to win an away Ashes since my dad was Man of the Series in 1986–87, and for good reason. We had a settled, winning team and our coach Andy Flower and his coaching staff had planned meticulously. Australia, in a rebuilding phase and uncertain of their best squad let alone best XI, were there for the taking and here we were in the second Test pushing for the victory that would put us into a 1–0 lead.

We had batted brilliantly, Alastair Cook scoring a hundred and Kevin Pietersen a massive 227, helping to open up a

375-run lead on first innings before declaring. I was bowling at third-wicket pair Michael Clarke and Shane Watson, in what was effectively my second spell following eight overs with the new ball split by a change of ends. In the first few deliveries, it felt like I was developing a stitch, but over the next two overs the discomfort got worse, to the point where it felt as if I had taken a heavyweight's punch to the ribs. At the drinks break, with Australia 120 for two and my figures reading 11–3–32–0, I walked off the field feeling over-emotional.

The heat was ferocious. Pouring with sweat, feeling all bowled out and in pain, I lifted my shirt as I walked through the long tunnel to the dressing room that gives Adelaide its unique character. There was already a residue of blood gathering in my side. When I showed Dr Nick Peirce my bruise moments later, he didn't say anything. He didn't need to, his look said it all. His experience told him what it meant. He wrapped me in his arms and I burst into tears. I was twenty-four years old and I knew this monumental tour was over for me before the obligatory scan confirmed ten weeks on the sidelines.

As my team-mates set off on a race to take the six final-day wickets required before the rain came – something they narrowly managed – I was coming to terms with my Ashes dreams developed over time being destroyed in a heartbeat. Was I ever going to play in Australia again? Who knew? And with the proud history of my dad, it really meant something to be there.

Sport then showed how brutal it can be when Phil Neale, our extremely efficient team manager, handed me details of my flight home in two days' time – Wednesday, 8 December. Wow, I thought. We haven't finished the Test yet and they've already booked me a seat on the plane. I got it. I was no use to the team any more, they weren't going to carry me around as a tourist, so they were packing me off. But I didn't feel ready to go, so stayed out for the third Test in Perth to do some media work. If I had left in the immediacy of the devastation, it would have had more deep-rooted effects.

Back home, I stayed at Dad's on Christmas night, stay-ing up to watch the Boxing Day Test, and it was that real throwback-to-childhood feeling. Nottingham, three degrees outside, but having started the series as one of the twenty-two players, it didn't possess the magical allure I felt as a kid. In fact, it was quite a lonely place now, and although I was excited when I woke up the following week to watch my team-mates celebrating the retention of the Ashes on a pres-entation stage in Sydney, having achieved the collective goal, personally, sitting on my own in the pitch-black on the other side of the world, it felt soulless.

BBC News asked me to go on the television to talk about the series win, but I couldn't. That wasn't me being selfish. It is what happens. If you have put everything in to be involved and then you're not, no matter how exciting it is for the team or the country, the achievement loses its lustre. Personal disappointment at missing out is natural. Jimmy Anderson had endured the same kind of experience earlier in the year when we won the final of the World Twenty20 in Barbados. All he wanted to do was go home and play for Lancashire.

During this unpleasant experience, I got lots of messages of support and good wishes. One more significant than the rest.

Pre-Ashes, I had done a sponsor's event and although it sounds outdated, I was asked to name someone I fancied. I said Mollie King from the girl group The Saturdays, not thinking too much of it. As fate would have it, the same PR firm was doing something with Mollie soon after I was injured and one of their employees recalled what I'd said. So one of their team asked Mollie if she would mind sending me a quick 'Get well soon' video message – something Mollie did without connecting who I was. It was the first time she'd heard my name. But it stuck in her head.

A few months later, out of the blue, she sent me a happy birthday message, telling me I shared it with her mum, Sue. It led to us chatting a bit, and we went on a few dates in late 2012, and spent New Year's Eve together in London with a group of her friends and a group of mine.

Typical of young professionals, though, we were all over the place. In early 2013, I flew off to India for some one-dayers and then on to New Zealand. Mollie went to film in Los Angeles, and despite really enjoying each other's company, being at opposite ends of the world didn't help us stay in touch. It is fair to say we were two people putting their careers first at that stage in our lives. I would never have guessed how big an impact she would have later on mine, not only as my partner and mother of Annabella, but my cricket, helping to alleviate pressure in my final five years with England.

Not long since returning to fitness, after missing the final three Ashes Tests and one-day series that followed, I was playing golf at Stapleford Park in Leicestershire when I got a call from Geoff Miller, the chairman of selectors, saying he wanted to offer me the captaincy of England's Twenty20 team. I was like, 'Oh, okay.' Without sounding disrespectful, I wasn't particularly buzzing with the news because it was never a goal of mine.

Later, I considered that the best man for the job had been overlooked. Having won a T20 World Cup in 2010, England's first ever global trophy, Paul Collingwood should have been given the right to defend the title as captain two years later. Collingwood had retired from Test cricket in January 2011, following the Ashes, and there was clearly a breakdown in communications, because this decision was made with a view to extending his white-ball career. Now, he had effectively been given the boot. If I had my time again, I would turn it down.

Along with a few other players, including Alastair Cook who would be appointed ODI captain on the same day of 4 May 2011, I had gone to Loughborough University a few weeks previously for what you might call leadership conversations. The decision of Andrew Strauss to stand down as ODI captain to focus on his Test career began the shuffling of the deck, and made all this necessary. It was the first instance of England having three different captains simultaneously. 'We don't know a hundred per cent whether it will work and be the most efficient system, but we're going to give it a try,' England coach Andy Flower said.

When asked about how I viewed things panning out, I spoke about the three captains creating a great synergy. We created nothing of the sort. The team I led on twenty-seven occasions between 2011–15 – winning 11, losing 15, with one no-result – could not have been any more like an addendum. Games were played every four months, and then we got a World Cup lobbed at us somewhere in the schedule, with no real opportunity to create any style of play or team culture in-between. A lot of the T20 series I captained were latched on to the end of a Test series, when everyone was exhausted. It should never have been split three ways, it should have been a two-way split like it later became under Eoin Morgan.

I'd had no leadership training and I struggled. I was twenty-four, hadn't captained since my early days at secondary school, and I was no Graeme Smith. Of course, saying no to the offer of a leadership position is not the done thing, but I had to 'manage up' and didn't have much of an influence. I wasn't even sure of the player I wanted to be, let alone the team I wanted to lead when I took over, and the fact I was not an official selector only added to the frustration. The best way I can describe the experience is to say it was like being made managing director of a business and not really being sure what the business was, or given your preferred staff.

Ahead of the 2014 World Cup, for example, I wanted Kevin Pietersen in the squad and was categorically told I couldn't have him. KP had been in that set-up the whole time I was captain. To me, it was illogical not to take him to a T20 World Cup. It was also a learning experience for me, because after making a strong pitch for his selection in a meeting with the ECB's director of cricket Paul Downton and James Whitaker, the chairman of selectors, telling them it made no sense to overlook our best player, especially when availability was limited due to injuries, I was met by a brick wall.

I knew there had been a breakdown in Pietersen's relationship with the England Test coach Andy Flower, but that had nothing to do with me. The first I'd heard about him getting sacked was on BBC News, and as far as I was concerned it was someone else's fall-out, not mine. The Twenty20 team had its own coach in Ashley Giles, who handled KP well, and I saw no reason why he wouldn't be on that plane to Bangladesh. Unfortunately, others did.

My appointment as England captain in one format provided a guaranteed place in the side. Ironically, it came at a time when I became less certain of it in another. The previous winter's Ashes mission had been completed successfully by a seam bowling attack of Jimmy Anderson, Chris Tremlett and Tim Bresnan, with that most brilliant of spin foils in Graeme Swann. But I knew I had credit in the bank as soon as I returned to full fitness. I had never let the team down and it was injury rather than a dip in performance that had knocked me out of it.

By midsummer 2011, however, we entered a five-match series against India with a leading topic in the media agenda being: will Stuart Broad retain his place? Was it time to move in a different direction?

How had it come to this? Simple, really. I'd been given a new role and one that I had neither been overly comfortable with or successful in delivering. I had taken eight wickets in three Tests against Sri Lanka as the attack's enforcer. The team management wanted to use my extra height in a new way, but banging the ball halfway down the pitch upset me more than the opposition batters it was supposed to. It didn't come naturally to me at all, even though it had been something I'd been asked to do in one-day cricket.

The day before we started the first Test against India, England captain Andrew Strauss came up to me on the Lord's balcony and said that he wanted to get rid of any doubts I had about my place in the team. I was going to play. That was good to hear, as I felt nervous and under pressure, but I now saw the opportunity to address the elephant in the dressing room. My enforcer tag had to be canned.

Back at Nottinghamshire, Andre Adams, the New Zealand international and a high-class technician when it came to the art of bowling, had challenged me about my displays against the Sri Lankans, reminding me what I did at my best – target the stumps. I had to be in and around them, he argued, as that was my strongest skill set. Yes, adapt to the situation of the game, but live and die by trying to be the best version of yourself, not the best version of someone else. The kind of job spec I was trying to form has only been mastered by one man, Neil Wagner, and at 5ft 9ins, there was a lot less of him to chug around for what is an incredibly demanding job physically.

Now, when I told Strauss I wanted to get up on length, he simply said, 'Yeah, bowl where you want.'

Gautam Gambhir chopped on to get me going and I never looked back, taking 25 wickets at 13.84 runs in a 4–0 white-wash of a strong Indian side, a statistic that combined with 182 runs saw me claim the Man of the Series award. Any young cricketers reading this should be aware that while you always have to adapt to what the team needs, being very clear what your own strength is can be such a positive thing.

My spot was in doubt and I was very strong. If they were going to leave me out after the first Test at Lord's, I wanted it to be because I had lived and died by my own sword. Gone out on my terms. Yes, there were times in my career when I was encouraged to bowl full and was reluctant. Was I stuck in my ways? Joe Root would say, yes, after he took over in 2017. I would say, no. So, that's probably a yes. But I always preferred working to a method that I believed worked for me.

I had developed my best training routine by the age of twenty-five, too. Previously, I did all the generic gym sessions recommended for batters and bowlers alike, but as I never liked heavy weights, had suffered a couple of issues with my side and due to my size was not overly mobile, squatting hurt my back and my hips. So I completely eradicated it from my fitness regime and placed the most essential ingredient of fast bowling, running, at its core. Credit to the fitness trainers the ECB employed over the years, because they were great with this and never forced me to do anything I didn't want to, trusting that I knew my own body.

Some players were keen on yoga for a while, and I joined in alongside Nick Compton and Will Jefferson on an England A tour of Bangladesh, but my willingness to experiment away from my staple routine was diluted when I saw team-mates pick up injuries trying different training techniques. I saw only risk in trying to force my body into unnatural positions.

My genes helped me too. As part of the ECB's research into the effects of fast bowling on the body, I underwent a DEXA scan, which revealed that my bone density was in the top 1 per cent of human beings. The equivalent of an Olympic weightlifter. I never had a stress fracture of the back. I can't think of many other seamers able to say the same.

Experience also tells you to spot the danger signs that a problem lies ahead. Fast bowlers play very few games at 100 per cent fit and you have to learn to manage your body, listen to what it is telling you and understand what you can push and what you can't physically.

Following that amazing Test series against India, we made a typically headlong dash into five one-day internationals against the same opponents, and we turned up at Lord's for the penultimate fixture on the back of just one day's rest. I was warming up by bowling a few balls into a mitt worn by Ben Langley, the England physio, when I felt something pinching in my shoulder. Ben asked me to explain the pain to him and started poking around when I showed him where it was emanating from.

I tried to shake it off and thought I would be okay. I could turn my arm over, but Ben questioned whether at 2–0 up in the series, it was worth the risk. Ten minutes before the toss, he called over Andy Flower, the head coach. I explained to Andy that it felt like something was nipping in my arm when I bowled.

His response was a terse, 'Are you fit to play for your country?'

'Yeah. I'm good. I'm fit to play for my country,' I said.

It was a tough question to ask a 25-year-old who had never hidden his passion of playing for England, and probably not the one to ask. But Andy was a tough taskmaster. I was never someone who pulled out of games, so of course I was going to say I was fit to play. It should have been a bit more considered, and probably would have been but for the proximity to the toss when it is panic stations, but I think I would not have played if Ben Langley, very much a caring man for his players, had got his way.

Adrenaline got me through until the final over of India's innings, when I bowled a wide yorker to Mahendra Singh Dhoni second ball and my lat muscle blew off the bone. I immediately left the field grabbing my arm, and Steven Finn sent down the last four deliveries to complete things. The pain was something never to forget. When I got in my car that evening, after a Ravi Bopara-influenced tied match, I went to close the door and that simple motion of pulling was absolute agony.

Medical advice was that it did not require surgery, and the only England action I missed was the final game of the series in Cardiff, as there was no cricket scheduled until a New Year tour of the United Arab Emirates to face Pakistan four months later. I was lucky, because on the rare occasions I did pick up a serious injury, a quiet spell tended to follow.

However, the bottom line was I should not have played. This was an example of me getting things wrong and it was a learning experience, because I became conscious of the difference between just feeling sore from bowling and the start of something with the potential to put you out of action.

I was even able to share the knowledge in this regard – a classic example being Mark Wood at the Wanderers on the 2019–20 tour of South Africa. He was sore, but talking to him it became clear over the space of a couple of days it was only a case of DOMS (delayed onset muscle soreness) from having played a Test match in Port Elizabeth the previous week. We all know that feeling, after you have done a workout or gone for a blitz on the bike, and wake up for the next day or two regretting it. This was one of those. He played, took nine wickets and claimed the Player of the Match award in victory. Bowling is a bit like lifting weights at the gym – something you need to do regularly to harden your body to its rigours. In that instance against India, I should have known that at the end of a long summer of seven Test matches and four ODIs, it wasn't DOMS.

Sometimes, though, getting your head around not being injured is hard. Like on the historic 2012–13 Test series win in India. We played a warm-up game at a new stadium in Navi Mumbai. Footholes out there can become quite crumbly and on this occasion it was creating a sizeable crater. Naturally, I began jumping wider on the crease to avoid it, only to be slightly off on one occasion, landing half in and half out as a result.

Any bowler that's bowled a lot would have suffered from a bruised heel and by the end of the day's play it was agony for me. Boots off, I couldn't put my left foot down on the floor, so I ended walking on my toes. Two days later, I went for a scan and nothing showed up, so I just cracked on, rubbing Voltarol gel on it to numb it, hoping the bruise would disappear over time. I've always had a good pain threshold. One of the best, I'd say, but I was struggling big time.

My impact in the games was zero, basically because I couldn't slam my foot down. Mentally you lose confidence in a situation like this. Picture yourself running in at about 80 per cent of your top speed and landing on an upside-down plug every time you release the ball. It doesn't take very long to lose the confidence of what you're actually bowling. All you're thinking about is that imaginary plug.

Wicketless in two Tests, the second of which also featured me battling a stomach bug, I got dropped for the third in

Kolkata. Alastair Cook, the recently appointed captain, was shaking as he pulled me aside the day before to break the news. He needn't have worried. It was the right decision. The spinners Graeme Swann and Monty Panesar were the main threats and Jimmy Anderson was more effective than me, because he swung the ball and was skiddier off the pitch. Steven Finn offered extreme pace.

When we got to Nagpur, where the task was to protect or improve upon a 2–1 lead, bowling in the nets was killing me. Even walking on the marble floor of my hotel bathroom was agony. I needed a secondary scan and because we were due to fly back on Christmas Eve, it was decided I would leave the Test early and get one done back in the UK before everything shut down for the festive period.

So I left after day two, got home and had the scan, and received a report informing me that I'd split my fat pad in half. The specialist had only seen it before in a water skier who landed funny. I taped my left ankle for the rest of my career, partly due to stabilisation, but it also brought my fat pad together to hold it as one. From the tour of New Zealand that followed in 2013, I also began wearing thick inner soles in my boots, which the All Blacks player Josh Kronfeld helped to design.

Let me share a secret. If Andy Flower called, I never answered the phone. I found him very intimidating, and I know others like Matt Prior and Jimmy Anderson felt the same. There was no lack of respect for him. He just had that old-school, football manager image. He wasn't a matey coach like Brendon McCullum, but he was brilliantly successful. Andy was a hard man. Few cricketers would have been brave enough to take a stand mourning the death of democracy in Robert Mugabe-led Zimbabwe, as he did alongside team-mate Henry Olonga at the 2003 World Cup.

He was also fiercely loyal. I felt like his player. I'm sure Manchester United players felt similarly about Sir Alex Ferguson. I would run through a brick wall for him. If I was wronged, he would back me up all the way, as I was to find out during the year of 2013, when an incident I had initially barely given a second thought to escalated out of control.

Ashton Agar, Australia's left-arm spinner, was bowling over the wicket to me in the Trent Bridge Ashes Test that summer and I got a fine edge that flicked off wicketkeeper Brad Haddin's glove end and thigh to Michael Clarke at slip. Australia didn't have any reviews left. Aleem Dar, the umpire, said not out and it didn't even cross my mind to walk off the field.

Why would I? Was I different to anyone else? There were multiple examples of players standing their ground across that series and the 2013–14 Ashes that followed, including Brad Haddin for the decisive wicket in the same match, when it took a review to confirm he had inside-edged off Jimmy Anderson and England had won by 14 runs.

It is a player's prerogative to allow the officials on the field to make the decision. In the circumstances, it was insane that my inaction should get all the attention. So, why did it become a thing? I put it down to the fact it was a month before the Premier League season re-started and as the only major sporting event in town, it had attracted the chief sports writers of the British press to Nottingham. I don't think any regular cricket writer would have criticised the decision and made it as big a story as it became. They would not have taken it out of proportion.

I would later develop a very good relationship with Oliver Holt, but at the time, writing in the *Daily Mirror*, he compared my actions of standing there and awaiting the judgement of the match officials to those of Lance Armstrong, who openly admitted to long-term cheating through the use of performance-enhancing drugs earlier in the year. Lance Armstrong? Cheating? That upset me.

I would come to have a good relationship with Ollie, because he later apologised and I respected him for that, but he was my number one bullseye target on a dartboard for a long time. He hurt me. But the level of criticism of which that was a part was so strong that even ten years later, with everything else I have done in Ashes matches, people in Australia still think about me for not walking.

Thousands of players through the history of the game have been involved in letting the umpire make a decision and yet this became a major thing in my life for quite a long period of time, and got considerably worse after the Australian coach Darren Lehmann went on Triple M, an Australian radio station, urging fans down under to make my life hell when we toured the following winter. He was here in England talking late at night to a breakfast show in Australia, and everything was taken in black and white by the listeners. It might have been meant in a humorous way – in the name of that neolithic beast 'banter' – but it added a lot of fuel to that fire.

'From my point of view, I hope the Australian public give it to him from the word go, for the whole summer. I hope he cries and goes home,' Lehmann said to hee-haws down the line, after one of my better career performances helped plunge his team from 174 for three to 224 all out at Chester-le-Street, and a defeat that ensured the urn would be in our keeping when we travelled that winter.

Relations were somewhat strained between English and Australian cricketers that summer following the first meeting of the teams at Edgbaston. We beat Australia by 48 runs in a Champions Trophy match at Edgbaston, and headed out for a few drinks in the Walkabout bar in Birmingham. The Aussies were there as well, and it got a bit late. My friend and former team-mate Harry Gurney always says nothing good happens after midnight and this was a couple of hours after midnight.

A green and gold Afro-style wig was being passed around the venue and people would dance with it on. A group of us were at the bar and Joe Root had it on his head, pulling it this way and that. David Warner, maybe meant as a joke, grabbed the elastic band under the chin and twanged it. Then, seconds later, he threw a punch that caught Rooty on the jaw. I was half a yard away. Thankfully, Clint McKay was also on the scene, because he is also well over six foot tall. He grabbed Warner and dragged him one way. I grabbed Rooty and dragged him the other.

It was a decent clonk. Not enough to knock him down or anything, but enough to really shock you after a few beers. Outside, Rooty was pretty emotional about things, like: 'What the hell just happened?'

I had recently secured Blackberrys for a number of us, as a friend of mine worked for them, and in his anger, Rooty threw his straight against the brick wall that faced us. 'No! Not the phone!' I yelled, as it shattered.

We disappeared back into the team hotel, 150 yards away, and were told next morning by our bosses to keep this kerfuffle under wraps. No one was going to hear about this, they said. We weren't to tell a soul. It was to be under the radar. A day later, it was in all the newspapers. Australia disciplined Warner, banning him for the rest of the Champions Trophy and the two Ashes warm-up matches. They also fined him £7,000.

Andy Flower, disgusted that an opposition coach could say such things about one of his players, wanted the same Cricket Australia hierarchy to take action on Darren Lehmann. So, he demanded a meeting with David Collier and Giles Clarke, the chief executive and the chairman of the ECB respectively, at the end of day one of the fifth Test at The Oval.

Up in the boardroom, Andy told them he could not let an opposing coach speak about one of his players like that. We needed an official apology from Cricket Australia. It got a bit heated, because the ECB clearly did not want to damage relations between the two boards. Andy let them know he couldn't give two hoots about CA, and that a lack of action was damaging relationships 'with my player; with your player'.

Lehmann was fined 20 per cent of his match fee by the International Cricket Council for making inappropriate comments, and apologised to me, explaining it was in jest, but faced no further censure.

It probably wouldn't have crossed my mind before Andy told me he wanted to get me a public apology, but not receiving one pissed me off. A few of the Australian players – Shane Watson, Mitchell Johnson, Ryan Harris among them – came to me that week and said they were so sorry, that what had been said was an absolute disgrace. It wasn't what the team thought.

That week on home soil passed calmly enough, but I had to contend with all sorts of nonsense in Australia. It was a disastrous tour from a team perspective, and contained some pretty unsavoury moments if your name was Stuart Broad, but it might surprise you to learn that I didn't find it as difficult as you might imagine on a purely personal level. Why? Because in anticipation of being abused, I had trained for it.

In the warm-up games at Alice Springs, Sydney, Hobart and Perth, I would walk laps of the ground with the sports psychologist Mark Bawden to prepare for when the real stuff began. The theory went that if you are playing in a packed 45,000-capacity stadium, you don't hear the individual abuse. The majority of the time it's just collective noise, but the kind of attendances that tour matches attract in Australia guaranteed individual shouts of, 'Oi, Broad, ya Pommie cheat,' being audible. I would become conditioned to it. Not let it rile me if my brain did process personalised shouts.

I knew it was coming my way from ball one at the Gabba. It would have been naive to think I wasn't going to get stick. But my training worked. I got six-for and took great pleasure in holding up the ball and showing it to the crowd when I reached the five-wicket mark on the opening day.

It still had an intimidatory factor, though. Never more so than, for the second consecutive Ashes Test in Brisbane, I found myself walking out to bat on a hat-trick. Four years earlier, I was one of the victims of Peter Siddle, and now I downed a can of Red Bull as the decision on Matt Prior, caught down the leg-side off Nathan Lyon, was reviewed. Come on, I thought, I need a pre-innings boost to get going. The boos were unbelievable now it was just me on my own. Wow. On the ring entrance four years earlier, I imagined the ground was shaking. That the crowd were singing: 'Kill, Kill, Kill.' It felt gladiatorial. Psychologically living up to its Gabbatoir nickname. I wasn't focused on the right thing. Siddle hit me on the toe and I was out.

Make sure you watch the ball, I thought. Bat on ball, I thought. I am so focused, I told myself. So focused that when Lyon bowled a wide one and I left it outside off stump, I didn't merely inquire, 'What the hell was that?' I literally shouted it, gesticulating with arms outstretched. Joe Root giggled at the other end, and Lyon sort of backed away like I was slightly mad. Australia had the last laugh, though, by refusing to relinquish the grip that they established from the second day of the series onwards.

Throughout the tour there were loads of instances of me coping with it, but the best from an individual came in Melbourne. Mum was with me. These T-shirts emblazoned with the slogan 'Stuart Broad's a sh*t bloke' were being distributed everywhere and walking past the Botanical Gardens to the England team hotel on Christmas Eve, I could see this fella walking towards me in the distance who was wearing one. Bright yellow, with green writing, you couldn't mistake them for anything else.

Oh, no. I don't want someone to abuse me when I'm with my mum, I thought.

I'm dressed casually, cap and shorts, flip-flops, and when we got up close, he addressed us.

'Excuse me, mate,' he says. 'Do you know where the entrance to the gardens is?'

'Yeah, sure. Just over there.'

'Cheers, buddy.'

He had absolutely no idea who I was, and that was a really good thing for me, because I was like, people aren't buying these T-shirts or people aren't in the crowd genuinely believing I am a sh*t bloke. It is only sports fans being sports fans. Shepherded into doing the same thing as the person sat next to them.

At the start of that tour, I sat in the Hobart changing rooms. Michael Carberry was doing cricket impressions in the corner, it was raining and I was reading a book by Sir Alex Ferguson.

In one passage, he talked about Patrick Vieira playing at Old Trafford, making the point that if the crowd don't fear you, they leave you alone, but if they feel you've got a bit about you and you can hurt their team, they come after you. I read it and thought: that's me.

I basically flipped Lehman's comments and the boos into being positive, which sounds very egotistical – but that's how I protected myself. During that first Test, the *Courier Mail*, Brisbane's local newspaper, refused to use my name. Under the headline 'The Phantom Menace', they carried a front-page story that told readers: 'England medium pace bowler skittles Aussies.' They whited-out my face in pictures. That week, I walked into a press conference with a copy of the *Courier Mail* tucked under my arm, as if to say: 'Is that all you've got?'

Psychologically, this kind of behaviour was good for me, but we struggled badly as a team thanks to the most influential performance of any series in which I played. That is pretty high praise. I played in fifty-five all told. We simply couldn't find an answer to Mitchell Johnson. In five matches, he took 37 wickets. He terrorised us with his pace and hostility.

He actually bowled like a drain first up, but after he had Jonathan Trott strangled down the leg-side just before lunch on day two, he steamrollered us. The chat in our camp from experienced players like Ian Bell was that the Gabba had almost slicked up a bit, so I knew he was going to be quick the first time I faced him. Left-arm, around the wicket, he bowled me this bouncer that flicked the metal grip earpiece on the outside of the helmet. Dink. The ball had flown past.

Oh my God, I thought.

I hadn't even had time to react. It wasn't like I saw it and swayed. The ball was upon me before any instinct to get out the way had kicked in. I looked down to the shiny surface below, that he was skidding these devilish deliveries off, and considered that I wasn't good enough to cope. I actually ended up scoring more runs (32) and facing more deliveries (45) than all of my team-mates barring Carberry, although it required two helmet changes.

Johnson was by far the most intimidating fast bowler I ever faced. Awesome. Ian Bell and Kevin Pietersen said it was rapid and I didn't have their skill set. To this day, Joe Root would tell you that Johnson is the quickest he's faced.

And we lost one of our best players of express pace when Jonathan Trott quit the tour due to a stress-related illness. Jimmy Anderson, Graeme Swann and I were in the changing room taking tape off our feet when Trotty went out to bat in the second innings crying. We all looked at each other, as if to say: Did you see that?

He was caught hooking soon afterwards, his last act of the trip. I was great mates with him. Still am. Love him to bits. We regularly played FIFA against each other. Yet I had no idea of the suffering that went on inside his hotel room. Some things are way more important than cricket, but we lost a gun player with his departure. One of the few with the ability to stop the Johnson onslaught carrying Australia to a 5–0 whitewash.

* * *

A blood-curdling blow from a fast bowler in the summer of 2014 severely reduced my capacity as a batter for several years of my career. Before being struck in the face by India's Varun Aaron in the penultimate Test of the 2014 summer, I averaged 24. Afterwards 13.

I came out after lunch on the third day at Old Trafford and struck my first two balls for six, but when Aaron switched to an over-the-wicket line, I lost sight of the ball and when it appeared again, it was almost upon me. It was as if time slowed down after the ball struck the top edge of my attempted pull and careered through my grille. Initially, I felt no pain whatsoever. To the extent that I twizzled and thought: where has that hit me?

My whole face was numb, but I couldn't feel a thing and, head bowed, I could see blood pouring from somewhere. Virat Kohli was first on the scene. The Indians were amazing. Highly caring opponents.

'Take your helmet off,' Kohli said.

'I'm fine,' I said. 'But have I still got teeth?'

The swelling made itself known as Craig de Weymarn and Rob Young, the England team physio and doctor respectively, came running out. They had clearly not finished lunch, because I could see food in their mouths as they chatted, explaining that I would be going off. The worst bit of all was getting into the changing room and the doc doing a quick stitch-up job to get me to a hospital. Again, I couldn't feel much, but my head was being tugged about like a rag doll.

As it was a Saturday, it turned into a shambles of an afternoon and I was thankful the ex-England physio Dave 'Rooster' Roberts came in to take charge of the situation. A lot of consultants at private hospitals were off, but he got me in his car and drove around, using his local knowledge to get me in front of a specialist. By the time we had found one, and I'd been checked over, the game was over. I was sitting in a waiting area when Rooster received a text telling him that I had been named Player of the Match for my six for 25 in the first innings. India had been bowled out for a second time in just 43 overs.

I was told that I'd got two broken cheekbones and a flattened nose, basically. The only advice I received in the immediate aftermath was to sleep upright that night in my Lowry Hotel room, propped up with cushions. Oh, and I had to call the doctor at 7 a.m. to confirm I was still alive. Pretty old-school, huh? I woke up with what felt like the biggest hangover of all time, without the pleasure of having a drink. Heading down to breakfast, I didn't want to open my eyes because the pain in my head was so sharp. I had to wear a Batman-style ice mask that pulsated in an attempt to reduce the swelling in my face.

Concussion was not a discussion topic at the time, so the main objective was to get me fixed as best as possible to play the next game. I had proper panda eyes and stitches down the nose, but I was given the all-clear. The only subsequent advice I received came from a specialist the day before the Oval Test match. He told me and Mark Wotherspoon, another of the ECB doctors, that the nose needed re-breaking to be reset, and it would require a hammer and chisel procedure immediately after the match finished.

Thinking about that process, and the pain I was still suffering, I couldn't accept it. I asked the doc how vital it was. Would it affect my breathing? No. But it might leave me with a slightly bent nose. I took the bent nose.

I got 37 off 21 balls, swinging from the hip in our only innings at The Oval in a match in which we clinched a huge victory and 3–1 win, but I felt nervous batting in an international for the first time and I really didn't want to be there.

The problem was exacerbated, however, after undergoing the knee surgery I had been booked in for earlier in the summer. I was a bit drowsy afterwards, had some painkillers to help my recovery and reduce swelling, and felt quite ropey for a couple of days. It was the start of some very weird episodes for me. I would jolt awake at night disturbed by visions. If you've ever been on a long-haul flight and got the nodding dog on, you will know something of the experience. A reflex kick of the legs and you come round. Every time I did, I would see that cricket ball hitting me between the eyes. I was haunted by it for months.

If I had just played on, I'd have been fine, I think, but stopping because of my knee meant I couldn't get back on the horse straightaway. By the time I got back to picking up a bat three months later, my feelings of 'I don't really want this' had grown even stronger.

It was not something I would ever have told a coach, but

facing Tim Southee when he took seven England wickets in Wellington during the 2015 World Cup, it felt like I'd never held a bat before. He was looking to pitch the ball up and swing it, but all I could think was, it's going to hit me. I just couldn't see it and, in no position to play any kind of strike, I was caught at mid-off from a leading edge. Batting at numbers 9 and 10 during a warm-up triangular involving Australia and India the previous month, I had faced three balls across the first three matches, and Mitchell Starc yorked me first game of the World Cup. I never got any rhythm. It wasn't as if I could go back into County Championship cricket and bat for an hour.

Before you get the wrong idea, it was not a case of being a scaredy-cat. I never lacked bravery. I just completely lost the batting process of being able to get my head towards the ball. I couldn't bring myself to make that forward defensive shape. Sadly, it remained that way for the rest of my career. Yes, I found a way to have an impact on games, but I lost something of my previous ability and it definitely changed me as a player.

When I started out with England, people would say that I was a proper batter, or certainly had the potential to be one. I would make the cut in bowling attacks because of my batting. But all that over-egged the pudding, to be honest. I was a decent number 8. No better. Those around me knew it.

After I marked my sixth Test appearance with a maiden half-century versus New Zealand at Trent Bridge, Michael Vaughan, my first England captain, said to me that I had to try to get a bigger stride in, and my head into the ball, if I wanted to take another step forward in the game. It was very constructive advice, but although I could time a ball, I had never been able to get a Matthew Hayden-size stride in and never did. I always looked at the finest players like Joe Root and Kevin Pietersen with envy, because they saw the ball so early and could.

So, even before the Aaron incident, my batting enjoyment came from triumphing in the moments of games, helping the team to a particular target. For example, at Eden Park in 2013 when I faced 77 balls, scoring six, alongside Matt Prior to secure a draw nine down against New Zealand. I loved it. Equally, I hated netting and I hated batting in the first innings with the team 200 for seven.

After losing my technical triggers, and no longer getting my front shoulder dipping towards my front knee, I was nothing, really. Neither able to get into position to play classical drives, nor to stop my back leg bending when a bowler dug it in, which meant I could not produce a stable hitting base to strike cross-bat shots consistently, as I once did.

I didn't want to make an issue of things when I was playing. You cannot be focusing on stuff that might be a hindrance, when only performance at the top level counts. That is what Peter Moores taught me during that Indian summer of 2014.

After Ishant Sharma blitzed us with seven wickets at Lord's, it became clear that the patellar tendonitis in my knee was leading my daily conversation, rather than how I was getting wickets. It needed to change and so I made a pact with

Mooresy that I was not going to mention it again around our England environment until the op I was booked for in September. Before each session, I put a hot water bottle wrapped in a towel around my leg to keep the tendon warm. Then, I would go out and bowl. I don't think there's any medicine behind that treatment, but that plus painkillers worked for me.

This was a good example of how a coach can influence how you are feeling. Mooresy was brilliant for me in this regard. Mega. One of the best coaches I worked with. He had a great ability to improve a cricketer. There were so many occasions when he helped me.

As I learned over this period of time, how you projected yourself was important. It showed others the type of cricketer they were dealing with. Of course there were indiscretions over seventeen years, but I hope people would say of me that I was highly competitive, fair and always preparing with full focus on the next task in hand.

CHAPTER SEVEN

HEADINGLEY is not the quietest place at the best of times and with no wiggle room left in our bid to win back the urn, I knew we would have to use its rowdy atmosphere to our advantage.

Yes, we were 2–0 down in the 2023 Ashes series after two pretty theatrical Test matches that lived up to what Ashes cricket is all about, but I knew that the Western Terrace would have more than a bit-part role to play in the next instalment against Australia. Looking around our changing room, I knew that most of our team had got a bit more performance left in us, too.

That was certainly the way I felt about myself, despite the fact that I was quite sore when I got up to Leeds with only three days' rest between matches. So, having arrived on the Monday, I considered what I needed to do to put myself up for selection. With each advancing year, you get better at working out the balance between appropriate preparation and recovery when faced with back-to-back Tests. This week, still feeling the fatigue caused by the mid-pitch pounding at Lord's over the previous weekend, I opted to spend lots of time lying on my hotel bed, weight off my feet, relaxing, and placed a real focus on hydration. I went and saw the physio, had a rub, and played a round of golf.

Selection is always out of your control as a player, but I wanted the people in charge of it to know that I was good to go if it fell my way, even though I'd bowled more balls than anyone else in the series at that point and had not contemplated playing four Tests between 1 June and 10 July. At the start of the summer, I genuinely meant it when I said I would be happy making one appearance. But that was then, this was now, and although I was taking things one game at a time, I had upgraded. My job now was to rest and recuperate.

I was in Zak Crawley's car as a passenger on the way to Jonny Bairstow's house for a barbecue on the Tuesday evening, when I got an inkling I would be retained. Flicking through my phone, I came across what appeared to be a leaked England team on social media. Jimmy Anderson wasn't in it, and I felt awkward as we arrived at Jonny's. Should I mention it to Jim, or not? I chose not to. It wasn't my position to do so.

That England side turned out to be the correct one and there were several changes to both XIs, in fact. Moeen Ali returned in place of the injured Ollie Pope, and Mark Wood and Chris Woakes, two men who would enjoy effective returns to Test cricket over the next few days, were in for Jimmy and Josh Tongue. I was already prepared for a slog in this match, because although they knew it was getting tiring now, I'd already been told to give everything I had. The fact I had been taking wickets persuaded them to pick me, and I was delighted to get the nod, honestly.

Australia were also forced into changes on fitness grounds after Cameron Green's back niggles resurfaced, meaning Mitchell Marsh came in for a first Test appearance in four years, while Nathan Lyon's calf tear at Lord's meant Todd Murphy got his chance in an attack that also included Scott Boland ahead of Josh Hazlewood.

From my perspective, I wanted to dictate things with the new ball – targeting Australia's most dangerous players. In this regard, what Ben Stokes said to me about Australia's batting line-up ahead of the series might surprise you. It was David Warner he was most worried about.

I found that interesting, not least because we'd done really well against him as a team in recent meetings, and personally I had developed a hold over him in 2019 that stretched into the away Ashes of 2021–22. At this stage, he was yet to score a hundred in thirteen away appearances against England and had averaged 9.5 on his previous tour of 2019.

Yet of their top six players, he was the one that Ben, as captain out on the field, did not feel he could control. Everyone who had watched world cricket over the past two decades knew Warner was so hard to stop if he got going, and it reminded me of exactly how I felt bowling at him in the period between 2010 and 2019. Even though I had created a dominance over him since, I still feared what he could do if I wasn't on top of my game.

Plenty of England supporters had told me in recent times

they felt confident every time I had the ball in my hand with Warner on strike, but his fear factor meant I had a slightly different take on things. It was such a different mentality in our changing room to that in the stands, because everyone knows and respects his danger.

Nowadays, in world cricket, you don't mind the batter who takes 300 balls to get a hundred, because you know if they make one mistake they're gone and the scoreboard hasn't really moved anywhere. It is the batters who can take the game away from you in two hours that are the concern. For all his struggles, Stokes's words were a reminder that David Warner – unlike his team-mates Steve Smith and Marnus Labuschagne – is one of those.

The way I bowled to Warner changed quite drastically from 2019 onwards, and not only because of a combination of his left-handedness and my willingness to go round the wicket.

For the first ten years of our tussles, he would use the differences in height between us to his advantage, by preying on a one-dimensional angle of attack from over the wicket. Because he's five foot six and I am six foot six, when I bowled into my natural length, he would routinely stay on the back foot and leg-side of the ball, cutting me through cover point for fun. It wasn't only me he did this to, of course, but as one of England's new-ball bowlers, I knew I couldn't afford to let it continue. I needed to find ways to counter his threat.

Even in developing my strength of going around the wicket to lefties, Warner could still open up that cover point region and find a way to strike the ball to the boundary with those powerful forearms if I dropped a touch short, so I needed to bowl differently at him. It led me to analysing his statistics. Where did he hit the ball? Research showed how off-side dominant he was. Generally speaking, other than pull shots, his boundaries came via strokes through point, cover point, cover.

Archetypal left-handers that flourished in international cricket like Alastair Cook tended to tuck you somewhere through the leg-side whenever you erred onto the pads. Warner didn't. Perhaps it was because he was a bit shorter, but he did not stand up on top of the ball, stay tall, and hit you for four through straight midwicket. His numbers showed this to be such a low-percentage shot in his repertoire. He literally never did it.

So then I started asking myself why? I worked out it was because of his desire to stay leg-side of the ball and feed his strength. Therefore, specifically to him, instead of having that mindset of nibbling the ball around off stump from around the wicket to the left-hander, trying to shape it away, I decided to bowl into the stumps, meaning that my 'miss' when my accuracy failed would be leg-side (a bowler's miss being the side you are prepared to err on if you do not execute the planned delivery perfectly). With him, if I bowled a ball down leg, so be it. Evidence suggested he was unlikely to punish me and it was certainly better than missing on the off-side, because he tended to murder width.

Remember, I hated bowling at Warner. But in the knowledge that he wasn't going anywhere soon, I knew I had to instigate change to alter feeling like this and so I spent a period spanning the 2019 World Cup experimenting, using the glut of left-handers on Nottinghamshire's staff that summer including the Bens – Duckett, Slater and Compton – as guinea pigs in the nets. The entire game plan being to take the off-side out of the equation.

After years of trying to attack him in a conventional manner, I was now aiming to hit middle and leg stumps rather than the top of off. I was to rely chiefly on wobble seam rather than swing. Forget getting him out. Primarily, it was about restricting his runs. I wanted him to know: you will not hit me through the off-side. It was designed to remove his strength, which was to score quickly, and then he might make a mistake trying to manipulate something.

Yes, he was a fine player, averaging 48 in Test cricket at that stage, but with a change of line, could the new unfamiliar angle I created lead to indecision? Could I get him to fine-nick? Could I nip it back into him for LBWs? Bowl him through the gate? These are the things I prepared to do. And when it came to it, I did. All of the above, several times over.

It should have been the most emphatic of starts to the new tactics, but when he nicked down the leg-side from the first ball of the series, we failed to hear it. No one appealed. Fortunately, we didn't have to wait long. For me to get him out three times in a row at the start of the 2019 series was massive. I knew I was on to something.

At Headingley, you look up not down at the toss. When the clouds are overhead it is a beautiful place to bowl, but when it is sunny the same can be said for batting. Sometimes when the weather changes, so does the rhythm of a match.

The 2023 Test match pitch itself was superb, containing both the pace and bounce to keep fast bowlers and stroke makers alike interested. The slips and wicketkeeper were always in play and I don't think there is a faster outfield in world cricket. If you missed the fielders, it was four.

The first ball, after Ben Stokes won the toss and decided to try taking advantage of the overhead conditions, summed up its characteristics. David Warner blocked me and as the ball sped to the boundary, I thought, Jesus Christ! I had hit the exact spot on the pitch I'd intended and it had cost me four runs. It was the right line, making the batter play, but nevertheless it led me to pull back my length ever so slightly.

The ball was literally flying through and so when Warner nicked the fifth ball, I thought it was through the gap for four, before I realised it was in the safe hands of Zak Crawley, moving to his left. It summed up how brilliantly he caught throughout the series.

No matter whether you are in your fifth or 165th Test match, taking a wicket in the first over is such an amazing feeling. Even though you've seen it all before, good and bad, you are still nervous when thrown the ball and asked to open an Ashes contest. I was buzzing as I ran off to celebrate with the West Stand. The crowd at that side of the ground provided such a rush of energy and it was almost a mixture of excitement and relief that I had set the tone.

There have been some famous Ashes overs that have gone

badly against English fast bowlers – like when Australian dasher Michael Slater crashed Phil DeFreitas square for four to open the 1994–95 series in Brisbane, and then repeated the dose later in the over. But I'd opened this one as I had intended, by killing two birds with one stone: extending Warner's misery and inviting the Leeds locals to raise the decibel levels around the ground. It was some roar.

In contrast to the other places we were to play over the five matches, Headingley also provided all the bowlers with energy, because the ground was rock hard. Every time your boots hit it, they skipped you forward – it was like running on a travelator. As a bowling attack, we would love to have taken these conditions with us around the rest of the country.

Warner was the first of four wickets to fall before lunch, but on a see-saw opening day, we had our worst spell just after it, when Mitchell Marsh was intent on gaining all the value for his shots and had the ball crying for mercy at times. Some of his drives simply rocketed across the turf. His run-a-ball hundred altered the balance of power further, after Ollie Robinson walked off the field with a back spasm.

There was little time for me to reflect on this setback as I had to finish his 12th over of the innings from the Kirkstall Lane End, but one thing I considered later was that you don't win many games when one of your seamers walks off in the first innings, not to return. I like Robbo, he's got a lot of great attributes – a really high point of release that exaggerates the bounce he extracts, skills to move the ball both ways, and the discipline to rarely bowl loose stuff. His accuracy means he is always at a batter. The combination of all these factors is why he entered the series having taken his Test wickets at a rate of one every 21 runs.

Unfortunately, though, his percentage of walking off the field is higher than you would want from an international performer. Exactly the same thing happened in the floodlit Ashes Test in Hobart eighteen months previously. His fitness has improved since then, because everyone's does when you get exposed to regular Test cricket. It has to, because it's a different type of fitness to that you require to play county cricket; matches are played at a completely different intensity. Only once you have played it, do you realise what you need from a physical perspective. He is a good bowler, a very good bowler, but he needs to be 100 per cent fit to fulfil his undoubted potential.

It was part of an under-par second session from us, having made Marsh walk to the crease at 85 for four when I located the inside edge of Steve Smith's bat. Marsh later joked that he had been the first player to score an Ashes hundred while on holiday. With Green the incumbent all-rounder, he had not expected to feature in the series despite being a member of the Australian tour party.

Ben Stokes rarely does rollickings, preferring to encourage players to relax rather than tense up, but he was clearly unimpressed with Marsh getting the deck chair and Ray-Bans out. We knew in advance that Stokes would not be a part of the attack in this particular match, because of the 12 overs in a row he had sent down at Lord's the previous week. It bust him, really. His knee pulled up so sore from that and this was the first of two sets of back-to-back Tests to finish the series. Had he been fit, this felt like one of those periods when he would have brought himself on. He has never been afraid to inspire through his own physical grind.

After Woakes got the wicket of Marsh on the eve of tea, with one that nipped back and found its way to slip off a combination of hip of batter and shoulder of bat, Stokes was straight into us.

'Come on, boys, that's not good enough,' he told us, back in the home changing room. 'We need to front up a little bit here. We have lost Robbo, and we are better than this. Fielders have gone missing. Yeah, we had a great morning. It was a good start, but this pitch is still doing enough. Every run counts from here and we don't know what a good score is until both teams have batted out there.'

Six wickets for 23 runs, starting with Marsh's departure, was how we turned the momentum of the match back our way. Mark Wood's extra pace proved vital in this regard. Australia's lower order simply had no answer during a final spell of the first day every bit as hostile as his first. He finished with figures of five for 34, including the spectacular uprooting of Usman Khawaja's leg stump before lunch. During that initial morning spell, his speed didn't drop below 91mph, answering the pre-match request from Stokes to 'bowl rockets'. A decision to limit him to three and four overs at a time aided the cause.

Of course, given the extra dimension he provides, we would all have Woody in our fantasy England XI every single day, but when you put your body through what he has to in launching those rockets, it is just not possible.

In this match, we were also grateful for his ability with the bat. Despite our early ascendancy, we were in danger of being completely knocked off course at 121 runs in arrears, with three first-innings wickets left – how did we mess that up on the second day, the best one for batting? – when Woody launched a counter-attack every bit as ferocious as his bowling, twice cross-batting blows into the stands in making 24 off just eight balls. It doesn't take much to get Ben Stokes going at Headingley, and this was more than enough. As at Lord's, he showed how he can change tempo at will. By the time he miscued one, Australia's lead had been reduced to 26.

By the close, they were 142 runs in front, with six second-innings wickets standing. The match was becoming another Headingley humdinger. Despite the glorious sunshine, we had managed to account for David Warner, to another fine catch by Zak Crawley, this time moving to his right, off me, plus Australia's top-ranked duo of Marnus Labuschagne and Steve Smith, sweeping into the deep and chipping low to midwicket respectively. Moeen Ali, who did an amazing job for us keeping it tight on that second afternoon, had claimed the pair of them as bonus wickets almost.

When Jonny Bairstow said, 'See ya, Smudge,' Smith nibbled back. Was that a sign that we were getting to Australia? Well, yeah. It appeared Smith misheard him, and I have no idea what he thought had been said, but it was nevertheless an indication of the tension that existed between the teams in the aftermath of the Bairstow stumping incident at Lord's.

Sometimes the weather gods are kind. On the third evening, they opened a perfect window for us to bowl and we took advantage of the most favourable of bowling conditions. Mitchell Marsh and Travis Head, Australia's two most attacking players, were at the crease overnight. With a lot of wet weather around, it looked like we were not going to get a huge amount of play in, but having looked at the radars, there was faith in the changing room that we might get a couple of hours' play towards the end of the day.

So we all stayed pretty switched on, and tried to relax as you do in a cricket changing room, chatting and playing cards, waiting for our moment. This was a really important passage of play, not only in the context of the match but the series, and because the rain limited the day's play to the equivalent of one session, there was no need for our three fit fast bowlers to hold anything back.

When it came to it, Chris Woakes led us superbly, putting his first real stamp on the series. He had taken three wickets in the first innings, but he was in his element here. Whereas the ball had not really swung for us the day before, suddenly it was doing so and it created plenty of indecision. Australia's players didn't know whether to play or leave. Marsh – fresh from his brilliant hundred – was caught behind withdrawing his bat and Alex Carey redirected another delivery into his stumps.

Earlier, we'd had a false start, bowling just six balls before leaving the field for a shower, with the team muttering a collective, 'No, come on.' Because we knew those conditions were great for us and equally that despite the fact Test cricket is a five-day game, you can get periods of an hour or so which can prove decisive. Our response to the dismissal of Marsh reflected this: more calm and considered than celebratory. We got together and talked about recognising the moments when you need to be right on the money.

Once Carey was out, Stokesy unleashed Wood. One of the secrets of using a fast bowler effectively is knowing when to hold them back, not just throwing them into the fray, and at Headingley the timing in both innings was perfect. Mitchell Starc and Pat Cummins did not last long.

We were convincingly on top, but Travis Head had played really well and, batting with the tail, he suddenly increased his level of aggression, hitting Wood for a couple of big sixes and generally looking to attack balls he was previously treating with restraint. He had farmed the strike cleverly, but when Stokesy brought me back from the Football Stand End, he was standing as non-striker and I had Todd Murphy in my sights. I met the pledge to seize the moment by beating him twice on the outside edge and following up later in the over with the one that nipped back.

One wicket standing, I was up against Head first ball of the next over, when I asked Stokesy, 'What do you think?'

Head was so obviously in one-day mode. He'd scored 43 from his previous 27 deliveries. Maybe slower balls? Yorkers?

Bouncers? The response was clear: 'Bowl round the wicket and try to throw the ball at the stumps and swing it out, because if you get into his stumps he will try to hit you leg-side, and if it swings away, there's a chance of it going straight up in the air.' Guess what? I did exactly as he said, it did swing and all Head could do was cloth it straight to midwicket. We were both buzzing, because while I wouldn't say we were rattled, runs were beginning to feel crucial.

Great captains are able to take the emotion out of situations like this by assessing things clearly, so that you are in no doubt what you are trying to achieve when you are running in to bowl. Decisive planning earned that wicket and we walked off to mumbling from Ben Duckett and Zak Crawley about not wanting to bat. Even though they are the most positive combination you could think of, no opening pair want to bat for five overs at the end of a day's play. Typically, they took 27 runs off our 251-run target by the close.

The introduction of Wood and Woakes at this point in the series, when it was shit or bust, was inspirational. It was clear Wood was never going to play five Tests given the physical demands of fast bowling, but from the moment he entered the series to its very last, he gave it everything and never let up in pace. The theatre he brought to that first morning at Headingley was incredible. The new stand at the rugby end of the ground is positioned in such a way that you feel as if the crowd is on top of you and they revved-up the atmosphere.

I'm not saying that Jimmy Anderson would not have bowled extremely well on a pitch that gave bowlers the most help of any in the series, but it was the right balance of team given the captain was not able to bowl a ball, and the rhythm of the bowling attack with Moeen coming back in after missing Lord's worked really well. Bowling-wise, it was our best performance of the series.

And so day four began with a gettable 224 runs required and all ten second-innings wickets standing. Time was not an issue, but it didn't suit us to play the long game any way. Asked on Sky Sports that morning how we would tackle things, I said, 'We take our chasing like a 50-over approach, and if you are chasing 250 with a 50-over approach, you're encouraged.' However, it was the most exciting pitch to play cricket on and, I would suggest, probably the most exciting pitch to watch cricket on, because both teams were always in the game. It was never going to be straightforward.

One significant thing had happened before we embarked upon the challenge of reducing the series deficit to 2–1. During the third day rain delays, Moeen Ali put his hand up and said, 'I will bat three.' With Ollie Pope out of the series, Harry Brook had gone in first wicket down in the first innings. But it was a decision that worked both ways for Mo.

Coming in at number 7 in the first innings, he had succumbed to a bouncer from Pat Cummins, and when you come in lower down the order, you can effectively put yourself down for a spell of short-pitched bowling. In contrast, if facing a newer ball, you tend to get pitched-up bowling.

Moeen's batting prowess should not be overlooked. He batted three for Worcestershire throughout his time at New

Road and only one player in that position had boasted a higher average in the County Championship over the previous ten years than his 57.32 – Marnus Labuschagne. Brooky was also more comfortable at five. Why wouldn't he be? He had scored in excess of a thousand runs there in just a few months as a Test cricketer.

In his very relaxed nature, as he does, Brendon McCullum accepted the proposal with: 'Sounds good to me, boss.'

That was the strength of this particular England changing room. It became a player-led environment.

It did not pay immediate dividends for Mo, but Brook showed his home crowd how essential he had become to this England side, and the characteristics that have made him such a good player on the international scene. The way he hits the ball. His stillness as a batter. He attacks good bowlers with brilliant shots, but he's also very calm.

Brook is lots of things, including feisty. He's not necessarily looking for a battle on the field of play in the way I always did, but beware if you do try to engage him in one. As Daryl Mitchell found out in Wellington in February 2023. The home team had taken three early wickets on a green seamer, but had turned to Mitchell's seamers during a burgeoning fourth-wicket stand.

'Come on, superstar, hit me over the top,' Mitchell chirped, trying to lure Brooky out of his bubble.

Next ball, he banged him for six down over long on, walked down to Joe Root at the other end and said, 'Ee's crap!'

He has a really simple attitude and simple technique. He

will be a great of English cricket, I'm sure. He doesn't over-think things, but he was really annoyed that he did not see the team over the line in Leeds when he was dismissed for 75 with 21 needed to win.

Throughout his innings, the nerves I experienced were horrendous. In fact, I'd say some of the worst I've ever felt. Mark Wood is one of the most nervous watchers of all time, too, as you can probably imagine from his character, and as we sat in the physio's room at lunch, he kept saying, 'Oh God. I am not sure about this.'

We needed 98 runs heading into the afternoon session, and then we lost a couple of quick wickets – Ben Stokes caught down the leg-side and Jonny Bairstow bowled by Mitchell Starc – so at 171 for six, Woody was scrambling to get his pads on, me my thigh pad.

'We can't afford to lose any more wickets,' he said, over and over again. He was next in at number 9.

'Hang on, you were great in the first innings,' I said.

'I know. But I'm not gonna do that again, am I?'

Most of the team were watching in the Dickie Bird viewing area, but every now and again Woody would come back into the changing room where I was sitting in my spot watching the action on the telly, intermittently staring at the floor, trying to process the fact that the series was on the line and we were a whisker away from being in a lot of trouble. Losing Harry Brook with 80 needed was not an option.

It was tense, my palms were sweaty. I had no idea why, because I don't normally get like that, but perhaps it was because I was thirty-seven, playing in an Ashes series that was destined to be my last, and I didn't want this team to be faced with two dead rubbers. There's no worse feeling than losing the Ashes with two matches to go, and being reduced to playing for pride. So I was building it up in my mind that everything hinged on this result, and I could not stop my hands from feeling clammy.

Joe Root uses dry chalk, the kind gymnasts put on their hands, to counter the effects of sweaty gloves when he bats for long periods of time, so for the first time ever I asked to borrow some. This was the scene as a fully kitted Woody popped back in from outside.

Both of us looked at each other nervously, and all I could think of saying to him, as I lifted them to show him the evidence, was: 'I've got chalk on my hands.' We both burst out laughing. And couldn't stop. You probably know the feeling when something so stupid sets you off and no matter how hard you try, it's impossible not to carry on. We howled until it got to the stage where it was virtually game over. That's when Woody went out to replace Brook.

Puffing out his cheeks, he gave me a look that said: 'For God's sake.' Then went out and blazed 16 off eight balls. it was brilliant, giving me more superb memories of what was a great Test match to play in, but primarily relief that the series was still alive.

The Player of the Match award went to Wood for his seven wickets and 40 quick-fire runs, while Chris Woakes finished unbeaten on 32, adding to his match figures of six for 141.

The pair of them had provided an injection of energy, while in contrast Australia had gained next to nothing from their two bowling changes.

Pre-series there was a lot of talk about Scott Boland and the impact he might have. He arrived with a big reputation, built on taking 33 wickets in eight Test appearances and conceding only 2.31 runs per over. But it was one of our game plans never to let him settle. Because he is so metronomic, you know exactly where the ball is going to be. When that is the case, as a batter you can put that to your advantage by using your feet, dropping deeper in the crease, or walking across off stump and clipping to leg – whatever is your preference.

Everyone had their own method on how they were going to play him, but as a team we wanted to attack him exactly the same way as the rest of their bowling attack. We weren't going to stand on ceremony as he plugged away. He went wicketless in this match.

Even more significant was Nathan Lyon tearing his calf at Lord's, because he had been a mainstay of their team for such a long time, as emphasised by the fact he was the first bowler to play 100 straight Tests. He played such a huge role for them, holding an end, and you can't dominate a bowler with close to 500 Test wickets.

So it was advantage us when they replaced him with Todd Murphy, a good talent but unable as a young bowler to apply anywhere near the level of pressure. It was clear that Pat Cummins did not want to bowl him at what historically is a seamer's ground, and when he did turn to him, it was arguably too late.

There was no massive celebration after Woakes struck the winning boundary. The changing room was relatively calm and the attitude very much that we still had a job to do. Yes, we'd won a Test match, but it was now 2–1 and we were focused on making sure the series came back our way.

We had some brilliant moments afterwards, though, that emphasised the relaxed mood. Everyone had family and friends there, and some of mine including my sister Gemma, Joe Worrall, the captain of Nottingham Forest, and football commentator Darren Fletcher, ended up having a game of cricket on the Test match pitch with one of the groundsmen fully kitted up having a bat, and me umpiring.

Playing on the Test match pitch, even when the game is over, is not something I had ever seen before, but Joe said it was one of the best experiences of his life running up the hill at Headingley to bowl. It was a scene that resembled a league cricket match as the young families of the Australian players ran around the outfield.

After the hullabaloo at Lord's, we had put some fun back into the series – and it was very much alive with us one down, two to play.

CHAPTER EIGHT

No one ever told me that I'd been dropped from England's white-ball sides or that I was to become a Test specialist. It just kind of happened.

The time in question coincided with the reset of our limited-overs teams in the aftermath of the humiliating 2015 World Cup and would trigger an unusual spell in my career in which periods of exultation would sandwich periods of despair. There were epic series wins over teams like Australia and South Africa, and the personal accolade of being the world's number-one ranked bowler, but they were punctuated by technical issues, overnight losses of form and unjust omissions. I was even dropped at the height of my powers – I never averaged more wickets in a year than the 4.75 per Test match I enjoyed in 2020, but it did not make me immune to the axe.

A lot of the joy had gone in the early part of 2015 when, playing a brand of cricket that would not have looked out of place when the World Cup had previously been held in Australasia twenty-three years earlier, we were eliminated by Bangladesh. But it was injected back into the country's veins with the takeover of the team by Australian coach Trevor

Bayliss, and the revolutionising of limited-overs methods by Eoin Morgan.

My natural inclination to improve, catalysed over the years by the busy mind of Peter Moores and the keen eye of Ottis Gibson, meant I kept developing parts of my game – albeit occasionally with detrimental knock-on effects. Downgrading from three international formats to one overnight provided me with both more time to think and more time to experiment. But I was to find that solving solutions one minute was creating problems the next.

I missed the build-up to the World Cup because I was still recovering from knee surgery to fix the patellar tendonitis issue that had dogged me for the majority of 2014, but you didn't need to be on the inside to see it was brimming with amateurishness.

Alastair Cook was sacked as captain the month before we were due to fly to Australia for a Tri-Series tournament warm-up, unable to ride out a disturbing 5–2 series loss in Sri Lanka, and no one was clear on either a style of play or the make-up of the team when Eoin Morgan replaced him. I wasn't on the Sri Lanka tour, but it was an unmitigated disaster featuring some extremely odd strategic calls.

Ben Stokes was picked intermittently and when he was, he batted at number 8 and bowled up to four overs an innings. Overlooking him for the fifteen-man World Cup squad felt like absolute madness, particularly given that he would go on to be Player of the Match in the competition's final four years later. The bowling generally was getting panned.

During the triangular Carlton Series, which featured a couple of wins over India but straight losses to the hosts Australia, I felt a bit off the pace. I had not played cricket since the previous September, and this was now January. I was lacking a bit of match rhythm and fitness, and it affected the control I needed when I was at the top of my game. But what stuck out for me was the batting line-up. No one had a clue who was batting where or what was happening.

Then there was last-minute tinkering to the first-choice XI right on the eve of the competition. Gary Ballance, who had broken his finger in catching practice during the tri-series preparation, would be batting at number 3, despite not much of a history there domestically or internationally, and the inevitable ring-rustiness that went with such a long lay-off – he'd not played since the previous September. We thought his injury was going to rule him out of the World Cup. Now, having managed to get back fit and without any cricket to speak of behind him, he was suddenly on the team sheet to face Australia in the first game.

Everyone in our camp was like, what? Ravi Bopara, who had been a regular feature for us, winning in excess of 100 caps, and capable of clearing the ropes in the middle order and bowling canny medium pace, was shelved. James Taylor found himself in the totally unfamiliar position of number 6. You don't win trophies without frontline spinners, but only once we were on the ground there did a theory develop that in Australia, James Tredwell didn't move the ball enough and people would often run at him and hit it straight down the ground. It was a poor squad. An old-fashioned squad.

In terms of style, we still had that mindset where you build for 40 overs and try to slog for ten, but the way the game was moving, we were miles off the pace. At the time, there was the stupid rule that restricted you to four fielders outside the ring across an entire innings, and so bowling at the death was impossible. There was always a gap and other teams exploited it. Five countries made totals in excess of 350. The twenty-one scores bigger than our best of 309 for six – in a match against Sri Lanka that we lost by nine wickets – were shared by ten different sides. West Indies' Chris Gayle and Martin Guptill, of New Zealand, made double hundreds.

So, did we have the squad to go and challenge for that World Cup? No. We didn't harness the style of cricket to challenge for it, either. What Eoin Morgan managed to do in the long-term was release the fear of failure so that batters would go out and play freely, because they knew they would get ten games to go and whack it, not dropped after three if they failed. Whereas we still had guys averaging good numbers, but it would be very safe all the time. Strike rates of 70 rather than 90, which got us nowhere, really.

Having said that, we should have won the Champions Trophy in England in 2013, and would have done but for a horror final. We had played great cricket throughout the tournament, and only came unstuck against India at Edgbaston after being forced to play a shortened game due to wet weather. The pitch turned square; Ravichandran Ashwin and Ravindra

Jadeja combined for figures of four for 39 in eight overs. We lost a 20-over-a-side affair by five runs, fielding a team not ideally suited to T20. But we should not have done, after needing 20 off 15 balls with six wickets left. If we had won England's first global 50-over tournament, things might well have been viewed differently, but I always felt as if we were one step behind during that period.

We treated white-ball cricket as a second-class citizen, too, always fielding a similar team to the one that proved successful in the very different pace of Test cricket. Andrew Strauss, Alastair Cook, Jimmy Anderson, Tim Bresnan, Graeme Swann and myself: we all played in both. Often heading into matches knackered immediately after playing a five-match Test series. Throughout my entire 121-match ODI career, in fact, they felt like add-ons.

For all our limitations, it was still a real embarrassment to be ousted from the tournament by Bangladesh in 2015. The Adelaide Oval was home to a flat pitch, and we kept them to a decent total of 275 for seven. A very chaseable one. Typical of our tournament, however, our innings was fraught with the fear of failure and the shackles were never truly released. I believed the chance of victory remained until I got out, leaving Chris Woakes stranded, but the record books showed we lost by 15 runs. For the remainder of that World Cup, incorporating a dead rubber win over Afghanistan and not much else, we were confined to our hotel rooms to avoid unwanted attention.

At the end of a four-year cycle you always expect there's

going to be change, but this was probably the one occasion when the fact that people often placed Jimmy and me in the same bracket – a bugbear of mine – really hurt me. Jimmy is four years older than me and this was a great example of selectors being unable to separate us as a pair, instead of treating us as individuals, identifying what our roles were, and what they should be in future.

As I say, I never got a phone call to tell me they were going to move on from me in white-ball cricket. But when I spoke to the chairman of selectors, James Whitaker, someone I liked and my first coach at Leicestershire, he said they were going for some younger options for the five-match series against New Zealand that would open the new era. I was twenty-eight. Then they picked Liam Plunkett, who had just turned thirty, so it was a little bit confusing.

For the majority of my career, I had no issue with Jimmy Anderson and myself being treated as a partnership. In fact, playing alongside him was the greatest pleasure of being a part of this era. However, I had briefly viewed him as a bit of a rival for a Test place at the start.

I had returned home from a tour of Sri Lanka featuring a one-wicket debut in Colombo in December 2007, and hung my England cap where the star would usually be on the Christmas tree at my mum's house. Mum found that quite funny, but there was a serious side to putting it on display. I wanted wearing it to become a feature, not a one-off, and there was a series in New Zealand in early 2008.

The first Test defeat in Hamilton became a changing of the guard for the England team's bowling attack. I was twelfth man and I thought it looked like it needed freshening up after we were plunged to defeat by the wickets of Kyle Mills. It would be in Wellington.

Jimmy had also been left out for the series opener and went to play a first-class fixture for Auckland. That's quite different, I thought, they obviously want him match fit and ready to go. I had a single Test appearance against my name, but I felt a bit annoyed that I had not been given the chance to do that. However, I reconciled that Jimmy was a more senior player than me and there was only one spot for such a venture.

I had a gut feeling that Jimmy was going to be playing the next game. What I didn't realise was that they would make a double change, until the day before the Wellington match when England captain Michael Vaughan came up to me before nets and told me I was in.

'I don't care if you don't take any wickets. I just want you to bring that sort of natural energy and enthusiasm that you have,' he said.

The fact that he wanted a bowler with youthful energy and drive suggested he felt such qualities were lacking in Hamilton, and I kept it in mind for future reference. Jimmy and I were replacing two bowlers in their thirties and I always pledged after that never to show a lack of enthusiasm or energy, because such perceptions worked against Matthew Hoggard and Steve Harmison at the time.

Maybe they had hit the heights of the 2005 Ashes success and nothing afterwards ever felt as good, or, like a lot of professional sports people, maybe they had come to the stage of their careers where they would not be getting any better. They had lost that pizzazz. Although Harmy did rekindle some of it, playing on for another couple of years, Hoggard never appeared again.

I had worked with England head coach Peter Moores on the academy at Loughborough, and I had a good connection with him, but I had not done much with Vaughan at all. I certainly didn't tear up trees in Wellington, but I picked up three wickets and we won. The great thing about winning Test matches is that the team generally stays the same for the next match, so Jimmy and I got an opportunity alongside the left-armer Ryan Sidebottom at Napier too. This time I was more prolific, bagging five victims, and we had turned the series around from 1–0 down to 2–1. It was the Branderson breakthrough.

There were times when we were irresistible together. Others when we were completely village – never more so than at Kensington Oval, Barbados, in 2009, when we got in a flap, fearful that stand-in Test captain Andrew Strauss was about to bowl first against West Indies, convinced that the best chance of any movement in idyllic batting conditions was day one.

'It's not swinging, it's not swinging!' we screamed from the practice pitches, as he got to within ten yards of the middle. It hardly mattered. England lost eight wickets for 879 runs that week; West Indies nine for 749. Slapstick it might have been, but it was an example of us working together, summing up conditions and preparing for the work ahead.

We had played together a lot by the summer of 2015, but over the course of the next twelve months, concentrating on only one format, we both reached the heights of our trade.

I began it as England's Twenty20 captain, until a one-minute phone call from the ECB's managing director of cricket, Andrew Strauss, informed me that the white-ball leadership was uniting under Eoin Morgan – an eminently sensible decision.

Then I took a match-winning wicket in a series against New Zealand that would provide us with a glimpse of England's Test future.

It came at Lord's where, with England 30 for four, the New Zealand captain Brendon McCullum packed the slip cordon, challenging the newly arrived Ben Stokes at number 6 to risk driving into the gaps created in the covers. Stokes hit 92 and then 101 off 92 balls in the second innings. The whole game was on steroids. Moeen Ali took a great catch to provide me with a sixth success of a 124-run win, tumbling high to his left at third man to dismiss Trent Boult with nine overs remaining.

'I thought we played our part in a tremendous Test match. That was a great advertisement for the game. Credit to England, they fought through the game, played an enterprising brand of cricket. We got 700 runs in the game and still lost by 100. It was a fantastic pitch, great crowds.'

Sound familiar? Those were the words of McCullum following England's first match since sacking Peter Moores for the second time. Paul Farbrace, in temporary charge until the Australian Trevor Bayliss arrived, said that he didn't want to have any real influence and we should 'just go and play'. We knew the Ashes was on the horizon, only two Tests away, so everyone was fired up.

I always enjoyed playing against New Zealand, a great bunch of guys who, without wanting to appear disrespectful, always punched above their weight. They upped the ante in the second Test at Headingley. And how. They scored at 4.84 runs an over in posting 350 and, after first-innings scores were tied, 4.98 for a total of 454 for eight declared in a massive 199-run win.

One passage of play off my bowling summed things up, highlighting what is truly possible in Test cricket with the necessary level of belief. Ross Taylor's departure, leaving the ball and literally walking for an LBW, brought McCullum to the crease. He charged me, hitting his first ball over cover for six. It was the most remarkable feeling, contemplating that I had got a batter out leaving the ball and then been smacked for six from a very similar delivery. Essentially, it showed how two different outlooks can be applied to the same scenario.

It was an unbelievably entertaining summer of international cricket. A 3–2 win in the one-day series against New Zealand opened with England's first ever score of 400; the enterprising style a far cry from the World Cup performances of only three months earlier. And despite being pegged back by the Kiwis, our Test team was a happy one as Australia landed. 'Hold Back the River' by James Bay became our theme tune of the summer, sung by us driving to and from the Ashes matches.

There was one day in which nothing could hold me back. It came in the pivotal match of five. Jimmy had hurt his side as we went 2–1 up at Edgbaston and so I knew that not only would I be needed, but even more would be required from me. Trevor Bayliss told the team the day before it, 'You will need to set the tone for this game.' He didn't want us to hold on to our advantage. 'Whoever's opening the batting or bowling, get your brain switched on now,' he added. He wanted us to hit the Aussies hard, not give them a sniff.

I felt pressure but in a good way. I had played 82 Tests before arriving at Trent Bridge, my home ground, but never before had I bowled the first over. As attack leader, I had told Alastair Cook, the captain, it was a bat-first scenario. Generally, it quickens up on day two for the nicks, but Cookie thought the pitch was really green. Ten minutes before the toss, I went to mark out my run-up and Shane Warne walked over to me.

'Looks like a bowling day,' he said.

If Shane Warne thinks it's a bowl-first day, I thought, I might be getting this wrong. You always want to be on the same wavelength as captain and opening bowler, and I had to let Cookie know.

At the five-minute bell, there was a Nottinghamshire tribute to Clive Rice, who had recently passed away. Clive was one of Dad's great mates, Mum was good friends with his wife Sue, and he called me during the previous home Ashes in 2013 to tell me how proud he was of me and to keep doing what I was doing. Although I didn't know him that well, I knew Dad loved playing with him, and this little ceremony stirred the emotions. It was a poignant moment for someone who meant so much to our club.

One other thing was significant before I embarked on a spell that would deliver my best Test figures of eight for 15. A smattering of rain fell, delaying the start but not lasting long enough to get the covers on. Edgbaston had a 12mm grass covering, this one was 8mm, but it felt zingy.

My first over was quite a nervous one, yet featured two wickets. Chris Rogers became my 300th Test victim when he edged one that angled in and nipped away from around the wicket. Then Steve Smith nailed me for four through cover point and I actually clapped. The ball was going all over the place and I thought, the number one rule is don't drive when it's like this here or at Headingley. When Smith nicked off, Australia were 10 for two.

Mark Wood bowled David Warner off the inside edge next ball and we were flying. Shaun Marsh had just come into the side, so my plan to him – a very good stroke player – was to make him play as much as possible. If you haven't played many games, you want to feel bat on ball. I wanted to make sure I made him play.

Then came the did-you-see-that moment when Ben Stokes,

at fifth slip, somehow clawed in a one-handed catch that appeared to have been behind him. The image of me, hands over my face in disbelief, when Ben took that belter to get rid of Voges, is probably one you can easily recall.

Michael Clarke announced his retirement later in the match and he looked shot to bits when he poked at one to give me figures of five for six. Three lower-order players followed. It was the greatest day of my international career, but it wasn't my best spell. It seems paradoxical to say, but I didn't bowl loads of wicket-taking deliveries. I wasn't nipping the ball back, bowling people through the gate. I just kept the ball up there, looking for movement. Australia's batters nicked it; we caught it. We maintained attacking fields and everything went to hand.

It also featured a period in the middle when, amid the mayhem, I completely lost my run-up. I could not for the life of me remember what foot I took off on at the start. Reading this, imagine having a line in front of you and not knowing which foot to put down first to guarantee staying behind the crease 20 yards away. It was the weirdest feeling when you have bowled thousands upon thousands of balls previously without thinking about it.

I was doing extra steps, shuffling, all sorts for a while. I threw one down the leg-side for four byes, it was awful, and then I remembered something that Glenn McGrath said once when it happened to him. He started singing a song when he got out of rhythm, and so I started belting out, 'Ah, one, two, three, four, five!' Reciting 'Mambo No. 5' over and over, the theme tune from the old Channel 4 cricket highlights programme, got me back.

It was a morning of elation, but the best feeling of all was making a cup of tea at 12.50 p.m., and watching Adam Lyth caress an extra-cover drive off Mitchell Starc for four from the second ball of our innings. I had bowled in an Ashes match and was enjoying a cuppa before lunch.

Joe Root's hundred on the same day was every bit as important as dismissing Australia for 60. If we'd have been bowled out for 120, we would still have taken a decent first-innings lead, but to close on 274 for four that evening put all doubt aside.

Jos Buttler said to me that evening, 'I've wanted to be an Ashes winner all my life, and it just happened in an hour and a half.'

We couldn't lose from there. The Ashes had been regained by virtue of an innings win secured on the third morning.

Next winter, we went to South Africa, and I performed as well as I had throughout my career. As a fast bowler, South African conditions were the best on the international circuit: pitches provided pace and bounce and slip catches carried. I like steak and red wine, too. So that always ticked a box. They were a tough team to play against in those days. I remember how pleased we were when we held them to a 1–1 draw in a really competitive four matches in 2009–10.

Despite his brilliance, for some reason I always had a really good record against AB de Villiers and I enjoyed my battles with him in 2015–16. He said he struggled to line me up and

I forced him to play when he didn't want to. A collection of 18 wickets, including match-shaping spells in Durban and Johannesburg, where James Taylor took two extraordinarily brilliant catches at short leg, were my high as an England cricketer.

By the end of that winter, I was officially the world's number-one ranked Test bowler and that meant something when I played in the same era as Dale Steyn – an absolute beast of fast bowling, who hurtled the ball down in excess of 90mph, swung it away, and knocked over tails for fun. To get to number one for just one week would have made me proud – and I could say that I got there.

It coincided with being my first year of not playing all the time, switching from red ball to white with limited time to rest or prepare between assignments. Being able to focus on one format meant I felt fresh. I couldn't say that in previous years.

Only two English bowlers in Ian Botham and Steve Harmison, on the back of his famously stunning West Indies trip of 2003–04, had sat at the summit before. Ironically, Jimmy Anderson would replace me to become the fourth later in the year. Neither of us were truly at the peak of our powers at the same time and that's what a really good part-nership is based upon – if one is hot, the other is slightly cooler. What you don't want is both to be hot or both to be cold at the same time. One supported the other. And we were happy to do so.

We also become better mates around this time. We always

spent time together, playing Call of Duty, that kind of thing, but for many years we each had other sidekicks. I hung around with Matt Prior. He would be with Graeme Swann. If we played golf, Jimmy and I would always pair up. Professionally, there was never any jealousy either. If he got five, I was buzzing. Vice versa. It was the same when he displaced me at the top of the rankings. Not all fast bowlers are like that. More often than not, they'd be thinking: I want his wickets.

The prolific Test series in South Africa took my tally to 69 wickets in twelve months, and led to me being asked to stay out for the one-day series following a spate of injuries to fast-bowling rivals Steven Finn, Liam Plunkett and Mark Wood. I was in form and on the ground, and adding me to the squad saved them an air fare.

Rested for the first three matches, following the Test exertions, I played at the Wanderers in the fourth match, dismissing Hashim Amla in my first over, and having AB de Villiers dropped on nine with the first ball of my second spell. He got hold of me after that, although I did bear in mind that I'd not played white-ball cricket for a year. I then bowled nicely at Cape Town in what was my last ODI on 14 February 2016. The other five England bowlers that day were all picked for the 2023 World Cup in India.

And that was it. After 178 wickets in 121 appearances, a return that placed me third behind Jimmy Anderson and Darren Gough among Englishmen, I was never asked again. I never missed it, either, to be honest. Physically, I found it quite hard work. Even when the lads came out on top in that

Super Over to win the 2019 World Cup, I wasn't wishing I was out there while I was watching it. Which was quite an interesting feeling, especially as I was still playing cricket. I didn't have any envy or jealousy. I had become conditioned to not playing, not hopping on and off a multi-format treadmill.

It wasn't as if I had not been viewed as a valued commodity in white-ball cricket. I had been captain of England at Twenty20 for four years and won a £250,000 deal to play for Punjab Kings XI in the Indian Premier League in 2011 on the back of strong international performances. I received my kit, but never actually went. In future years, I probably would have done a bit of rehab out there, but at the time the ECB didn't want that lack of control and a side strain kept me out.

The thing that was really disappointing was that Adam Gilchrist was captain and I was looking forward to playing under him. When he called me to ask how I was, I told him I thought I would be okay, but he said that they needed to sign a replacement if I wasn't fit. Punjab even retained me for 2012, but another injury cropped up, and it was different then for England players, as the IPL was not something in the calendar that you really targeted.

The one overseas Twenty20 competition I did feature in was the Big Bash League in 2016–17, and I enjoyed playing for Hobart. The following summer, I finished with a winner's medal for Nottinghamshire in the Royal London Cup. My last ever game of white-ball cricket was watching Alex Hales dismantling the Surrey attack with an innings of 187 at Lord's.

Partly through being categorised as being older than I was,

my limited-overs career was wrapped up a week after my thirty-first birthday. I still believe that with my record and the way I bowled, I was suited to being in England's 2019 World Cup squad. After all, it was the batting that changed massively via the 2015 reset, not necessarily the bowling.

If I look at T20's skill sets, could I have successfully worked on my bowling skills and tried to whack it out the park for five balls? Potentially, yes. Yet I wouldn't change anything I had in my career. For anything. I absolutely loved Test cricket and in reality, if I had carried on trying to juggle three formats, I would not have been playing it at thirty-seven. There would have been no 2023 Ashes memories. Everything happens for a reason.

The focus on Test cricket had one significant benefit: the extra preparation time it afforded me to work on technical and tactical aspects of my game.

For example in 2015, the Australians were coming over with more left-handers than normal. In the build-up, it was anticipated that David Warner, Chris Rogers, Shaun Marsh, Mitchell Johnson, Mitchell Starc and Josh Hazlewood would all be involved. It was reasonable to assume that five would potentially play in each Test, and I knew my average was in the high 30s against left-handers in Test cricket. Vastly inferior to my record against right-handers. Ottis Gibson was pretty blunt.

'Look, mate, if you're going to average 37 against left-handers, you might find yourself under pressure for your place,' he warned. 'What's your game plan?'

I told him it was to bowl over the wicket, try to move the ball into the stumps and if the ball held its line, I would get a nick. It wasn't a manifesto dripping with conviction.

Gibbo began a second spell as England bowling coach that year and came to see me at Trent Bridge in May, not long after we returned from a series in the Caribbean most memorable for Jimmy Anderson passing Ian Botham's England record Test wickets tally of 383. My southpaw scheme wasn't going to work, he persuaded me. At six foot six, trying to swing the ball back into the stumps, there was a good chance it would go over the top of them when I did. The danger I would create felt limited.

We toyed with being a bit more like Glenn McGrath, bowling from the same over-the-wicket line and concentrating on getting the ball to move across all the time, targeting the outside edge. The other option, though, was to emulate what Andrew Flintoff did with reverse swing, predominantly in the 2005 Ashes. Flintoff's ability to bowl round the wicket to the left-handers, angling the ball into the stumps and then getting it to tail away, proved devastating.

So, we began messing about with a bit of string in the nets, trying to recreate the ball's ideal arc between release and hitting the wicketkeeper's gloves. It was the start of something. But it wasn't a quick fix. It took me three months of grooving to get comfortable, and in the first Test against Australia at Cardiff, I started off over the wicket before coming round and nicking Rogers off in the second innings.

Leg before wicket dismissals from round the wicket were

pretty rare pre the Decision Review System being introduced in late 2009, as an umpire's tendency was to assume that the ball would naturally go on with the angle and miss leg stump, but as was later shown, you only need to move it the other way a tad off the seam or through the air, straightening its path in the process, to be in with a shout. I certainly took my fair share from 2015 onwards and my gain was definitely pain for David Warner.

Let me repeat that Warner had spent his early international career tormenting me, but the occasions upon which he hit me through cover point reduced massively over the final eight years of our head-to-head combat, and by 2023 he was much more likely to drive me as I tried to get the ball further up to him, having completely dried up his preferred scoring area. And it wasn't just me dismissing him seventeen times that hurt him.

For a great player, Warner will be left to reflect on a career record in England that was not great – an average of 26.74, not a single hundred in 35 innings – and I honestly think that angle was everything to do with that. I later watched the Indian guys like Mohammed Shami go round to him, and Kagiso Rabada, of South Africa. It started affecting him everywhere.

When I came through as a junior, everyone bowled over the wicket to left-handers, and that was true all the way up to the top. No one really latched on when Flintoff did it so successfully in 2005, but ten years later when I copied him, it became more common. I certainly didn't create anything earth-shattering with my decision to switch, but I had an influence on how other bowlers around the world thought going forward. With four left-handers of our own in the England Test team during that period – Alastair Cook, Adam Lyth, Ben Stokes and Moeen Ali – it was a double whammy.

Very soon, however, my greatest strength was to become my biggest weakness. As quickly as things came good, they went bad. By the summer of 2016, the repetition of pushing the ball into the stumps and moving it away from that newly created angle had altered my body shape on the point of release to a position where I was falling away and softly angling it into the batter when I was confronted by right-handers. I began pushing the ball down the wicket rather than bowling it. My contributions to the cause reflected it as well: throughout 2017 my strike rate was up at 78.4.

For a couple of years I was surviving in international cricket rather than thriving. Naturally, I worked hard to get things back on track, but that was not always easy. Not least because it took some time to understand how the technical faults had crept in. I also confess that I was not always inclined to keep my frustrations to myself. Newsflash: fast bowlers can be grumpy. Later, thanks to the positive energy that flooded the England environment under Brendon McCullum, I was able to look back through a different lens, realising there were occasions – even though I was down about my worrying form – when I could have done more to tackle my inherent grumpiness in the middle of Trevor Bayliss's tenure as coach.

During times when things don't go so well, it is important to take pressure off yourself by evaluating performances properly. Sitting in hotel rooms at night, you might reflect that you have set the tone, created pressure, chances for wickets and been positive around the group. As I confess, that was not always the case. Fast bowling is a grind. An achy pursuit. Some days you are fatigued in the morning before you've even pulled on the boots. The footholes are crap. The pitch has no pace. Travelling has left me stiff. Net? Nah. Don't fancy one. Like enthusiasm, negativity is infectious. I knew it was a weakness of mine.

There were times that I was annoyed for good reason, though. Like in the day-night Ashes Test of 2017–18 when we bowled first and after the opening day's play, the coaches told me and Jimmy that we had bowled too short. Our on-field assessment had been that we felt it was tricky to get the ball away from back of a length, but when it was fuller you could score. Regardless of the difference of opinion, however, what really irked me was the timing of this.

Don't tell me at 11 p.m., after we have left the field for the close of play, tell me live. The horse has bolted.

I was someone who was generally open to new ideas, but the coaches I worked with needed to provide evidence backing up their theories if they wanted to instigate change. It was no use coming to me with information lacking backbone. If you told me, 'Broad, you should bowl fuller', I would always ask why. I was never someone who listened to opinions and took them as read. I always needed an argument with solid

Being hit for 36 in an over by Yuvraj Singh in Durban in September 2007 hurt, but it was arguably the making of me as an international cricketer.

Receiving the applause from my home Nottingham crowd after taking five wickets in an ODI v South Africa in 2008.

Celebrating the first of my four Ashes series wins after winning the Player of the Match award at The Oval in 2009.

Back at The Oval in 2013, after England made it three Test series victories in a row over the Australians.

Raising my bat for my solitary international hundred – against Pakistan at Lord's in 2010.

On my haunches after being struck in the face by a bouncer from India's Varun Aaron at Manchester in 2014.

Arguably the most famous image of my career: Ben Stokes has just dismissed Australia's Adam Voges with a catch off my bowling at Trent Bridge which, as my reaction suggests, had to be seen to be believed.

England's triumphant Ashes-winning team of 2015, captained by
my close friend Alastair Cook.

Appealing for the wicket of Mohammad Rizwan in the first Test of a 1–0
series win over Pakistan played in Covid conditions in 2020.

My mum Carole was so influential on my career, always asking whenever I played: 'Was it fun?'

Brendon McCullum – not only a tactical master on the cricket front, but just an all-round fantastic person.

I had the best seat in the house for Ben Stokes's 155 against Australia at Lord's during a century stand – unfortunately it came in a losing cause.

I loved my career battles with David Warner: the second innings of the Headingley Ashes match of 2023 was the 17th and final time I dismissed him in Test cricket.

A little thank-you tap to the bails after I switched them for good luck, immediately before dismissing Todd Murphy.

Exiting international cricket with Moeen Ali at The Oval, 2023, was a special moment: I'd known him longer than any of my other England team-mates.

Indescribable feelings when Annabella was born – she has enhanced our lives in every way. Annabella brings us both such joy and happiness.

How lucky am I? Happy days on holiday with Mollie.

structure. When I left Oakham School, Frank Hayes, the cricket master, told me to make sure I always used the best filter possible and what he meant by that was take all the information in from coaches, but filter the bits that are supporting you.

Mentally, the technical work on a collapsing bowling action had taken a greater toll on me than I was prepared to admit, and at the end of that Ashes tour, I considered calling it quits. The thought of playing cricket again was the last thing on my mind while I was on a week's holiday in Noosa on Queensland's Sunshine Coast with Jimmy Anderson and my best mate, Sean Reddington. I hardly needed reminding about my day job. We had just lost 4–0 to Australia.

So, I was not in the best frame of mind when my seven days away was disturbed by a call from the chairman of selectors, James Whitaker. He was calling with what on face value was good news. But my heart sank. I had been picked for the tour of New Zealand. My next two days were spent thinking, oh, no, there must be something better.

Eighteen months previously, at the end of the 2016 international summer, I had been on the Oval balcony talking Jimmy Anderson out of what would have been a massively premature retirement, so he knew what would be going through my head. It was Sean, however, who proved more influential. He is a successful businessman and because he doesn't know cricket, he provides uncluttered, honest opinions.

He persuaded me to bide my time rather than act rashly, give it a week and follow my heart. That I was on a comedown post-tour and needed a detox from cricket. He was right. I just needed to stop thinking about the England environment temporarily. When I touched down in New Zealand the following month, I was fully motivated.

I had not stopped trying to add menace to my bowling throughout my times of trouble. Indeed, before he left us in the second half of 2017 to become head coach of South Africa, I had told Ottis Gibson that I thought my best out-swinger routinely beat the bat and so I worked on placing wobble seam, nipping the ball back into the stumps, at the heart of my repertoire. It was an art generally frowned upon for decades, because it suggested you were a bowler who couldn't present a good seam. But if it was a good enough staple method for someone of the calibre of Curtly Ambrose, it was good enough for me. The key to this mode of attack was accuracy. Hitting a spot around off stump. It's not what a ball does, it's where it does it from, Gibbo used to say.

Through all the deconstructing of my bowling, and looking at others for inspiration, I also began to admire what Jimmy Anderson had done in reducing his run-up. So in late 2018, I got in touch with my dad's former Nottinghamshire team-mate and New Zealand great Richard Hadlee to ask about why he shortened his approach to the crease.

Aside from swearing by the physical knock-on – 'I did it at twenty-nine, and it gave me ten more years of bowling at the top level,' he wrote in an email – there was a technical aspect, too. The shorter the run, the more efficient your running pattern tended to be. It encouraged shorter strides and the benefit of a shorter delivery stride over a lengthier one was that it led to a higher release point: maximising the bounce you would extract from surfaces.

Mine had become stretched and slow. I wasn't creating enough momentum through the crease, so I drilled a 16-yard sprint throughout the 2018 tour of Sri Lanka and by the tour of West Indies in 2019, my geekiness when it came to fast bowling was feeling ready to bear fruit.

Operating from this reduced run, I felt as though I was flying in the warm-up period in Barbados in January 2019, taking four wickets including a hat-trick for not many runs in one of those games in which the touring team remains in the field all day and the home batters keep returning to the crease.

I felt my rhythm was great. Then I got left out of the XI for the first Test match at Kensington Oval. A couple of things annoyed me on the morning of the game. Firstly, I didn't know if I was playing or not, because a team of twelve had been named, and then literally five minutes before the toss, Trevor Bayliss wandered over to me and said, 'We're going with two spinners, you're not playing.'

Historically Barbados is quite a good place for tall people to bowl, and it is the most iconic England versus West Indies game on a tour of the Caribbean. So, I was gutted to miss out. Sam Curran had been selected to take the new ball ahead of me. I kept my disappointment to myself, although I decided to request a talk in private when it was convenient for Trevor. I asked him if we could have a drink that evening to discuss what was going on. But he simply said, 'Nah, mate, I'm not coming to that.' When pressed, he implied that the decision had nothing to do with him.

Basically, my understanding was that he got overruled by the chairman of selectors, Ed Smith. Trevor wanted me to play and Ed didn't, so Trev would not even discuss it with me. Upon departure that evening, I got Ed off the team bus. I only wanted five minutes and I tried to talk to him, as I wanted to know why I wasn't playing. But he just stared at the ground the whole time, did not make eye contact, and had no reasons for me. Nothing.

The Test match went down as a shambles. Eight wickets, after losing the toss, represented a pretty good day, but the England team looked a bowler short and then got dismissed for just 77 by a four-pronged West Indies pace attack on day two. Jason Holder followed up with an unbeaten double hundred before the Windies declared. England lost by 381 runs inside three days.

My first experience of Ben Stokes as England's 81st Test captain was not a good one.

When it was announced that he would lead the team against West Indies for the first international match of the summer in Southampton in 2020, while Joe Root was on paternity leave, he provided a lovely snapshot of what he envisaged his captaincy would look like, suggesting his first field setting would be nine slips and a gully. Naturally, it left people wondering whether he was going to sacrifice the wicketkeeper or the bowler, but all joking aside, it summed up perfectly the mindset of the leader we saw develop a couple of years later. Brimming with attacking intent.

Inside our camp at the Ageas Bowl for the first fixture of our biosecure summer, there was an expectation that he would be as adventurous in his leadership as he was as a player. However, his first act left me crestfallen. I was called to the team room at 6 p.m. the evening before the match and was told by Ben that I would not be playing, because they wanted extra pace in the forms of Mark Wood and Jofra Archer.

To be fair, I felt quite emotional, and he was quite emotional telling me too. It was as tough a week personally as I ever experienced in my career, not least because of the environment we found ourselves in. Under the COVID arrangements for playing Test matches, we could not leave our 'bubble' of the Hilton Hotel and I felt imprisoned with my feelings.

The arrangements in Southampton, though, allowed me to release those feelings ahead of the third morning's play. Sky Sports had set up an interview studio not dissimilar to the diary room of the Channel 4 TV show *Big Brother* – and Ian Ward's remote questioning provided me with an opportunity to vent my frustrations.

It was an unusual situation to be sitting alone, in front of a single camera on a Friday mid-match, discussing my omission. That environment can make you feel like you are talking to yourself when you are actually engaging with hundreds of thousands of people sat in armchairs at home. I had no pre-conceived ideas of what I was going to say. However, I found the chance to speak my mind was therapeutic. I was never going to go in and tear down trees, because that would have been a potential dressing-room distraction and detrimental to what the England team were trying to achieve on the field, but neither was I willing simply to toe the party line when not agreeing with the decision.

The frustration I felt during this particular week stemmed from a belief that the shirt was mine. I had worked hard to make things that way. Statistically speaking, I didn't think I deserved to lose it, and the fact I had done so was down to opinions winning out over facts. It was a tough pill to swallow, when I considered that I was England's leading wicket-taker in both the previous year's Ashes and the tour of South Africa in 2019–20, and effectively had not been selected next up.

There was nothing I had to prove. Those wickets were already there, on paper, in the form of my statistics: 485 career wickets, as prolific as any pace bowler in the previous couple of years. Having not been left out in a home Test since 2012, I was not used to being in such a position and in some ways that made it harder. So did receiving more messages of support than I had in congratulating me for my eight for 15 against Australia.

That was an antidote to my general mood. I struggled to sleep for a couple of days after being told I was not playing, and it was only human, I guess, to start catastrophising. I felt as if I had done enough previously not to consider my spot was under pressure. Now the pressure was on, because

I was not in the side. Arguably, that would bring the best out of me.

I also had to hear from the mouths of the national selector Ed Smith and the England coach Chris Silverwood the truth of the situation. If the reality had been that they saw no future for me, that would have been that. It is the nature of professional sport. But they said they did. It was of no comfort whatsoever that, like in Barbados, England lost. You always want your team to win, regardless of whether you feel personally aggrieved.

Stokes was exceptional. On the second night of the match, he knocked on my hotel room door and asked for a chat. He said, 'This is nothing about cricket. I just wanted to know how you're feeling.' That was a classy touch and the sort of thing that leads teams forward. The type of conduct we would come to expect from him when he became permanent Test captain. He is not only an exceptional cricketer, but a real people person.

I came back into the team in relentless fashion. My speeds were up and I was a constant threat when the series moved to Manchester. Six wickets were mine in the first of two wins at Emirates Old Trafford, and there was an innings of 62 to complement the ten wickets in a Player of the Match display in the second. The 2020 season had featured a horrid start, but as I maintained my form against Pakistan, I didn't want it to end. Every time I got the ball in my hands I was expecting to create chances, and every time I walked out to bat I wanted to have an influence on the game.

It was against Pakistan, of course, that I hit 169 at Lord's back in 2010 – the highest score by an England number 9 – helping us to recover from a position of 102 for seven. The Test was later sullied by revelations that Pakistan had bowled deliberate no-balls, bringing lengthy bans for three of their players, Salman Butt, Mohammad Asif and Mohammad Amir. However, I don't believe my performance was tainted. Spot-fixing – the arranging of micro-managed moments in a game like wides and no-balls – is not the same as match-fixing. And I always had a good eye, which is why the Night Hawk role was primed for me.

That my upturn in fortunes with the bat occurred in another year in which Pakistan toured was down to Peter Moores. During that lockdown summer, I worked on the tactical side of things with Moores at Trent Bridge, where we practised in small training groups.

When it came to batting, he said, attack was my best form of defence. I assessed my previous dismissals and felt that I was losing sight of the ball and getting bowled, so I changed my guard, moved more onto leg stump and tried to access it more freely.

As a coach, Pete always liked to use other players as examples so that you can visualise what he is talking about, and he used Shane Warne's slightly unorthodox batting in the 2005 Ashes as a template. The bowlers didn't know whether he was going leg-side or off-side when he was putting bat to ball. Equally, he could have used other slightly awkward tail-end batters like Daniel Vettori or Mitchell Starc. What did help me to emulate some of their results, though, was the fact that my head was now still at the point of the bowler's delivery. That seems an obvious thing, but bad habits had crept in.

One-day cricket also prolonged my Test career in 2019. With ill feeling still festering from the away series against West Indies at the start of the year, I told my manager Neil Fairbrother that if I was left out of the XI for the first Ashes match at Edgbaston, that would be it. Crucially, however, Jofra Archer was carrying a niggle from England's glorious World Cup campaign, which had concluded only a fortnight earlier. I was in – and after Jimmy Anderson damaged his calf on the first morning, I transformed from a selection permutation to a permanent pick. As an ever-present, I finished as our leading wicket-taker with 23.

It was a series that was defined by one of England's great innings. Ben Stokes rated his unbeaten 135 at Headingley in late August, which kept the Ashes alive, as better than the one he made in hitting a double hundred against South Africa in Cape Town in early 2016, and the World Cup final effort that defeated New Zealand.

We won the toss and bowled in beautiful bowling conditions. The Leeds lights were on, it swung and we bowled Australia out for 179. We were absolutely delighted to be beginning our reply on the second morning. I was buzzing, because it looked like perfect batting conditions, and we had the chance to put a score on the board and get ahead of the game, which is exactly what you need to do at a ground as capricious in its reaction to the elements as Headingley. When the clouds are out, wreak havoc. When it's warm and dry, go big with the bat.

Jofra Archer had taken six wickets during a first day of murk and then spent the evening into the early hours playing Call of Duty in his room. We turned up together at the ground and he told me he felt knackered. All I could think was: I hope we don't have to bowl today. Somehow, we contrived to be bowled out for 67.

I hurled my bat in anger when I arrived back in the changing room, unbeaten on four, because I felt that my top-order colleagues – players I had the utmost respect for in terms of ability, whom I had watched construct brilliant innings against different opponents all around the world – had rather thrown their wickets away. It didn't feel as though we were making the Australian bowlers work very hard at all. And I knew, contrary to my earlier hopes about resting up, that I would now have to get out there and put in another shift. Despite what you might think, having to go out and bowl because the batters were out cheaply did not get to me that often over the course of two decades as a professional, but this was one of these occasions.

We should be batting still, I said. The odd swear word thrown in. I couldn't stop thinking that we had thrown away an unbelievable opportunity. To be fair, Jonny Bairstow pulled me up on my behaviour and straightened me out of my wobble. I knew then that I had to get my head on, because if we were to have any chance of remaining in the game, we needed to bowl Australia out cheaply, too. I got Warner leg before in my first over, the second of the innings, and taking six in all by the close kept us in the hunt for history making. Stokes, whose real moments of class were yet to come, bowled a marathon spell up the hill in setting up the 359-run target.

English cricket fans tend to know what came next, but although Joe Root rightly gets credit for his scoring 77, the innings that tends to be forgotten was Joe Denly's half-century. He battled his way through four hours and some pretty testing spells from the Australians to wear them down a little bit. We only ever talk about that undefeated last-wicket partnership of 76 between Stokes and Jack Leach – and it's the best one that you will ever see. But without Denly that would not have been possible.

When I walked out to bat at 286 for eight, I tapped gloves with Stokesy. He was in one of those glazed-over moments in which he is really focusing. Just like the one he had at Lord's in 2023. He simply said, 'Stay with me.' Unfortunately, James Pattinson hit me on the toe second ball. I had stayed with him for two minutes. Pattinson is a legend of a bloke, someone I loved to bits when he played with us at Nottinghamshire, but a proper snotty Australian all the same, and he was shouting, 'Cheerio, Broady, we've got the Ashes now,' as I trudged off.

No offence to Leach, but I thought he was right and the game was done. Of course, I did. Everyone did. Not because of the loss of my batsmanship, but the chances of the bloke at the other end being able to do unbelievable things with only one wicket standing. So I took my place for what I anticipated being the last rites. Sitting next to Jos Buttler and Joe Root in Headingley's cramped indoor viewing area, it was understandably a bit glum. But once Stokes got the requirement under thirty, with a series of scoops and hauls to the leg-side boundary, we suddenly thought, we've got a chance here.

Jos and Joe couldn't bring themselves to watch and I was doing the commentary for them. Both faced forwards but they were peeping through fingers or looking at the floor. Nobody moved. There was that heart-in-the-mouth moment when the ball looped to third man and Marcus Harris grassed the ball diving forward, but Stokes had fully engaged the crowd and the atmosphere was bananas.

Then, there was the one that came to long off from the bowling of Nathan Lyon with eight to win. It looked for all money as though it was going to be caught and I was shouting, 'Get up, get up, get up!' Urging the ball to clear the fielder one minute, bellowing, 'It's six, it's six, it's six!' the next. Then time stood still as Lyon fumbled a run-out chance and every one of us demanded to know, 'Leachy, what are you doing?' Next ball, Stokes would have been LBW – my naked eye has always doubted Hawk-Eye on this – had Australia not burned their reviews.

But we all know those shared things, don't we? What makes this great piece of British sporting theatre so special, however, is remembering where you were after Leachy clipped a ball from Pat Cummins off his armpit for one and set up one of the most beautiful moments in my memory.

As Ben Stokes rocked back and the ball hit the middle, I knew that was it. I jumped instantly and my head went through the temporary tiles on the home changing room ceiling. In the commotion, the metal leg of the stool that Jos was sitting on went straight into my shin, causing a gash. The chaos was wonderful. To be out there with that atmosphere, as we raced out onto the pitch to celebrate, was so unbelievable and a taste of what would come again on a couple of occasions four years later.

I took a picture of Stokes back in the changing room with a cap over his face – the realisation of what had just happened sinking in underneath. To doublecheck we weren't dreaming, we watched the highlights back before we left the ground that evening.

Metaphorically speaking, I also knew exactly where I was in the game at this point. Test specialism had crept on me by stealth, but I was sure happy it had at times like these.

CHAPTER NINE

I F ever anyone wanted me half an hour before the start of a Test match in which I was playing, they would know where to find me. Standing five yards from where the toss would take place.

Watching the coin go up from close quarters was a routine of mine that I never changed. I loved the sense of anticipation around the ground over what the winning captain would choose to do, and as someone in the privileged position of being able to witness that decision in this way, I always did.

With heavy rain forecast during the fourth Ashes Test at Old Trafford in 2023, the toss in Manchester took on extra significance. So when Ben Stokes won it for the fourth occasion in a row and said, 'We're going to have a bowl,' the majority of England supporters would have been thinking, oh good. However, after Michael Atherton's snap interview with Ben to provide his reasoning, I thought, Oh God! Atherton told him that no other captain had won the toss at Old Trafford, bowled, and then won the game.

As a rule, Stokes likes to bowl first. Setting up fourth-innings chases is a style of cricket that he prefers, but as the pitches in Manchester historically have deteriorated, it has always been a bat-first place. Had conditions been dry, that would have been my preference, but because of the potential for reduced time in the game due to the weather, it was the most sensible option.

We knew that we would have to go even harder in this match in the pursuit of victory, as at 2–1 down, only two victories over Australia would do if we were to achieve our mission of returning the Ashes to English hands for the first time in six years. We might have to win inside the equivalent of three and a half days, and that potentially meant bowling out the Australians twice and batting only once, depending when the showers materialised.

Australia's response to this scenario was to lengthen their batting, recalling the fit-again Cameron Green as a second all-rounder, neglecting to play a frontline spinner and asking Travis Head to fulfil the role as a part-time one. With such a defensive decision, we would not only have to make the running, but slog uphill on what was an unforgiving pitch to the bowlers.

While we are on the subject of pitches, here's a thing. Why in a week like this, in a series that had moments to match the vintage Ashes summer of 2005, were we not producing a green seamer? The long-range forecasts had made for pretty unequivocal reading – it was going to be a heavily disrupted match. Why, then, not use the home advantage and produce a sporting surface to increase the chances of the contest ending in a result? Therefore increasing the chances of an England win and setting up the enthralling prospect of an Oval decider.

It was not as if doing so would guarantee victory – there are two teams out on the field after all, and the Australians had won two of the first three. But the fact it wasn't on the menu highlighted the disjointed relationship between the England team, the ECB and the counties. The players occasionally want co-operation, whereas the suits consistently think corporate. Too much focus was placed on the unlikely prospect of a fifth day, when it should have been on increasing the probability of an unbelievable fifth Test. In the circumstances, we gave it everything in the conditions presented to us and only just fell short.

To bowl Australia out for 317 showed great spirit, determination and adaptability. It had poured down on the eve of the match, and I thought my feet were sinking in an opening spell that was frankly a pile of crap. My first ball could have gone anywhere, but David Warner made sure this particular long hop ended up exactly where the first one I'd bowled to him in Leeds had gone – to the boundary. Early on was a real struggle. I managed to nip one back to get Usman Khawaja leg before, but I couldn't find any real rhythm, and fortunately Jimmy Anderson bowled very tightly at the other end, highlighting the strength of our partnership.

Jimmy also used his local knowledge to help the rest of us in the bowling attack. We started off with wobble seam, but balls were almost sticking in the pitch, giving the batter too much time to react. So he told us that his home ground for Lancashire could sometimes be like that, and if we bowled more traditional seam-up, it might kiss off the rope and feel quicker. From a few overs in, we all held it bolt upright. It was a good example of how the two of us worked in unison over the years.

As a friend and new-ball partner I felt a bit for Jimmy, because he did not take the wickets he would have liked during the series, but cricket can be a weird beast, and nothing summed it up more than the fact that on the opening day the Aussies couldn't score off him, or nick him for that matter. Then, having walked off the field that first evening wicketless, with a lengthy list of plays and misses, he began day two with a wide half-volley that was slapped to cover by Pat Cummins.

You could see how buzzing the lads were when Ben Stokes took that catch and everyone ran to Jimmy and celebrated with him. We knew how frustrated he was getting, not taking the wickets he probably deserved. He'd had a couple of dropped catches at Edgbaston, and numerous spells when it seemed only a matter of time until his luck changed. It never did, and he was the only one within our squad that could say they didn't have the kind of impact we were all looking for – either going big with the bat or ball.

Our style was not about consistency. It was for someone to have a great day at some stage in the series. And at some stage, everyone did. Whether it was with two wickets in a spell or a great knock that changed momentum. It was only Jimmy that did not. Obviously that was familiar territory for him previously, but as he said himself, the pitches of 2023 were his kryptonite. Edgbaston and Lord's were lifeless; he didn't play at Headingley where it did carry, and he would have bowled great there.

I had other reasons to celebrate in the first over after tea, when I joined a pretty mega club of which Jimmy Anderson is also a member. When the ball was in the air travelling to Joe Root at fine leg from Travis Head's bat, not for one millisecond did I think about it being my 600th Test wicket. What was swirling in my head was the plan we had come up with at the interval: to bump Head.

Then, as Joe closed his hands on the ball, it hit me. I'm not a numbers man and I was not one to play for milestones, but following Muttiah Muralitharan, Shane Warne, Anil Kumble and Jimmy was special. It was nice to take my 600th from the end at Old Trafford named after him, but Jimmy wasn't on the field at the time, so the congratulatory handshake had to wait. Nor was it a landmark I had considered to be attainable by its seventh month when 2023 opened, but with that record-breaking run of five or more wickets in seven successive matches, I had made it.

Five of the wickets in this first innings were taken by Chris Woakes, who returned to the England fold as if he'd never been away. It was easy to forget, given his seamless return to success midway through this series, that he had been on the outside when it came to the Test scene, stretching back to the Caribbean tour of fifteen months previously. His ability to move the ball both ways and get it to rise sharply in the process added another dimension to our attack.

That was no mean feat either, because of the state of the Dukes balls we were using. They went soft and then subsequently out of shape quickly and we found it quite frustrating that the umpires' ball rings used for testing were not the same carried by English county umpires. The International Cricket Council ones are universal, accommodating the products of different manufacturers, and you can fit a beach ball through them. It made requesting checks irrelevant at times, although you had to go through the process to express how unhappy you were. If we had played county cricket with the balls we used against Australia, they'd have been getting changed every 20 overs. There was a huge change in the quality of Dukes post-coronavirus and it was clear some pretty major issues remained.

In this match, Zak Crawley was hell-bent on making those balls less spherical. Not one to be critical of opposition teams, but I thought Zak made an Australian team crowned world champions only a month earlier look very average, hitting boundaries at will. The innings he produced, of 189 from 182 balls, showed everyone why so much faith had been invested in him. He had been picked for performances like this. It was complete vindication of the unflinching faith shown by Brendon McCullum and Ben Stokes when people were asking why a player that averaged under 30 as an opening batter remained in the side.

Only Crawley, Stokes and Joe Root had played every game since English cricket's entertainment era was launched. This was the embodiment of putting pressure on your opponents.

He looked so confident in what he was doing and wherever Australia put the fielders, the ball went into a gap elsewhere. Often, the place where a man had just been. It was as dominant an innings against an Australian bowling attack as I have seen, and proved the cornerstone of an innings of 592 at a rate of 5.49 runs per over.

Crawley's runs made him the leading run-scorer in the series, but it was a performance worth so much more than that. It was the style of play, the showmanship, and the enjoyment he gave to others watching, but ultimately, it was the way he took the game forward at a rate. In future years, when he is re-living it, he will be able to tell people what I told him at the match's first drinks break.

'This pitch is right up your alley, Creepy, you're getting 150 on this,' I told him, after my initial new-ball spell. Why so confident? Because it was such a true pitch to hit on and I thought his power and presence would make him really difficult to bowl at. So it proved. To be fair, I also said that Joe Root would get a hundred – something that looked on until he got a shooter from Josh Hazlewood only 16 runs shy.

Our top-order batting was a pleasure to watch. But not the most enjoyable period of our innings. For it was here in Manchester, despite the gloomy mood that its infamous climate cooked up, that we experienced our favourite period of the series. To paint the scene, it is the third afternoon and I have just been dismissed, trying to score some quick runs ahead of a declaration. We are 526 for nine, and one ball away from the innings being concluded.

Jonny Bairstow, who has been struggling for a score since beginning with a rapid half-century at Edgbaston, is unbeaten on 41, and has been joined at the crease by Jimmy Anderson. We knew by this point that in all probability we only had time to bat once, given the deluge shaping up for the following day and Sunday, so as many runs as possible in the first innings would be beneficial.

When your number 11 is at the crease, you are generally trying to rev up your energy for bowling and fielding, in expectation of a change of innings, but for the next forty minutes we were like giddy sixth-formers in a common room, each of us in turn offering their best impressions of Jonny.

Perhaps earlier in his career, he might not have taken favourably to people taking the mickey out of him, but since turning himself into such an integral and valued member of the side, we say to him, 'Alright, Jonny, how ya getting on, lad? Cracking.' And he loves it.

On the back of playing at Headingley two weeks previously, it felt like Yorkshire accents had been drip-fed into our blood-streams. To a man each of us got involved, with varying levels of success. I won't out the absolutely horrendous ones for fear of being sued, but suffice to say that Moeen Ali and Ben Stokes, our best impressionist and Arthur Shelby imperson-ator par excellence, were the best. Joe Root obviously didn't need much help with the accent, but his best trait was providing the content, because he knows Bairstow so well.

Jonny has a tendency to get angry at anything he perceives as negative media coverage, taking things very personally at times, and some of us had witnessed a key pre-play moment on the first morning of the second Test at Lord's when Michael Vaughan, who had been heavily critical of Jonny's wicket-keeping at Edgbaston, was on the outfield.

Jonny was receiving some simple under-arm taps into his gloves from Brendon McCullum – the kind of catches you would give to a youth-team keeper to warm up. After one such, Jonny looked straight at Vaughan and said, 'You see that? You watching that?' Fixing him with a steely look. 'Yeah, I can see that,' Vaughan replied.

Now, here we were at Old Trafford with Jonny belting sixes into the stands, turning that awkward moment into a comedy one.

'Pat Cummins sets off from his mark, running in with Michael Vaughan in his hand,' someone would say, in their best Jonny. 'And Bairstow thumps him into the crowd. Twenty rows back. He really meant that one!'

At one point, the television cameras panned round to us on the balcony, and we were laughing and smiling and it looked like the team spirit was very high. It was, of course. All to do with the Bairstow caricatures – meant very much as a compliment to him. In more recent times, he has joined in with the Jonny-against-the-world joshing. As his team-mates, we were more likely to joke about it than bring his attention to things in a more serious way.

I will level with you here, I'm really bad at impressions, but my one strength is Yorkshire, because of mimicking Geoffrey Boycott over the years. I have heard him so much and adapted some of the things he's said to me and my team-mates for material.

For example, during the 2019 Ashes, Ben Stokes, Jos Buttler and I were playing golf at Geoffrey's club, Wetherby. We had walked off the 18th green and he was just about to start his round.

'You,' he said, turning to Jos. 'You! Get in, before they get you out. Get dancing, get those feet moving, come on!'

It was not the kind of environment where Jos might have expected a dressing down, but because of my toss habit I was also present when Joe Root received some rather loud and public Geoffrey advice at the end of that series.

Joe, batting at three that summer rather than his customary four, was waiting with the Australian captain Tim Paine in the middle at The Oval and Geoffrey, whom we had not really seen all summer, was on the pitch in recognition of being knighted. There he was, suited and booted, taking the acclaim of the crowd, with Joe waiting patiently alongside Michael Holding, who was doing the toss presentation for Sky Sports.

Suddenly, Geoffrey piped up with, 'Joe, what number are you batting?'

'Three, Geoffrey.'

'Oh, no, no, no, no, no, you're not a number three. I've been saying this all summer. You shouldn't be batting three, you haven't got the technique. You've got to get yourself to four.'

He was dressing down the England captain in front of the Australian one!

We've always had fun with the old maxim that a Yorkshireman says what he likes, and likes what he bloody well says, and back on the Old Trafford balcony, someone was pretending the ball was Alex Carey as it pounded off one of the concrete terraces.

'Run me out at Lord's, would you? I'm gonna have you here, mate! Bosh!'

The records will say Jonny finished on the cruellest score possible of 99 not out, but we roared him back into the changing room in acknowledgement of his contribution. When a team is nine wickets down, Bairstow is the best batter in the world, because he is such an amazing boundary hitter. Ben Stokes is a good rival, but Jonny has probably done it a bit more in recent years and he is so dynamic in those situations. He has such an amazing ability to clear the rope, even when nine Australian fielders are positioned on it.

Until this point, the series had been a difficult one for him. There were big question marks over his wicketkeeping and he was right, he had not done the job regularly for a long time. Three years, in fact. Remember, his previous run in the England Test team had been as a specialist batter.

Jonny's frustration came out in the press conference that evening. Aimed at people who weren't taking his full story into account – that he had fractured so many bones in his leg and ankle in an horrific accident on a Harrogate golf course that his surgeon had doubted he would be able to recover sufficiently to get back to the top level at all, let alone make 2023's main event against the Australians.

Regardless of the extent of his damage, I don't think anyone would have been fit with the amount of cricket he'd had in preparation. Eight months out for a bowler can take anything between six to eight first-class matches to get back up to speed, and it is exactly the same with keeping, a physically demanding job requiring mobility and movement. Jonny lacked that at the start and some of the nicks he missed were going low. What you might call tough chances.

By its very nature, though, Ashes cricket is not designed to settle you back in slowly. You've got to be good to go. This is sport at the very highest level, so I could see things from both sides. If, as a pundit, I was watching a match, I would not necessarily be assessing the history of individual players, so that if a catch was dropped, I could provide an excuse for why it happened. I would be reporting the facts and the ramifications of hurting a team in the present.

Jonny's agility undoubtedly improved throughout the series, in line with his match fitness, and his reawakening with the bat at Old Trafford was arguably sparked by the stunning first-innings catch to dismiss Mitchell Marsh off Chris Woakes. With all-rounders, one suit feeds the other, and if someone does well in the field, it can carry confidence into their batting. In this instance, it was a stupendous low grab that catalysed things.

Of all the players I came up against, the biggest example of someone transferring the feel-good factor from one to another was Mitchell Johnson. If he scored runs, you were thinking he would bowl well, too, because he was someone who fed off the energy of both disciplines. It's a confidence thing and Jonny is a bit like that in terms of character. We saw how incredible his batting was across 2022 when he played as a specialist batter and there were no question marks, stresses or strains caused by his keeping. He simply concentrated on one discipline and smashed it.

When we claimed four wickets at Old Trafford by the close of the third day, we'd probably had the most perfect first three days we could have wished for. Now, we just needed a bit of luck from the Manchester weather gods.

Sitting in the changing room watching the rain fall on Saturday morning, it felt so unjust that the weather might have a decisive say after such an incredible few weeks. Typically, Brendon McCullum came up with a phrase to keep me calm.

'Boss, we're too lucky to get wet,' he had said, when we'd arranged to play golf in the build-up to the match and, despite a horrendous forecast, we only had to contend with a light smattering of rain.

'Boss, we're too lucky for it to rain all day,' he said now, as he did his crossword. He was right again.

We weren't supposed to get any cricket in on the Saturday, according to the forecasts, but we squeezed in a 30-over window of play. It was not a fruitful one, though. Usually the overcast conditions, and use of the floodlights, lead to the ball moving around a bit, but unfortunately it got wet and then went soft, negating any such prospect. Mitchell Marsh and Marnus

Labuschagne, the overnight pair, had been playing quite nicely, but after finally being granted a ball change following a couple of false starts, we wanted to test them out with a spell from Mark Wood. We hoped the new one might swing and that is always hard to combat when delivered at high pace.

The response from the umpires Nitin Menon and Joel Wilson that it was too dark to do so caught us completely by surprise, not least because the latter was wearing dark glasses. He later clarified that his chosen eyewear were light enhancers, but it did not feel in the slightest bit dark out there considering what we'd had to contend with batting at Edgbaston, when we lost Ben Duckett and Zak Crawley for two runs at a similar time on the third afternoon.

'This is absolutely ridiculous,' I told Joel, relating this fact to him. 'What was the light reading of that day, because visibility is much better today than then.'

His answer summed up why I get so frustrated with the ICC – an organisation I have a connection with, remember. My dad works for them.

'I didn't do that match,' Joel replied.

To me, that was irrelevant. It shouldn't matter who was officiating. Only that the rules are applied consistently. If one rule was applied one week, it should also be applied the next. If it is okay for one team to bat with a reading showing such-and-such, it is okay for the other team to do so later in the series.

Forced to bowl a diet of spin, all we had to show for being 'lucky' was the wicket of Labuschagne – who for the first time in the series showed the kind of form that had taken him to the top of the Test rankings in mid-year – caught behind by a juggling Jonny Bairstow off Joe Root. Australia were still 61 runs behind at the close and we left the ground hoping for one more mini-session on the Sunday. One irritation as we left the field that evening was that the hours of Test cricket in this country are so inflexible. We had just entered a dry spell. But the close can only be put back by one hour under the current match regulations.

I was probably like every other England cricket fan on the way back to the hotel that evening, checking the weather apps and bracing myself for a tense wait. Despite anticipating Armageddon, I still held out that rarest of hope when you are spending time in Manchester that the clouds would somehow skirt round the city and miss you. A chance it could slide to the side.

But as I thumbed through my phone, I also saw a statistic of Old Trafford featuring a full day washed out every 2.7 Tests. It was the second most rained-off Test venue in the world behind Sydney by one day. Sadly, they levelled up.

Because the British Open golf was being held down the road at Hoylake and the wind direction was coming from Liverpool, we were watching it on television on the fifth morning, hoping to see the sky clearing. Unfortunately, they kept putting more and more rain jackets on. The picture looked bleaker and bleaker.

It was almost an act of defiance when a large group of us went out in the drizzle as lunchtime approached to play PIG – our football keepie-up game. Trying to show the people gathered in the stands, wrapped up in blankets and arched under umbrellas, that we really wanted to be out there. We did not want the rain to beat us. It was our way of sticking two fingers up at the clouds above us.

A brief flurry of activity from the ground staff around 1 p.m. suggested they spotted an opening, but it didn't last and the outfield was sodden by now. We got drenched, there was no gap in the cloud and no movement. We hadn't got a prayer.

The one image I have of that afternoon, with us taking shelter back in the dressing room by this point, is of one lady, a lone wolf, sitting at the very top of the 8,000-capacity temporary stand, exposed to the elements. She sat there all day and didn't move. Until about four o'clock. I watched her through the window and when she got up and walked down the stairs, I said to Rupert, our statistician: 'Mate, we are done.'

The mood inside was that we could not have done any more. We had played the game as hard as we could and dominated for three days. I didn't feel angry. Just a bit sad. That we'd had five full sessions washed out when we had trodden Australia into the ground. The weather meant we had now lost the chance to win the series and regain the Ashes. It was such an unemotional way for this most passionate of series to be defined.

Down the corridor, Australia celebrated. Pat Cummins said that it was 'a bit weird' and that his team had not retained the Ashes 'in the circumstances we would have liked'.

Let's face it, they were happy for rain to ruin the game, as we probably would have been if the shoe was on the other foot. It saved them from certain defeat. We were very confident of not only winning in Manchester, but following it up at The Oval to make it 3–2. From Leeds onwards, we had felt like we were on a steam train that was gathering pace and no one was getting off. We just kept adding more fuel.

England's dominance had also changed the way Australians were viewing their team and its leader. Despite his side going 2–0 up a couple of weeks earlier, Cummins was suddenly under pressure and there were questions over whether he was the right man for the job, because very rarely do you see captains chasing the game as much as the Aussies were in that match. To be honest, it felt like the theme for the series. As we had anticipated before a ball was bowled, it would be our team that did all the running, and the Australians the chasing.

It was all a bit subdued back behind the door with 'home' on it. We shared a beer in the changing room and sat around, chatting about how we could lift our spirits for The Oval. Forget about regaining the Ashes, we agreed. That had gone. But let's make sure we bring a similar style of play next week, because it was noticeable that the Aussies had gone. In the field, they were broken.

Everyone felt focused on this, because there is such a huge difference in the feeling and the sound of 2–1 and 2–2, and we sensed that there would be a huge difference in the public reaction to drawing or losing. A shared series was the least our performances deserved. We did not contemplate defeat.

We knew we wouldn't lose at The Oval. A 3–1 scoreline never crossed my mind.

Back in the hotel bar, a few of us got together to share the two nice bottles of red wine the team had presented to me for reaching the 600-mark in Test wickets. A very quiet ending to a weekend that could have been so different had the weather played its part. Next morning, I hopped on a 6.45 a.m. train to London. There would be one final career landmark left to toast.

CHAPTER TEN

I T was the spring of 2022 when I changed my career goal summary to 'take control of your own destiny'.

Career goals naturally change over time, reflecting key points in a career and relating to targets in the not-too-distant future. For example, one I penned while in New Zealand in late 2019, simply read: 'Next away Ashes is my Olympics'. I have always set them in this way, because I am very much a short-term process character.

At this point, others had made decisions that left me feeling unjustly treated and angry. I couldn't change what they had done, but I had to alter my mindset going forward. I had mulled over my shelf life as an international cricketer throughout my thirties, but being dropped for England's Test tour of the Caribbean meant someone else thought that, at the age of thirty-five, I was past my sell-by date. This provided my playing days with a completely different dynamic.

It felt as if I had been made a scapegoat for the 4–0 thrashing in Australia. Personally, I had taken 13 wickets in three appearances, and only Mark Wood with 17 in four was more prolific among our squad. Yes, we had all felt hollow in Hobart at the end of that 2021–22 Ashes tour, and as a senior player I so wanted to play a constructive part in altering the England team's fortunes. Coming out of COVID conditions would help in that regard, I believed.

I was actually discussing what had gone wrong in Australia, and what could be done to put things right in the Caribbean in early February, at the end of a round of golf at Sunningdale in which Zak Crawley, Rob Key and Tim Henman were my playing partners. It was a candid conversation. One of English cricket's failings, I said, was looking so far ahead all the time. We were always focused on the next Ashes, when what we needed to do was pare it down to game by game and picking the best XI each week.

Cue dramatic irony. Within seconds of getting into my car to drive home, I had a WhatsApp call from Andrew Strauss, the ECB's interim managing director of the England men's cricket team following Ashley Giles's sacking just days earlier.

It was a terrible signal, which therefore led to a very brief, broken conversation, beginning with him informing me that unfortunately, I would not be going to the Caribbean.

'Oh, interesting,' I said.

Of course, it wasn't interesting. It was infuriating. Nobody takes being dropped lightly.

'We're going to go with a younger bowling attack,' he told me.

What was I to say? I was a novice in such situations. These phone calls were usually of the good-news variety. I'd had plenty of pre-match, hotel door knocks to inform me I had not made the eleven taking the field, but a full tour squad?

'I'm assuming with that comment that Jimmy is not going either?'

Strauss confirmed I was right. I put the phone down, with a compulsion to tell someone immediately. Perhaps it was the state of shock I found myself in. I couldn't keep it to myself. So I called Rob Key, who I was now following on the M25.

'Mate, you can forget that chat we've just had. I'm not actually going to the Caribbean.'

'Yeah, I know,' he said.

At the time, Rob was working for Sky Sports. I didn't ask how he'd found out, but the fact that he had, flicked a switch. Yes, there was intense frustration at not being picked, but it had now developed into full-blown fury. The first whispers are already out and I didn't even know about it.

When I got back to our flat in London, Mollie was out and so I called Jimmy Anderson. I told him I wasn't in the squad, he said ditto and we discussed our surprise at some of the players that had been called up, agreeing that these had been some massive calls for an interim appointment to make. Jimmy had received his own devastating news as he picked up his daughters Lola and Ruby from school.

Although the official announcement was not until the following day of 8 February, I'd been prepared for the news of our omissions to leak into the public domain, because if Key knew, others would too, and it was soon being debated on social media. The fact that people were saying they found it hard to comprehend only served to wind me up even more.

Naturally, lots of calls followed between senior players and player management representatives, and one of the suggestions was that a couple of different squads had done the rounds, and that my name was included in the one that the England captain Joe Root had asked for.

Whoever made the casting vote was inconsequential, but in the circumstances, I felt it was very much a statement call, and a massive one to make, as I don't believe in handing out England caps. Especially in big series, and this *was* a big series. We had not defeated West Indies away for eighteen years, and only once since 1968.

Nothing personal against someone like Matt Fisher, or any doubting of his talent, but I found myself logging on to Cricinfo to find out a bit more about him, poring over his statistics to discover he had played only twenty-one first-class games.

I asked myself: 'How is he better than me?'

My mind was a maelstrom. The more I tried to get my head around the situation, the worse it hurt. Naturally one thought developed into another, and I didn't consider solely the immediate consequences, but the longer-term ones.

'Hang on, have I just received a five-minute phone call that ends my international career? Out of respect, someone ought to have driven to my house and told me in person after sixteen years of service.'

Back on the phone later that night, Jimmy and I agreed

that we needed to calm down and get away from things, so we booked a golfing trip to Scotland, staying at the Old Course Hotel in St Andrew's for two nights during the third Test in Grenada.

But calming down was not easy. The news was like being tasered. I had been stunned, stopped in my tracks, and for the next two weeks I wanted to vent my anger and hit back. Neil Fairbrother, my manager, talked me out of putting an inflammatory response to the squad announcement on Instagram, and my first newspaper column with the *Mail On Sunday* was heavily edited by the ECB – as was their prerogative as my employers.

Not that I heard anything else from the organisation over the next few weeks. Professional sport moves on very quickly. It can be a ruthless world. I've got mates that are footballers who are in the first-team squad one day, training with the Under-21s the next. It is part and parcel of the industry. But accepting that doesn't make it any easier when the music stops and you discover you are the one without a seat on the plane.

The whole episode meant that I retained a bit of a dark spot for the ECB for a decent period of time, stretching deep into March. Yet when I say ECB, I don't really know who I mean by that. I certainly had no beef with the employees of the ECB. I still loved the England badge. People within the Test team set-up, both players and coaches, were lifelong friends. So where exactly was I directing my ire? Was I still angry at Strauss? Yes, definitely.

My mood began to change during that trip to St Andrew's when one day over breakfast, I exchanged some messages with Rob Key. News had come out that he might be interested in the England director role that Strauss was keeping warm. I was surprised, because I thought he had a great job with Sky Sports. Not many names had been linked with the ECB position, but the presence of his felt out of kilter, so I began some banter with him.

'You won't be able to play as much golf, mate!' I joked. 'Those clubs will have to be consigned to the garage.'

Key is not only someone into golf, he is one of those players who is fully into the technical side of things, analysing and practising different techniques. He would have his hands full running the English team. There would be no downtime.

He'll never take it, I thought. Not for the first time, I was wrong.

In the nicest possible way I was ready for a leadership change and I don't mean any slight on Joe Root at all in saying that, because I played a lot of very, very successful Test matches with England's most-winning captain. Truthfully, it felt the right time for the whole group, and for Joe himself, when he resigned on 15 April. International cricket captaincy is often talked about in four-year cycles and Joe had done five.

He called me the day before he stepped down and I was naturally sorry to hear the news, because he'd been in the job for such a long time and that meant we had shared a lot of memories. I was not prepared to let recent events distort that.

The fact was that he had overseen one of the toughest periods with the team. The challenges on and off the field were huge.

But my overriding feeling was it was a good decision, and the right decision. I told him that he had given everything to the England Test captaincy, and I could tell that leading through the COVID years had left him very weary. It had also restricted how much time he spent with his family. At this point I did not know for certain if I would ever play alongside him again, but regardless, I felt the team needed freshening up. No doubt that was the intention of Strauss when he dropped playing personnel like myself, Jimmy Anderson, Dawid Malan and Rory Burns. However, above and beyond any kind of squad shake-up, the team required both a new style of play and mindset.

'Congratulations on being an amazing captain for England,' I said. Because let's face it, he had led the team to some magnificent highs such as a thumping home win over India in 2018 and the away triumph in South Africa. Not many visiting captains win a series in Sri Lanka. He did it twice. 'But I can tell in your voice, you're just very ready to be a player again. Come back into the ranks. Fit back into the group.'

In short, we were getting our old Joe back – the cheeky chap, the fun, smiley guy that had gone missing through the most testing of times – but not necessarily losing any of his leadership qualities. You always need strong senior figures within a changing room to offer support to the captain and guidance to younger players making their way. He sounded ready to fit back into the regiment and be a strong lieutenant.

This particular conversation was probably the starting point for me buying into a new beginning with England. One of the reasons I hurt so much was that I cared so deeply and had done for such a long time. This had been my team since December 2007 and would always be my team, whatever happened next. If the new environment involved me, great. If it didn't, so be it. I just knew English cricket was ready for something different. And so was I.

Did I fear that my career was over? Yes, I did. Moreover, I had been mentally preparing for it over the previous eight weeks. Not long after my omission from England's tour of the Caribbean, I began sessions with the Nottinghamshire psychologist Chris Marshall on my mindset. We spent a lot of time talking things through. As a professional sportsman, you have to accept you are being controlled by others, and our work together was about taking control of my own destiny for what was left of my playing days. So, whether I finished for Nottinghamshire at Trent Bridge or for England at The Oval against Australia, both were going to be acceptable options.

One phrase had been swirling around my head: 'Always jump before you're pushed.' There was a determination in me to play on and allow my own actions to decide the timing of my exit. I had come close to being pushed out, but now I would take back the responsibility from the ECB by dictating my own terms. How? By staying fully focused on enjoying my day job of playing cricket.

Nobody knew at that stage in which direction the England

Test team would go, and who would be included, so to concern myself with that outcome was expending energy better used elsewhere. So, I flicked through my proverbial book of cliches. From now on until the end – whenever I chose the end to be – I was going to play every day as though it was my last.

'I am going to attack each week, and give my heart and soul,' was a phrase I repeated regularly in press conferences going forward.

Whether it was going to last sixteen days or sixteen months, I refused to look further ahead than the following week. I vowed to treat every single game like it could be my career sunset, giving it absolutely everything until the dying of the light.

On 17 April 2022, three weeks after that exchange of messages I'd had with Rob Key as I sat eating breakfast at St Andrew's, he was appointed as England team director.

One of the things I had done during my soul-searching sessions with Chris Marshall was draw a mind map to delve into what I was really thinking about my England career going forward. The positive green entries outnumbered the red and among them was the prospect of regime change. With new personnel coming in and the chance to impress fresh pairs of eyes. So, this news felt like a good first step.

Key called me almost straight after his unveiling, the first contact I'd had with anyone official from the England management since Strauss delivered his devastating news more than two months previously. It was not a long conversation. Could we meet for breakfast, he wondered. Sure. We arranged a date for the Ivy in Cobham.

The fact there was no discussion on what he wanted to see me about added to the intrigue, but I was less inclined to worry about such things now that Chris had persuaded me to adopt this new outlook on my remaining playing days. My mind was in a more positive place with regards to the future, which, of course, I wanted to be with England. My new boss wanted to talk, and I was mildly excited about what that might entail.

Only at the last minute did my mood change, and negative thoughts creep in. As I left the house, turning to Mollie, I said, 'Well, this is either one of two things. I am either getting sacked here fully, and never playing for England again, or he's going to have half-decent news for me.' As I shut the front door, I had zero idea which way the coin would fall. The half-hour drive to Cobham was the most nervous imaginable.

Along a fifteen-mile stretch of the A3, I began building up so many conspiracy theories in my mind. I've seen it in films, I reminded myself. People always say if you're going to sack someone, do it in a public space, so you avoid a big kerfuffle. No one likes creating a scene.

My fears were allayed as soon as I got there and Key was . . . well, very Keysy.

'Thanks for meeting me. I'd like your thoughts on a few things.'

It was a chat about his role, essentially. Did I have any opinions on who should be the next England Test captain?

Did I have any opinions on coaches? Obviously, at the time, this was highly confidential.

We chatted about all things cricket and I lay on the table what needed to change. There was nothing about style of play, but I did reel off things I had previously aired when I was asked to a meeting four months earlier with the then ECB chief executive Tom Harrison in Sydney, ahead of the New Year's Ashes Test.

One of my focuses in that discussion had been inconsistency of selection. By the end of January 2022, we had made forty-seven changes of personnel in the previous fifteen matches. Name me any team in any sport, I said, where such a lack of continuity works. It might happen, but it was not a recipe for success. We had to start picking consistently and with clarity so that players knew what they were doing.

These were the things that players needed to perform. Not a team announcement taking place on our WhatsApp group the day before an Ashes match with Ollie Pope or Jonny Bairstow in one of the eleven positions. The uncertainty felt amateurish. People needed to know whether they were playing or not as part of their preparation and I argued that the naming of England teams should take place two days out whenever possible for that reason.

It was also necessary to treat members of the England team better, I continued. Undoubtedly, this made me sound a bit like a diva, but I informed him that we were staying in lower-budget hotels representing our country than those enjoyed by the Hundred teams. While we were at the Regent's Park

Marriott, the London Spirit were housed at the swankier Landmark. It was a minor thing, but it was nevertheless sending the wrong message to the 500-plus male professional cricketers wanting to play at the highest level.

Great as it was that the Spirit were enjoying the comforts of superior accommodation, my point was that if Test cricket really is the pinnacle of our game, you have to treat your players better. Leave them in no doubt that it is. Remember, this was coming at a time when some players were sacrificing significantly more money elsewhere to remain loyal and play for England.

Ben Stokes was the man for the captaincy, I said – although I'm pretty sure the decision had already been made. Ben is one of my best friends, I went on, and you must take all other responsibility off him. What weighed Joe Root down, pushing him to levels of exhaustion, was all the extra Zoom meetings, sitting on committees, being pulled into areas away from the cricket side of cricket. Someone else would have to pick up all the crap that comes with the England captaincy going forward. Let Ben lead on the pitch.

Key also mentioned the name of Brendon McCullum to me when discussing the vacant head coach position. Interesting, I thought. An amazing captain, I offered as an observation. But someone not easily prised out of the Twenty20 franchise world, in my opinion. Aside from Gary Kirsten, written up as hot favourite by the British press, there were not many other rival candidates being mooted. After all, coaching England, a team on a run of one win in seventeen matches, was hardly an attractive proposition.

I left breakfast that day uncertain whether I would be welcomed back into the squad at the start of the summer, or whether I had a future at all. It was not Key's place to make any promises ahead of appointing a new coach and new captain. That would be their domain, not his, but I made it clear that I was as keen to play as ever.

Within days of the coffee in Cobham, Ben Stokes was appointed England Test captain and one of the first things he said after taking on the responsibility was that Jimmy Anderson and I would be coming back into the fold.

Confirmation of my return to the England Test squad came on Tuesday, 17 May, when I received a mobile phone call from a New Zealand number as I walked to the City Ground for the second leg of the Championship play-off final between Nottingham Forest and Sheffield United. Or more accurately, on a walk to meet Joe Root – as passionate about the Blades as I am about Forest – for a pre-match beer.

'Congratulations, you're in the squad,' Brendon McCullum told me. 'See you in a couple of Sundays' time.'

'Thank you so much, Baz. I'll give you everything.'

Football on my mind, I also wanted to check the meet-up details for the first Test there and then.

'What time and where, please, Baz?'

His answer, typically of him, was casual, 'Some time Sunday

evening. We might just get together for a soft drink, so travel down and be ready to train on the Monday.'

I saw my opportunity. As I said, my football team mean a lot to me.

'Nottingham Forest could be in the play-off final at Wembley that day, with the chance to get back into the Premier League for the first time in twenty-five years,' I said.

'Who are Nottingham Forest?'

He found out the answer to that, after granting me permission to go to a match with a 4 p.m. kick-off, when I checked into the hotel on the morning of Sunday, 29 May. We had agreed to meet for coffee in the hotel lobby. Him, bleary-eyed from a long-haul flight from New Zealand. Me, sporting a Forest shirt, with a scarf around my neck. I felt a bit of a prat meeting England's new coach for the first time in this way, but was soon to learn it very much aligned to the laid-back ethos of McCullum's coaching mantra.

Despite Ben Stokes tweeting, 'Someone make sure that he gets home tonight,' after Forest defeated Huddersfield across London, I afforded myself only one celebratory glass of champagne, and didn't even finish that, trying to maintain a high level of professionalism ahead of training the next morning.

The most stark element of the changeover from one regime to the next was the contrast in styles between McCullum and previous England coaches I had worked under. Firstly, there was no PowerPoint presentation. No books in sight. Or handing out of sheets of paper punctuated by bullet points.

As the lads strapped their boots on, Baz told us how delighted he was to be here, and that he judged the culture of his groups in cricket on a few simple things:

1. Take the positive option.
2. Chase the ball as hard as you can in the field (and I mean like sprint, all the way to the rope).
3. If ever there is danger in the game, run at it.

It struck me immediately that running towards the danger was a really good saying and it was clear from the word go that we would not die wondering on McCullum's watch.

It sounded fun. These messages, reminding players to be brave, were built on over the next few days and weeks, and were followed by another with Kiwi traits before we went out onto the field against Ireland on 1 June 2023: 'Enjoy yourselves, I'd love you to be on the back pages, but never on the front – so no dickheads.'

I had not socialised with Baz much in the past and when I played against him, I was a little bit in awe, in all honesty. He was one of those players that had a real aura. How could you not have the utmost respect for how he went about his business captaining New Zealand? He was a hugely fierce competitor to play against, but a lovely man, and he was asking us to play in his image. Be positive when it was possible; flick the ball back before it hits the boundary; embrace moments of jeopardy in matches, don't fear them.

I was approaching my thirty-sixth birthday, but buzzing

to be there that week. Weirdly, I was also more than a bit nervous for training, despite having been through net practice processes for the past fifteen years; chiefly because it felt like I was reintegrating in a sense.

Neither did it help when Ben Stokes did his best to denormalise it by absolutely smoking every ball I bowled. His intention was to hit every delivery for four, so there was no holding back. It was not that he wanted to humiliate me. He wanted everyone to notice what he was doing, and balls flying out of cricket nets tend to get people's attention. He was making a statement to back up the assertive nature of the play that he and McCullum wanted to instil.

One other thing I noticed straightaway as we practised on the nursery ground at Lord's was how relaxed Baz was in our training environment.

'You won't see me on the tools,' he had warned us in advance.

In other words, he would not be flicking balls to batters, providing throw-downs. But he would always be there with the team. Available for each individual player in a one-on-one capacity. His way of working was very different to those that had gone before. From that first day, and at pretty much every training session going forward, he made it his business to speak to every player in turn, sidling up alongside people to ask: How are you getting on? Feeling good? Have you thought about this? What about that? Reckon we can get this working this week?

Everything with McCullum is tactical; nothing technical. In fact, I have never heard him say anything technical whatsoever.

His style, while striking me as unusual at first, was nevertheless very refreshing. I am pretty sure it would break every rule in the ECB's level-four coaching manual, and in truth he is more of a sports psychologist than a cricket coach. Most importantly, though, he was 100 per cent the man that English cricket needed.

Baz doesn't care if you have a trigger movement or not as a batter, whether your head falls across slightly, but he does care about brains being exactly in the right frame of mind to deliver. It was clear he saw his remit as someone to take as much pressure off the players as possible, so they could just go out and play, and enjoy playing.

One thing has always rung true to me. You should play cricket for England like you did as a twelve-year-old kid opening the curtains on a Saturday morning, praying it wasn't raining. He was tapping into that ethos.

A quick word about B-ball. I warned you some time ago that I wouldn't call it by its other name. What is it? What does it mean? What are its targets? Are you trying to score 400, 500, 600? And if so, how quickly? Do you need to score at a rate of X? Is there an optimum number of overs to bat for? Well, I have kind of covered much of this in previous pages, before even mentioning anything of what became the most glorious of twelve months under Brendon McCullum.

In terms of style, factors like this were never mentioned. Everything was so organic. Baz hates meetings, hence we literally had five-minute chats first thing in a morning. From then on, it was just constant positive messaging throughout the whole Test match.

Never was this better exemplified than in our first match at Lord's in June 2022 when, after bowling New Zealand out for just 132, we began the chase positively before experiencing a horrible collapse. At one stage on the opening evening, we lost five wickets for eight runs, and as changing rooms tend to do in such circumstances, we all went eerily quiet. Remember, despite all the upbeat attitude, this England team had failed to secure victory in sixteen of the previous seventeen matches.

Baz walked in as relaxed as anything, and said, 'Jeez, boys, it's quiet in here,' and put some tunes on. He wants to instigate life, for batters to contemplate possibilities going forward, not be staring at the floor because they got out.

It was a reminder that playing cricket was supposed to be fun. Thanks to Joe Root's hundred, we won that match. Of course we did. It set the tone for what was to come.

Victory at Lord's had been the perfect start, but it was day five of the second Test versus New Zealand at Trent Bridge that proved to be the biggest, most influential one we had in the transformation of the team's mindset.

When we arrived at the ground that morning, we needed to take three wickets to dismiss New Zealand second time around, and potentially set up a victory chase that had not appeared even remotely possible when our opponents made good use of an excellent surface to post 553 all out first time around. They resumed 238 runs ahead.

Jonny Bairstow had suffered a bit of a wobble in his first three innings of the series, struggling to get going and contributing scores of 1, 16 and 8. Now, however, the team was to benefit from Baz's attention to detail with individuals. Those little chats reminding players how good they were and how even the most seemingly insignificant numerical contributions could be huge positives for the team.

It had struck a chord with me at Lord's when, in the immediacy of our victory, it wasn't Joe Root's brilliant, match-defining innings that Baz focused on in his debrief. Or even Ben Foakes's supporting role in an unbroken 120-run stand for the sixth wicket that carried the team to its 277-run target. Instead, he picked out a certain person that had not been mega-successful, but who had tried to do things his way. They had tried to be true to the attacking mantra.

After playing international cricket since 2006, it felt incongruous compared with previous post-match round-ups to hear Baz focusing on Jonny Bairstow, who had scored only 16, but had struck a couple of really crunching fours.

'Fantastic shots, mate. They were seriously high-end, mate. Just keep doing that.'

It is fair to say in my own experience of Test cricket that no one had ever been congratulated for hitting a boundary or two before. Certainly not ahead of a bloke steering a team that had forgotten what it was like to win over the finish line with a high-quality and their own maiden fourth-innings hundred, as Root had managed.

But Jonny is someone whose mind can wander all over the place, often thinking the worst in situations. Someone who needs a lot of building up, and the public pumping of his tyres was paid forward over a week later when, after two low scores in the opening match of the series and a failure on what is known in the trade as a 'road' in the first innings, he turned up on the fifth morning at Nottingham. Initially, I sensed he was on edge.

To paint the scene, I was sitting in my usual spot in the home changing room at Trent Bridge, tucked away in the corner, and Wayne Bentley, our South African team manager, was drinking a coffee, perched on a stool. Just the two of us. For those unfamiliar with the lay-out at my Nottinghamshire headquarters, the changing room is split in two – the bottom half where we were located leading onto the stairs, down into the pavilion and onto the pitch. I became aware of activity in the top half: it was Jonny putting his pads on over his training kit, readying himself for a pre-play hit.

As I was putting spikes in my boots, I had been quite preoccupied when suddenly, I become aware of his presence directly in front of me. He was staring directly into my eyes as I lifted my head. After fixing them for a couple of seconds, he turned the same steely gaze at Wayne, without saying a word. Then he turned to leave like a soldier going into battle. A reminder here. He was going out for a net. Chest puffed out as wide as you could imagine, he took a huge inhalation of breath through his nose and declared, 'Right then, Jonathan Marc Bairstow, it's your day.'

Without so much as a glance back, he was off down the stairs, leaving myself and Wayne looking at each other as if to check: what the hell just happened there? Of course, we couldn't help smiling, but that was the making not only of Jonny, but given his integral role, the success we enjoyed as a team throughout the summer of 2022. He was fired up and it was going to be his day.

It took us just over an hour to dismiss the New Zealanders for a second time, leaving a target of 299 in 72 overs. At tea, Jonny was in, alongside Ben Stokes, with the score 139 for four, meaning 160 runs were required in a minimum 38 overs during the final session. It was now that Ben Foakes, sipping tea and nibbling on something or other, piped up with what was a very reasonable and routine question, given he was next man in.

'Guys, if we lose another wicket, are we blocking for the draw? Are we going to shut up shop?'

It drew a critical response. Not only for that afternoon, but forever as far as this particular England team was concerned. It would form the fabric of future attitudes.

'Everyone come in,' McCullum said, urging people to meet up on the same level. 'Just so we're all aware. We're going for the win. At all costs. We will have the mindset that we're going to chase these runs down, because I would much prefer to lose this game giving it everything than draw.'

He made the point that it was a beautiful sunny day and a full house had turned up to see us hit boundaries. Not block. Run towards the danger . . .

Emphasising that he wanted to take the New Zealanders on until the last batter walked to the crease, Baz looked at Jimmy Anderson and continued, 'Jimmy, if you get in, I want to see you hitting boundaries. Let's chase this game.'

The game plan could not have been any clearer. Our new coach was not interested in drawing games. Even if it cost us a defeat, we were going for the win. There was no doubt in his voice.

When play resumed, Matt Henry signalled his intention to open a period of bouncer warfare, beginning with a delivery that Jonny ducked. Ben Stokes walked down the pitch and quizzed his partner, 'Jonny, why are you not hitting that for six?'

Perhaps taken aback, Jonny said, 'Oh . . . well . . . I just wanted to have a look at one.'

'Well, you've had a look at one now. I want you to hit the ball.'

In the first five overs of that session, five sixes and five fours flew off Jonny's bat alone. Bang, bang, bang, bang, bang.

This period did not only kick-start Jonny, it unequivocally spelt out the style of play for a transformed England team. It got everyone talking. People down the supermarket, at the petrol pump and in the pub were discussing what an exciting Test match had taken place in Nottingham. Jonny came off as a hero, having struck 136 off 92 balls – one of the best hundreds I've ever seen.

As part of our new post-match routines, Baz had introduced feedback from all the players, going round the room, asking players for their thoughts, starting with the youngest. As team-mate after team-mate covered ground that I might have done, with their reflections on a performance that had emphatically sealed a series win over the reigning world Test champions with a match to spare, I thought, bloody hell, I haven't got anything left to say here.

It had been a very student-heavy crowd, following the decision by Nottinghamshire to open the gates for free on the final day, and some of the lads provided cover versions of songs about downing pints as we sipped bottles of beer and laughed.

Then, Baz let me know my turn had come.

'Broady, you got anything?'

Jumping to my feet, I went and got Jonny's bat from the next level up and re-created the morning episode that only Wayne Bentley and I had witnessed. I am not much of an impressionist, but I pulled this one off. The fact that everyone was guffawing told me so. The stare, the bulging chest, the big gasp. And to the delight of the room, the man himself stood up to deliver the punchline, adding, 'Just so you know. It's Marc with a C!'

Funnily enough, I had said to him at lunch that if he went on to win us the game, I would forever call him Jonathan

Marc Bairstow, and I would re-enter him as such in my phone. Mollie had not really met him before, but whenever the name Jonny came up after that, she would check she had got the right person by reciting his full name.

There were no real rules to the way we were being asked to play, more a case of anything goes. Warm up how you want to warm up – you're the pro, you're the one who has to go out and do it on the field. You decide. What do you need to feel ready?

There are so many restrictions on international sports people through pressures imposed from outside, but this release from convention meant the most important person doing the judging was yourself. The refreshing message has been to live how you want to live, play how you want to play, knowing you will be backed through your failures.

For a bowler like me, someone who has played so many different roles over the years – all roughly based on the principle that you are trying to restrict batters, to grind them down, to induce errors – it took a leap of faith to accept that being struck for a boundary could be a positive thing. That instead of drying up fours, offering them could be beneficial, because if a batter finds the rope and then attempts to play the same stroke again and gets out, you've won. No longer is anyone talking about the four you conceded.

There have been a lot of ways to plan bowling, and loads of them have been very, very successful in their own time. England's strategy under the captaincy of Andrew Strauss was to go at under 2.7 runs per over as an attack, building pressure collectively, because if we bowled 90 overs in a day, and kept opponents under 250, we calculated that we would create enough chances within that window to dismiss them. We would then back our own batters to upgrade on whatever the opposition posted.

It was a very different way of using time and interpreting its constraints. Under McCullum's method of removing draws from the equation, you have to create time in the game by taking your wickets and scoring your runs at faster rates.

Interestingly, evidence showed we were still taking 100 overs to bowl Test match teams out, because that is how it tends to be at the top level, but crucially by hunting wickets directly rather than relying on stealth, we bowled opponents out with regularity. Indeed, we took all ten wickets in 26 consecutive Test innings before losing to Australia in Birmingham in 2023.

No longer was it acceptable to bowl a spell of seven overs for seven runs. The only question Ben Stokes tends to ask when you are standing at the top of your mark is: what field do you need to take a wicket? Typically, if you tell him the pitch is a bit slow, and the ball's not moving about, that you won't require more than one slip, he will demand that two close catchers are placed elsewhere. You might get a short midwicket and an extra cover. Under his captaincy, there's never been a conversation about how to stop the scoreboard moving. Only to stop the batter by sending him back to the changing room.

This more positive approach was certainly influential for me. Massively so. Just look at the evidence. I finished on the winning side in Test matches ten times out of fourteen matches – my previous ten wins for England had spanned forty months. During this period I became the first English bowler to take five or more wickets in five consecutive matches, extending the overall tally to seven during the 2023 Ashes.

On the flip side, the one time I didn't fully commit to the plan, against India at Edgbaston in July 2022, I got hurt. Or at least my figures did.

As a bowler, I don't mind getting in on a bouncer barrage if invited, but prefer doing so bowling with the old ball as opposed to the new, because if a batter top edges, it generally doesn't reach the boundary, which brings the possibility of catches in the deep into play. It's a clear wicket-taking option. If you do it with a new, rock-hard ball, that top edge flies for six, and so I don't like it anywhere near as much.

In this particular instance, in a Test match that completed a series held over from the previous summer, Stokes announced we were going to bowl bouncers after India resumed the second morning on 338 for seven. I accepted it, but told him I wasn't wild on the idea, reminding him that the ball could easily fly to all parts.

'I don't care,' he told me. 'Go for as many runs as you want.'

I am not sure he expected me to take him so literally.

The first ball in an over that would cost me a Test record 35 runs resulted in a half-chance when Jasprit Bumrah helped the ball to the finger ends of Zak Crawley, diving forward at fine leg, the ball going for four to add insult. To Stokesy, however, such an outcome was a vindication of the plan. He wasn't looking at the end result, but the fact we had immediately created an opportunity through its implementation.

The reality is that it was not the most expensive over I have ever bowled in a match – I got that one in before you did – but I didn't think it was the right plan and neither did I execute it very well, bowling a no-ball and harshly being called for five wides.

There is no chance I would've continued with it had us bowlers not vowed to commit to a wickets-first policy within our greater tactical plan. The old me would have rejected suggestions to stick with it out of hand, and ended up in a heated difference of opinion with my captain.

But as a leader, Stokes was not going to let me change. I had created that wicket-taking moment with the first ball of the 84th over. What was to say that I wouldn't create another with ball three? No longer was the main consideration how many runs it would cost, only how long would it take to get someone out.

Stokes and I had ding-dongs a couple of times, but we also had a great relationship, so cross words were forgotten about within minutes. Rarely does every single person on a team agree with every other one of their team-mates, and that was the case for successful, happy teams like us too.

The most regular phrase Baz used at this time was: 'I'll just say a few quick words before I pass to the captain.' He started every single group discussion with that. The focus was always on what we had done positively brilliant, and how we could win the game from the position we were in.

The win over India at Edgbaston was an example of no target being out of reach. Previous England vintages might have approached an equation of 378 runs required for victory and 147 overs remaining in the contest a lot more defensively, but, having knocked off an average target of 291 in our three victories over New Zealand at the start of the 2022 summer, recent history was on our side, even if this was taking it up a notch.

Once again, there was a positive vibe regarding our task within our team environment, and one of the interesting observations about how positive intent works is that it alters the best-laid plans of opponents. As we found out during a seven-wicket romp to victory through Root and Bairstow's unbeaten centuries.

Playing such attacking cricket can scramble the thinking of others. Here, we had one of the best left-arm spinners in the world, Ravindra Jadeja, reverting to bowling over the wicket on a fourth- and fifth-day pitch – a player that takes his Test wickets at a cost of 24 runs. He was no longer focused on his own strengths, concerning himself instead with negating those of others.

When opponents act in this way, you know you are onto something. Setting the agenda in some ways felt un-English. Being part of a team like this after the start I'd had to the year almost felt unreal. But it sure felt good.

CHAPTER ELEVEN

I T is not how you start, it's how you finish. That is a well-worn sporting phrase, of course, but never did it feel more apt than when applied to my final week in an England shirt. It really could not have gone any better.

The best views come after the hardest climb is another one, but sometimes there is beauty in the mundane. Being able to clamber up those steps at The Oval, sit under my peg in the changing room and stare at the floor, reflecting on one last win over Australia and one final wicket from me to complete it, it felt magical.

There were several occasions in the past when my career might easily have ended in less salubrious circumstances, and the opportunity to make the perfect exit had only been a possibility for 72 hours. I reached The Oval that week with only one thing clear in my thoughts: I wanted to add to the dismissal of Travis Head at Old Trafford, the 149th of my career versus Australia, which propelled me past Ian Botham to the top of England's Ashes bowling chart.

I had actually started thinking about retirement after day one of that Manchester match. The series had gone so quickly and my overall feeling was that if the Ashes was to be my last involvement in cricket, I had only a week to get my head round that fact. Crikey! A week. I needed to make a call on this, and soon.

One thing bothered me, though. Whenever I had spoken to former international team-mates about calling time – people like Eoin Morgan and Alastair Cook – they had said, 'When you know, you know.' Problem was, I didn't know. Genuinely. Then I began questioning the hackneyed theory itself. 'Hang on, do I actually want to know?' Because, I reasoned with myself, if you're saying that you know, then you're already over the hill, and I never wanted to have the feeling that I had 'gone' as a cricketer. That future meeting with a twenty-year-old telling me I was a has-been was something I could live without.

Could I still perform at the top level? One hundred per cent, I could. In a way, I wished I was bowling crap, then the decision would have been easier. The truth of the matter was I was still bowling really well and taking wickets. I was the first seamer to claim thirty Test victims in 2023.

However, I was determined not to invite distraction mid-series, so I kept my own counsel in Manchester, aside from one conversation that developed not of my instigation. Brendon McCullum and I were lying on the floor in the Old Trafford changing room, wishing the rain away, watching the golf on TV. Everyone else was occupied, playing cards.

'How you feeling?' Baz asked.

I was like: 'Yeah, I'm good.'

Perhaps it was the location that made me connect what on face value was a very innocent question with my future, because it was at Old Trafford twelve months previously that I'd told Baz I would walk away there and then if he wanted me to. I would understand if he viewed the end of the 2022 summer as a time to bring in younger bowlers. If he needed to create space within the bowling group for that to happen, I could move aside. He was adamant that he wanted me to stay.

'I've got a bit of a decision to make coming up, but I'm trying not to think about it too much right now and hopefully the gut tells me,' I told him.

'Obviously, I want you to stay,' he said.

That was nice to hear. Let's face it, if he'd come back with the opposite, I would have thought, oh bugger!

Baz creates a hold over you that is hard to describe. He is a hard man to say no to. That's a phrase you have probably already heard in relation to him. But the only person I was now answerable to was myself.

Alastair Cook told me when he retired that whenever I was thinking about the issue, if choosing to confide in others, I should keep the circle of trust extremely small. Discuss it only with a select few, because even if you're only thinking about it, if your bosses become aware, they will assume you now lack motivation. Which, in the instance of you carrying on, might lead to them not offering you a new contract.

It stands to reason that the more people you tell, the more chance there is of something leaking out, and I had now given Baz an inkling. He had seen me commit fully to twelve months since making my step-aside offer, but equally that I'd been prepared to do it in the first place.

Away from cricket grounds, I considered some facts. I had just turned thirty-seven. Then again, in the next thirty appearances Jimmy Anderson made after his thirty-seventh birthday, he took 107 wickets at under 21 runs apiece. Statistically, he got better. When I considered that, I genuinely believed I also had 100 left in me.

Once the final Test began, I didn't want any of these thoughts occupying my head space at all, so I called Cookie over the practice days. Moving on from the international scene is something you have experienced relatively recently, I said. How did you feel in the lead-up? He said that ultimately he just couldn't tell anyone. Not even Alice, his wife. He was so emotional that instead of discussing things with her, he ended up texting her, saying, 'I'm going to retire.' She texted back: 'I know.'

Psychologically, I felt in that same place. We discussed the fact I had no internal signposting one way or the other. He told me that one of the nicest feelings he'd had carrying on in first-class cricket with Essex for five years was people saying to him: I wish you were still playing for England. Memories of him scoring that farewell hundred at The Oval against India had left people wanting more.

Taking a leaf out of my mum's book, Cookie said he would never lean me towards one way or the other, but would ring me back later with further thoughts. He texted back instead, simply saying: 'I think you know. I honestly reckon you won't regret going six months too early. You have achieved everything you wanted to achieve and you're the only cricketer I know who can say they thrived in and delivered in every big moment. Surely, that's the best feeling ever?'

Cookie was always a trusted confidant. Everything I've ever told him remained on his farm. Nothing got out. He'd been a good sounding board.

But there was one more person I wanted to run things by. I had known Paul Monk, best mate of the late Bob Willis, for five years. We occasionally play golf together and eat together. I am my mother's son and so she is always the one I ask for advice, but if I want someone from outside my family and cricket bubbles, it's him.

The conversation lasted the length of an Uber journey across London; me telling him I was considering the possibility of this week's game being my last, and asking what that looked like from his perspective. He told me that he knew I had more to give, that I could go on and play another year or two and enjoy a lot more success. But that it was my call. We were still chatting as I got out of the car, and the driver, who clearly had no idea who I was or what I did, but sensed I was about to make a big decision in my life, simply smiled and told me, 'Follow your heart.'

My heart. In recent times, there were new people in it. Maybe Mollie and I starting our own family with the arrival of Annabella would prove to be an influence.

Mollie and I got back together in early 2018. Apart from

her ringing to see how I was when I got hit in the face by Varun Aaron, we had not really spoken in the meantime, but sitting with her mum Sue at Christmas, she said she was going to drop me a text. I was on the Ashes tour, so we agreed to get together when I returned from that lads' holiday in Noosa with Jimmy and Sean. We saw each other a couple of times before I went off on another tour of New Zealand.

Oh no, not New Zealand again, I thought. I didn't want the same curse of five years previously striking once more, and with me living in Nottingham, Mollie in London, it could have shaped up as being another, I go away, she goes away, situation.

It felt like we needed to have a couple of nights and some time together to make a call on whether we could make things work, so two days after I got back from New Zealand, despite being worried about the jetlag, we were on our way to Paris on the Eurostar. We walked around the streets, sat and drank coffee, everything we could do in London. But somewhere else.

Things were not always straightforward. They never are when factoring in international cricket schedules, and COVID meant we were away from loved ones a lot, but I knew Mollie was the one and so I arranged for her parents Steve and Sue to come up to Nottingham in late 2020. I bought all the food, everything we needed, and then the prime minister Boris Johnson cancelled Christmas with six days' notice, instructing everyone to resist the urge of travelling and stay at home.

With this nationwide cancellation, he had also postponed my personal plans.

I had been thinking of asking Mollie to marry me with her parents around on Christmas Eve, as I thought there would be no way she would want to tell her news without being able to hug them. So I delayed it. Driving to Loughborough on 27 December to attend an England team training session, ahead of our tour of Sri Lanka, snow began blanketing the ground, and I had an idea we should go to Wollaton Park and I would propose surrounded by deer. But I wanted it to be perfect, and it didn't feel so without her family close by.

Mollie was working at Radio 1 on New Year's Day 2021, and that allowed me to line things up exactly as I wanted. We travelled back to London on New Year's Eve and that's when I thought, right! Our favourite spot in London is Richmond Hill, at a point where you can see a gorgeous view of the Thames and the City. Mollie and her two sisters Laura and Ellen used to play there as kids, so I proposed that we got up early and started the New Year with a nice walk. My plan was to get towards the top of the steps, and allow Mollie to go ahead so that when I called her name and she turned around, she saw the view while I was on one knee. What could possibly go wrong?

I had calculated that it was early morning, everyone would have been out partying the night before and lying in. They were. Apart from one bloke sitting on the park bench exactly in the spot where I wanted this romantic moment to take place: reading his paper, having a coffee. I was like: aaargghh! I gave him the eyes to suggest he moved on but, after doing another loop of the park, he was still there. So, I persuaded Mollie to go round once more. Next time, he'd gone.

We had about 15 minutes of enjoying the moment together before we walked up to the highest point of the hill and, much to Mollie's surprise, we were greeted by her mum and dad, who I'd arranged to be standing waiting at the top so she could share the excitement of the moment with them. I suppose you'd call it a celebrappeal proposal. I was pretty confident she would say yes.

Steve was also due to come to the first day of the South Africa Test match at Lord's in August 2022, but when Mollie and I went for our regular dog walk with him that week, up to the Windmill pub, grabbing our usual bacon sandwich and coffee, we noticed certain things about his behaviour. He seemed to be repeating himself a lot and this was odd, because he was very switched on, an accountant by trade, a clever man as well as being a very fit one. He had run loads of marathons, and still walked miles daily before most folk were out of bed. It had been hot and he said he'd been feeling a bit dizzy in the afternoons. Maybe I need to drink more water, he said.

Two days before that match, we discovered he had a brain tumour. Sadly, he did not have long to live and we felt that he was hanging on for Annabella's arrival. It was of great comfort to Mollie that despite this horrible disease, Steve was able to hold Annabella in his arms. He died, surrounded by his girls, eleven days after she was born. It was an unbelievably emotional time for Mollie – having the incredible joy at the birth of our beautiful baby, while at the same time dealing with the grief of the devastating loss of her dad. I really don't know how she managed it – I'm in awe of her inner strength and how she coped with both emotions. She's truly amazing.

But it also reinforced some things for me. To be honest, even if I had not initially pulled out of the Pakistan tour because of our daughter's November due date, I would have remained at home once we'd received Steve's brain tumour diagnosis. Aged twenty-three, that's a very different proposition, because you are trying to fight your way into a team and you don't know what opportunities you might be giving up, or presenting to rivals, if you say no. But at thirty-six, you become very aware that family is infinitely more important than your day job.

As the partner of an England cricketer, Mollie trained herself for me having to be away for long spells, but despite retaining the hunger to play Test cricket, I felt less inclined to be away as our relationship went on. Did I want to be away again in 2023–24? No, I knew I didn't. It was one of the red crosses on my mind map as I contemplated the pros and cons of playing on or otherwise between the fourth and fifth Tests.

I still loved cricket, though, so walking away was one of the hardest decisions I would ever have to make. Equally, it was my goal to finish at the top.

* * *

The fifth match of the series began in the manner of those that had gone before. An unchanged England team playing with haste and purpose – although the glass-half-full merchants might have claimed we showed too much of the former and not enough of the latter after being inserted and posting 284. But we knew we had to get the game moving forward with more showers forecast.

In contrast, Australia appeared intent on playing very cautiously. They scored only eight runs with the bat in the final ten overs of the first day and 13 runs off 15 overs to start day two. I put it down to the steam train momentum of ours as much as any Australian failings. We thought we were bowling in a way that they could not attack us, not giving them any freebies, and with that pressure, the wickets would come.

We bowled beautifully during that first session of the second day and all we needed was a change of luck. My decision to alternate the bails just before lunch coincided with that moment, when Mark Wood nicked Marnus Labuschagne off the next ball for nine – the 82nd he had faced in his innings.

In Test cricket, you talk about building pressure over a period of time, and then your luck will change. We had bowled well in the first session but didn't really get any rewards. Then bang, three came in the first hour after the interval. Striking at the start of spells was definitely a feature of my performances in my final few matches, and I continued the habit when I accounted for Usman Khawaja first over, and then got Travis Head out, caught behind. When Jimmy Anderson bowled Mitchell Marsh soon afterwards, we were on a roll. Alex Carey and Mitchell Starc didn't last long either. Suddenly, everything was going our way – or nearly everything.

Until just after tea, which was taken with Australia 185 for seven, when third umpire Nitin Menon deliberated for an eternity over a potential run-out of Steve Smith. The incident occurred a couple of overs before the second new ball became available, when Smith, on 42, took on the arm of substitute George Ealham, the son of my former Nottinghamshire team-mate Mark – you really should know it's time to go when you have been on the field with a father and son – who sprinted in from deep midwicket and produced a rocket-like throw that was collected by Jonny Bairstow, who took the ball cleanly, but partly dismantled the stumps in the process.

It appeared that Smith was short of his ground, but on subsequent replays, Menon ruled that the spigots of the one remaining bail had not been completely dislodged from its groove until Smith, who had pulled out a full-length dive, was in his crease. To level with you, despite playing inter-national cricket for seventeen years, I had to confess while chatting to the on-field umpire Kumar Dharmasena that I did not know the rules in this regard. He explained to me that if we had been using the flashing zing bails prevalently used in one-day cricket in England, Smith would have been given out.

I know it is said that there is no such thing as benefit of

the doubt for batters in that situation, but it has to be a not-out if the officials are not sure. Had it gone the other way, Australia would have been facing a considerable deficit, but as it was, we trailed by a dozen on first innings.

From there, we had only one thing on our minds. To entertain with the bat and see where it led us. By now, despite some early scepticism, people truly accepted this was the way we played and it was the best way for us to play. I lost count of the number of older generation, traditional cricket lovers, who came up to me during the series, saying what a brilliant series it had been, and how the whole family was sitting down to watch it, enjoying the fun. Keep going, they'd said, when we were 2–0 down. People had almost forgotten the significance of the result. They were just enjoying the cricket.

Professional sport has always been about winning and losing for me and people of my generation. I liked winning; I trained to win. And I hated losing, which is why my mum imposed that 24-hour rule to snap me out of my disappointment. She could always tell when I'd lost games because my voice was different. I could never hide my emotions in that regard.

Yet the possibility of defeat no longer hung as heavy, the end result was not at the forefront of our minds, and that is why playing for this particular England team was so unique. Letting go of my inhibitions had a significant impact on my cricket. Of course, we remained desperate to win every match, but entertainment was at the heart of the whole ethos, because ultimately fans want to buy a ticket and watch us play and, win, lose or draw, leave the ground saying that was fun, wasn't it? Getting rid of the fear of failure improved their experiences and our results exponentially.

I told my team-mates that this latest push for victory would be my last alongside them on the Saturday morning, the third of the match, before our second innings began. My intent with the bat was exactly the same as with the ball – if I got a chance, I always believed I could change the momentum of a day's play by getting the crowd going, lifting the Barmy Army and giving my team-mates more energy.

On this occasion, thanks to half-centuries from Zak Crawley, Joe Root and Jonny Bairstow, the skills of the Night Hawk – the alter ego of the Nightwatchman, a player who plays with abandon when expected to show restraint – were not needed until a final few minutes saturated by the fall of wickets. My departure from the field preceded my announcement on Sky Sports that my countdown clock had 48 hours left to run.

I treasured two things next morning. The first was a guard of honour from the Australian team as I walked onto the field alongside Jimmy Anderson. It was very kind of Pat Cummins, and very patient of him, too. We left them waiting a couple of minutes at the boundary edge because I was handing Jimmy his 41st birthday card in the changing room.

'I tried to contact one of your previous captains to come in and present this to you,' I said. 'But W.G. Grace didn't get back to us.'

Having a laugh with my old mate and 10th-wicket partner

was glorious, and the applause that greeted us did not cease on the walk down onto the pitch, through the tunnel of Australians, all the way to the middle.

The second was managing to haul a delivery from Mitchell Starc into the stands over deep square leg before Jimmy was dismissed, ticking off the first leg of my memorable double. Finishing with a six as my last scoring stroke in a Test career tally of 3,662 runs was pretty cool.

It was not the most significant blow of the day, though. That was the one to Usman Khawaja's helmet in mid-afternoon from Mark Wood's thirteenth delivery. Australia had moved smoothly to 126 without loss at that point. They were dominant. We had barely encouraged a play-and-miss and had reverted to bowling off cutters with fielders in front of the bat, looking for a chip to mid-off or mid-on, until Wood, who was nursing an increasingly sore ankle by this stage, was finally unleashed.

Khawaja ducked and the ball hit the metal bit where the grille attaches to the main part of the helmet, completely splitting the ball open. It was unusable. And it proved to be the biggest stroke of luck that we got, as it led to another ball being picked out for us by the umpires.

It drew a 'Wey aye, man. Happy with that, like,' from Woody on first inspection. The replacement was definitely newer than the previous ball and slightly darker, but not to the extent some people suggested later by comparing the rough side of the old one we'd been preparing for some reverse swing with the shiny side of the new one.

The ball change would be debated for days, with some suggesting it was not like for like and others that it was not even year for year. That somehow one from an old batch of balls had found its way into those provided to The Oval as used spares from 2023.

Conspiracy theories that the England team were somehow something to do with all this were quite frankly ludicrous. The fielding side gets what they are given by the officials in such circumstances. Yes, there is no doubt that the replacement offered more assistance to the bowlers, but light rain, starting later in that Wood over and intensifying in the next, meant we did not get to see how it would benefit us until the next day. Australia had reached a premature close on 135 without loss.

Determination and confidence were the qualities that were noticeable among our group next morning. In our minds we still knew that 384 was a big score. The pitch was offering turn, and it felt as if Moeen Ali or Joe Root would be able to do a job as the innings wore on, so we were being patient, trying not to leak runs. Moeen had tweaked his groin earlier in the match, keeping him off the field for a period and forcing him to bat at number 7.

He was never not going to bowl, though. Even if it was off one yard. The same with Mark Wood. He was crying inside every time he bowled, he was in that much pain with his heel, but he gave everything he had. We knew that after this sixth innings in a short period of time, he'd have no more to give.

First up, however, it was Chris Woakes who made the impact, with a ball that didn't stop moving around until my attempted in-swinger to Alex Carey completed our win by 49 runs.

Woakes has always been a brilliant cricketer, but in the last eighteen months he had struggled so much with his fitness, requiring knee surgery, and didn't bowl a ball in the summer of 2022. Set on trying to play in the Ashes, he had not made himself available to go to the Indian Premier League in 2023, and to finish as Man of the Series and have the influence he did in two winning Test matches paid that decision back.

He is one of those bowlers who needs workload in his body, and if he doesn't have it, he is susceptible to injury. Physically, he was hardened by July, and when he came in at Headingley, he didn't look back.

Psychologically, it could have been quite tough when he was left out against Ireland at the start of the summer, to provide Josh Tongue with Test exposure, but he's a fairly pragmatic character and probably recognised he was just slightly down the pecking order, having not played Test cricket since the Caribbean.

I think he knew that there was always one injury cloud or another hanging over us as a bowling unit, and that a chance would come. That is one of the reasons why we carried a bigger squad than usual into this particular Ashes. In the past, the bowlers not making the match XI had been released, but personally, I was keen on keeping all the bowlers around all of the time. Not that it was my decision, but I

expressed to Brendon McCullum that I thought it was important for everyone to feel a part of things if we were going
to be successful.

So instead of heading off to play for Warwickshire or Sussex
or Worcestershire as soon as the coin tosses took place, as
had been the norm in the past, they stuck around. If you
leave, you feel less connected to the series. This way, if you
were called in, you wouldn't be asking how so-and-so got
out the previous week. Well, you were there, watching. You
tell me. You have been in the bowlers' meetings, in on all the
changing room chats and on the team bus every day.

Would Chris Woakes have played a lot more Test cricket
over his career if Jimmy Anderson and I had not been around?
Probably. He is such a solid operator as a seam bowler. Someone
who moves the ball, and who bowls wicket-taking deliveries
to right- and left-handers. He doesn't have a particular strength
or weakness in that regard. He formed a good bowling partnership with me, in the fact that I liked to bowl around the
wicket to the lefties, releasing the ball from a higher point
given that I am six foot six; he did so with a preference to
bowl across them. He accounted for David Warner and Usman
Khawaja in successive overs, and our pursuit of ten wickets
was under way.

Mark Wood claimed a third, having Marnus Labuschagne
held in the slips for a second time in the match, before what
felt like a massive moment on a gripping last day before lunch
with Steve Smith on 39 in a score of 237 for three. Moeen
was bowling when Smith gloved the ball down the leg-side,

Ben Stokes reached up to complete a one-handed grab at leg slip, and went to throw the ball up in celebration, but what some of my team-mates and I saw was different to those watching at home on TV or at The Oval itself.

I was fielding at point. So I saw the glove. I saw the ball disappear into Stokes's hand and turned to look at the umpire Joel Wilson, asking, 'How's that?' There was no reaction. 'Mo, it's one hundred per cent glove,' I said. Review, review, review, was the mood. I wasn't the only England fielder who had not witnessed the sweep of Stokes's arm and the ball inadvertently coming out of his grasp, after striking his knee.

We got to see it first time on the big screen, and despite looking sheepish, Stokes's reasoning for challenging the not-out call was, 'They might think that I've got control of it.' The replay confirmed he wasn't in control, and like Mitchell Starc's grassed effort at Lord's, the right decision was made. Having survived becoming the series' first run-out victim earlier in the match, Smith had been reprieved once more.

Fear of an Old Trafford repeat might have struck some when the inclement weather caused a severe delay to proceedings and it would have been so different for me to finish my Test career, shaking hands in the rain, for a draw to lose the Ashes. But after being forced off without bowling a ball after lunch, I knew we'd get back on. Two and a quarter hours later, we were.

There were 146 runs required and 52 overs remaining. It was an equation that still looked in Australia's favour until a flurry of four wickets in as many overs and an overall demise to 294 for eight. I was thrilled for Moeen that he took three of them. At Edgbaston, after he sent Travis Head back with a beauty for his first wicket since reversing his Test cricket exile, I ran to him from point and the smile on his face was massive, beaming. It was a sign that he had made the right decision to come back. These are the moments you play for, I told him. He agreed with me. Oh, to be twenty-two again, we'd said.

A remarkable story emerged about a woman who sent Mo a special gel made from honey to hasten the healing of his blistered spinning finger after his first first-class bowl in eighteen months. It's amazing what people will do in an Ashes effort.

Mo's successes played their part in allowing me to shape those wonderful last memories on a cricket field. And I was so proud of my own execution when it mattered most. Remember, I had just one ball left of my spell when I got that delivery to leave Todd Murphy and brush the edge of the bat for the ninth Australian wicket. For a long time, the media perception of me was that I was this streaky bowler who would be quiet for six Tests and then strike, but over the final five years of my career, I became so much more consistent.

Experience told – all the ups and downs, controlling my emotions, composing myself, pumping those legs efficiently and knowing how to deliver under pressure. My dad said to me when I was sixteen years old that Test cricket was 80 per cent mental and 20 per cent technical. I didn't know what he meant. Now, after playing 167 games, I did. Only, I would say the ratio is more like 90 and 10 per cent. Because if you're not fully switched on and focused, you can't perform.

But the kid in me never left. I hope you saw that with the way I aeroplaned around the square on dismissing Alex Carey, before finally landing in a Jimmy Anderson embrace at mid-off. After all we had been through together, it was great to share that moment with him. Then the hugs from others. The exchange with our very own Nostradamus, Jonny Bairstow. He had told me how my journey with this team would end.

I'd had wonderful times with this team throughout, and in terms of success, winning thirteen of eighteen Test matches, it would have to be up there alongside the Andy Flower-coached era of 2009–13. No one could ever claim that Andy's style didn't work. He was coach the only time England reached number one status in the world Test rankings. His coaching style was hard, disciplined and authentic to his own characteristics. I just don't see that style having longevity for a team now. The one under Brendon McCullum feels sustainable. Players so want to be part of it.

It will always feel like my team. I care about it so deeply. I even worry about how some of them will cope now I'm gone. Not for the on-field stuff, mind. You see, every club team has a handyman or two and I was England's go-to for bowlers. 'Broady, you got any spare spikes? Stud tightener?' From the batters, Joe Root would get, 'Any tape? Got a grip, please?' No one is organised enough to carry a tool kit, so after finishing up writing this, I will donate mine.

Going forward, I will be watching from the commentary box. Just two days after the final Ashes Test, I was on duty for Sky Sports, covering a Hundred match at Lord's. Attempting to get into the ground, I zapped my player pass at the gate. It was declined. I had been deactivated.

Time moves on, but the memories remain.

CAREER STATISTICS

ENGLAND:
TEST MATCHES:

Period	Matches	Runs	Avg	High	Wickets	Avg	Best	5wkts	SR
2007–2023	167	3,662	18.03	169	604	27.68	8/15	20	55.7

BY OPPONENT

	Matches	2007–2023	High	Runs	High	Bat Avg	100	Wkts	Best	Avg	5wkts
Australia	40	2009–2023		1,019	65	18.87	0	153	8/15	28.96	8
Bangladesh	3	2010–2016		26	13	8.66	0	8	2/31	39.87	0
India	24	2008–2022		470	74*	17.40	0	74	6/25	28.51	2
Ireland	2	2019–2023		24	21*	24.00	0	13	5/51	14.76	1
New Zealand	23	2008–2023		479	64	14.96	0	94	7/44	28.21	4
Pakistan	19	2010–2020		539	169	23.43	1	67	4/36	22.53	0
South Africa	25	2008–2022		573	76	17.36	0	89	6/17	27.83	2
Sri Lanka	12	2007–2021		202	54	14.42	0	33	4/21	36.66	0
West Indies	19	2009–2020		330	62	20.62	0	73	7/72	24.90	3

ONE-DAY INTERNATIONALS:

Period	Matches	Runs	High	Avg	Wickets	Avg	Best	4wkts	5wkts	SR
2006–2016	121	529	45*	12.30	178	30.13	5/23	9	1	34.3

BY OPPONENT

	Matches	Runs	HS	Bat Avg	100	Wkts	Best	Bowl Avg	5wkts
Afghanistan	1	–	–	–	–	1	1/18	18.00	0
Australia	20	69	24	6.90	0	28	4/44	34.71	0
Bangladesh	6	30	21	15.00	0	8	2/43	32.75	0
India	19	148	45*	29.60	0	24	4/51	37.62	0
Ireland	1	–	–	–	–	0	–	–	0
Netherlands	1	–	–	–	–	2	2/65	32.50	0
New Zealand	17	86	23	9.55	0	26	4/39	25.50	0
Pakistan	13	16	8*	5.33	0	21	4/81	26.23	0
Scotland	3	0	0*	–	0	2	2/35	54.00	0
South Africa	12	29	13	5.80	0	25	5/23	18.68	1
Sri Lanka	12	52	20*	13.00	0	16	3/36	36.62	0
West Indies	16	99	28*	19.80	0	25	4/46	27.84	0

STUART BROAD

TWENTY20 INTERNATIONALS:

Period	Matches	Runs	Avg	High	Wickets	Avg	Best	4wkts	SR
2006–2014	56	118	7.37	18*	65	22.93	4/24	1	18.0

BY OPPONENT

		Matches	Runs	HS	Bat Avg	100	Wkts	Best	Bowl Avg
Afghanistan	2012–2012	1	–	–	–	–	2	2/10	5.00
Australia	2007–2014	8	38	18*	12.66	0	8	3/30	30.12
India	2007–2012	4	6	3*	6.00	0	2	2/37	77.00
Ireland	2010–2010	1	0	0*	–	0	–	–	–
Netherlands	2009–2014	2	4	4	4.00	0	4	3/24	14.00
New Zealand	2007–2014	10	14	6	3.50	0	14	4/24	20.42
Pakistan	2006–2012	10	8	6*	8.00	0	15	3/17	15.26
South Africa	2007–2014	7	28	18*	28.00	0	7	3/37	24.71
Sri Lanka	2010–2014	4	1	1	0.50	0	5	3/32	22.20
West Indies	2007–2014	8	18	10*	9.00	0	7	2/26	28.85
Zimbabwe	2007–2007	1	1	1	1.00	0	1	1/29	29.00

FIRST-CLASS:

ALL MATCHES:

Period	Matches	Runs	Avg	High	Wickets	Avg	Best	5wkts	10wkts
2005–2023	265	5,840	19.08	169	952	26.71	8/15	32	4

LEICESTERSHIRE:

Period	Matches	Runs	Avg	High	Wickets	Avg	Best	5wkts	10wkts
2005–2007	27	515	19.07	91*	93	29.44	5/67	5	0

NOTTINGHAMSHIRE:

Period	Matches	Runs	Avg	High	Wickets	Avg	Best	5wkts	10wkts
2008–2023	53	1,319	20.60	60	201	23.17	8/52	6	1

PHOTO ACKNOWLEDGEMENTS

Photo Section 1

Page 7 bottom: © Matthew Lewis/Getty Images

Page 8: © ADRIAN DENNIS/AFP/Getty Images

Photo Section 2

Page 1 top: © Hamish Blair/Getty Images

Page 1 bottom: © Reuters

Page 2 top: © Tom Shaw/Getty Images

Page 3 top: © Tom Shaw/Getty Images

Page 3 bottom: © Stu Forster/Getty Images

Page 4: © Laurence Griffiths/Getty Images

Page 5 top: © Philip Brown/Popperfoto/Getty Images

Page 5 bottom: © Dan Mullan/Getty Images

Page 6 bottom: © PA Images/Alamy Stock Photo

Page 7 top: © Mark Cosgrove/News Images/Alamy Stock Photo

Page 7 middle: © Stu Forster/Getty Images

Page 7 bottom: © Ryan Pierse/Getty Images

Page 8 top: © Gareth Copley/Getty Images

Page 8 middle: Gareth Copley/Getty Images

All other photos are from the author's own collection.